Teach
yourself
about
shares

Teach yourself about shares

A Self-Help Guide to Successful Share Investing

Roger Kinsky

THIRD EDITION

WILEY

This third edition first published in 2020 by John Wiley & Sons Australia, Ltd
42 McDougall St, Milton Qld 4064
Office also in Melbourne

First edition published by Wrightbooks (an imprint of John Wiley & Sons Australia, Ltd) in 2003.
Second/Revised edition published by Wrightbooks (an imprint of John Wiley & Sons Australia, Ltd)
in 2009.

Typeset in Liberation Serif 11/14 pt

© John Wiley & Sons Australia, Ltd 2020

The moral rights of the author have been asserted

ISBN: 978-0-730-38494-6

 A catalogue record for this book is available from the National Library of Australia

Cover design: Wiley

10 9 8 7 6 5 4 3 2 1

Disclaimer
The material in this publication is of the nature of general comment only, and does not represent professional advice. It is not intended to provide specific guidance for particular circumstances and it should not be relied on as the basis for any decision to take action or not take action on any matter which it covers. Readers should obtain professional advice where appropriate, before making any such decision. To the maximum extent permitted by law, the author and publisher disclaim all responsibility and liability to any person, arising directly or indirectly from any person taking or not taking action based on the information in this publication.

Contents

Preface

I wrote *Teach Yourself About Shares* because very few share investing books contained worked examples or exercises that enabled the reader to learn while reading and put the ideas into practice. After many years working as a trainer and TAFE teacher, I'm firmly convinced that the best way of learning is self-guided learning, where the learner has input into the learning process and the trainer acts as a mentor or guide. I've adopted this principle in this book, so you can reinforce your learning about shares through self-learning.

I'm pleased to report that the first edition of this book was successful, justifying the reasoning behind it. After some years, a second edition was produced and now this is the third edition. In this edition, I've tried to make the book even more user-friendly by simplifying the explanations and by including additional worked examples and learning exercises (with solutions). Many of the worked examples and learning exercises are based on real-life cases, but fictitious names and codes have been substituted to give them a timeless value considering the rapidly and ever-changing nature of financial markets.

To gain maximum benefit from this book, I strongly suggest that you attempt the learning exercises at the end of each chapter without referring to the solutions until you've completed them to the best of your ability.

This book complements my book *Online Investing on the Australian Sharemarket*, which is devoted specifically to online investing. I believe that *Teach Yourself About Shares* will have value for all types of share investors and traders. If you use the internet for research or trading, this book can be used in conjunction with my online investing book for maximum benefit.

Every effort has been applied to make the book error-free but perfection is very difficult to achieve. My email address is rkinsky@bigpond.com and I'd like to hear from any readers who detect errors or have any constructive comments or suggestions.

I hope that this book proves to be truly useful in improving your understanding of shares and your success as a share investor.

Roger Kinsky
Woollamia, NSW
May 2020

Chapter 1

Getting to know shares and securities

In this chapter, I outline the various types of shares and securities you can invest in. I also discuss some important terms and concepts, so you'll be able to understand the information available.

Understanding financial investment instruments and securities

A *financial investment instrument* is something of monetary value that can readily be traded; that is, bought or sold. These are also known as *securities* because of their monetary value, which allows them to be used as security for a loan.

Shares

Shares are a popular type of investment instrument or security.

The idea of share ownership originated in the early days of English exploration, when expeditions were mounted to far-flung regions in search of riches. For those prepared to take the risks involved, a successful expedition could make them large profits. However, such ventures were very expensive and often relied on royal patronage (funding). In addition, private investors might contribute; for example, if a venture cost £10 million to mount, this might be obtained from 10 investors, each contributing £1 million. Funds obtained this way became known as *equity capital* because investors were part owners; that is, they had an equity in the enterprise.

Notes

- Capital is just another name for money or cash used for business purposes.
- Shares are also known as *equities*.
- Apart from equity capital, a business can also obtain capital by means of loans from banks or financial institutions. This capital is known as *loan capital*.

The idea of issuing shares to obtain equity capital for business ventures caught on in capitalist economies. Soon, several refinements were introduced. These included:

- Issuing shares with smaller monetary value. That is, instead of raising £10 million by issuing 10 shares of £1 million, the same capital could be raised by issuing 10 million shares at £1 each.

- As shares had a value, they could be traded between willing sellers and buyers. Indeed it was possible to make a profit by trading shares without actually participating in the enterprise. Originally, share trading was done at the Royal Exchange and then in coffee houses where investors gathered, but by 1748 share trading was so popular that a dedicated stock exchange was set up in Threadneedle Street, London. Soon this idea spread throughout the world and today most countries have their own stock exchanges.

Stocks and shares

The words *stocks* and *shares* are often used interchangeably but really they have slightly different meanings. Shares are the smallest equal units of division of ownership in a business enterprise, whereas stock is the sum total of all those shares. For example, all shares issued by Woolworths comprise the total Woolworths stock. If you buy some Woolworths shares, the number of shares you own determines the extent of your equity in the company—in this case, Woolworths.

Company

A company is a legal entity in its own right; that's to say in law it is regarded as a body that's distinct from the owners. This legal body is known as the 'body corporate' and it can do many things a person can do such as:

- enter into legal contracts

- sue or be sued

- buy or sell commodities

- hire or fire personnel

- own assets, including stock, machinery, real estate and cash.

For business purposes, the great advantage of a company is that the owners cannot be held liable for the debts or contracts of the company. This is different from business enterprises such as sole proprietors or partnerships, where there is no body corporate and the owners are liable for contracts and their assets can be used to repay debts if necessary.

Public versus private companies

As the name suggests, a public company is one where anyone can buy shares in the business and so be a part owner. This is different from a private (or proprietary) company (Pty Ltd), which is limited to 50 shareholders and the public at large can't become shareholders unless the company 'floats' (that is, converts to a public company). Public companies are listed on a securities exchange so the shares are available to all, whereas private companies are not listed and you cannot become a part owner unless invited.

Public companies are limited companies so their name ends with 'Ltd' (although this is sometimes left off in abbreviated share listings). The word *limited* means that, in the event of liquidation, the liability of the shareholders (owners) is limited, and the shareholders' personal assets can't be used to repay business debts (unlike in the case of a sole proprietor or partnership). To be precise, shareholders' liability is limited to the amount of any unpaid calls on contributing shares (if any).

A special type of listed company is the no liability (NL) mining company. NL means that there's no liability on the shareholders for unpaid calls on contributing shares (if any). (I discuss calls and contributing shares later in this chapter.)

Businesses that don't issue tradeable shares

In Australia, there are far more businesses that don't issue tradeable shares than those that do. Sole proprietors, partnerships, cooperatives and proprietary (private) companies are some of the business enterprises that don't issue tradeable shares.

Notes

- Public companies are usually larger than private companies but this is not always the case. For example, in Australia, Woolworths and Coles are public companies but Aldi is a private company of similar size owned by a single family.

- BHP is the only public company in Australia allowed to use the word 'proprietary' in its name, despite not being a proprietary company.

Initial public offering (IPO)

In order for a business enterprise or private company to convert to a public one, it must comply with legal requirements and also the rules and regulations of the exchange. This conversion occurs as an initial public offering (IPO) or 'float'. The issuing company must prepare a document known as a *prospectus*, which outlines all relevant commercial and financial information about the business (including investing risks). Investors can obtain shares only by completing the application form in the prospectus, and an investor obtaining shares in this way is said to have 'subscribed' to the issue. No transaction costs are usually incurred when shares are obtained this way.

Most floats are underwritten, which means that an underwriter (such as a large broking firm or financial institution) guarantees to take up any leftover shares if the issue is undersubscribed. On the other hand, if more shares are applied for than are available, the issue is oversubscribed and investors may not obtain as many shares as they applied for.

The price at which shares are offered is determined through consultation between the floating company and the underwriter, who are trying to obtain the maximum price consistent with full subscription. From the day of listing onward, the shares can be traded on the securities exchange in which they are listed. If the market considers that the issue price has been set too low and/or the issue has been oversubscribed, the price will usually take off on the first day of trading. If the issue price is too high and/or the issue is undersubscribed, the price will usually fall on the first trading day.

Notes

- You might wonder why a business would go to all the expense and hassle of 'going public'. One reason is that the business wants to expand and needs more capital and can't get sufficient capital from a limited number of private investors. The other main reason is that an entrepreneur wants to bring a new product or service to the market and needs considerable capital to do so.

- Company law, exchange regulations or reputable underwriters do not of themselves guarantee investors that any new listed company will be profitable and that buying shares in an IPO will prove to be profitable.

- Investors who subscribe to an IPO and sell the shares on the first day of trading hoping to make a quick profit are known as 'stags'.

Considering different types of shares

Several types of shares are available, which I will now discuss briefly.

Ordinary shares

The most common type of share by far is the fully paid ordinary share (FPO). The adjective 'ordinary' is often dropped and because nearly all shares are fully paid, you can also usually assume that the word 'share' means 'FPO share'. Ordinary shares are essentially 'plain vanilla' shares without any frills or special conditions attached.

Preference shares

Preference shares are superior to ordinary shares in some defined way, usually because they have first right to a dividend. This dividend is often set at a predetermined rate, such as at a certain margin above the prevailing bank bill rate. However, preference shares don't usually carry voting rights.

Convertible shares or hybrids

Some preference shares are convertible; that is, they can be converted to ordinary shares at some time in the future. These convertible shares are also known as *hybrids* and acronyms are often used to denote them — for example, PERLS (for preferred exchangeable resettable listed shares). They are often issued by the major banks as a means of obtaining more capital at a lower rate than otherwise obtainable.

Contributing shares

Contributing shares are issued at a price that's payable immediately along with a balance due by instalments at a future date. These future instalments are known as 'calls'. Contributing shares are rare nowadays and are usually issued by mining companies only.

Listed investment company shares

Listed investment companies (LICs) are companies that don't have a product of their own but aim to make a profit by owning and trading shares and securities in other businesses. Many have been in operation for a long time and include shares such as Argo Investments, Milton Corporation and Platinum Capital.

Buying shares in a listed investment company is an easy way of diversifying a portfolio. Although you own only one stock, you're really distributing your capital over a large number of different companies according to those the LIC has invested in. The downside is that you lose control of the mix of ownership and, because of administration and management expenses, your overall return is necessarily lower than that achievable from direct ownership of the same shares.

Company-issued options

These options are issued by companies and give the holder the right to acquire a certain number of fully paid shares at a stipulated price at any time in the future time up to a date limit known as the expiry date. Naturally, the options are not treated as shares until the options are taken up and converted to shares. The option holder is not obligated to take up the option, but options not taken up (exercised) by the expiry date become worthless.

It's important to realise that though the word 'option' is often used by itself, actually two different types of options are available. As well as company-issued options, there are exchange-traded options (ETOs), which are an investment instrument known as a 'derivative' (discussed later in this chapter).

Rights

After obtaining the initial equity capital needed when a business enterprise goes public and issues shares, the business may want to obtain further capital later on to fund expansion or to reduce debt. One way of doing this is to issue rights, which are similar to company-issued options except that the time period is usually shorter and rights are issued to existing shareholders only. The number of rights issued to each investor is in proportion to the number of shares already held, and the issue price is usually at an attractive discount to the current share price.

Bonus shares

Bonus shares are additional shares issued free of charge to existing shareholders in proportion to the number of shares held, as a kind of reward for them. This type of issue was once common but is now relatively rare.

Note

Rights, options and bonus issues and their implications for investors are discussed more fully in chapter 7.

International shares

With the trend toward globalisation, many securities exchanges throughout the world have linked trading facilities, so investors in any nation can place orders through their brokers to trade shares listed on an overseas exchange. Of course, currency exchange rates apply and the trading cost is usually relatively high but international investing opens the door to trading opportunities not available in Australia.

The Australian market tends to be strongly influenced by international markets (particularly the US market). You can understand why when you realise that Australian shares account for about 1.5% of the total world sharemarket. In recent times, the Microsoft Corporation in the United States had a higher value than the entire Australian stock market! Indeed, we are only small players!

Note

International investing has many complications, so unless you're a very experienced investor I suggest that you stay away from direct investing in international shares until you become confident and experienced. A much easier way of getting exposure to international shares is by means of an exchange traded fund or investment company that issues shares listed on an Australian exchange and that invests in international shares.

Sector groups

Shares can be classified according to the main type of business the share-issuing company is in. These are also known as *sectors*. The broadest sector groups are just two, namely:

- industrial

- resource (mining and oil).

These two sectors can be broken down into more precise groups and these are discussed in chapter 12.

Working with risk and potential

Shares can also be grouped according to market perceptions of the risk and potential associated with them. Some of the common ones are now outlined.

Blue chip shares

These shares are regarded as solid and low risk. The name derives from the fact that blue chips are the most valuable in a casino.

More specifically, the term *blue chip* applies to shares issued by a company that is relatively large, stable and well known, with very small risk of folding (going bankrupt). The products or services provided by the business have good market acceptance (high market share) and the business has a stable and reputable management history and has been in operation for some time. The business usually makes a good profit and rewards shareholders with significant payouts (usually in the form of dividends). Investors usually buy these shares and hold them for the long term.

Examples of blue chip shares are those issued by the major banks, listed investment companies, large retailers, property trusts and large miners such as BHP, Rio Tinto, and Woodside Petroleum.

Green chip shares

Green chip shares (also known as a *second liner* or *near blue chip*) are solid shares that don't quite qualify for blue chip status. The company is generally smaller than a blue chip one, or could be relatively new on the block or have products that don't yet have a high market acceptance. Naturally, investors perceive a higher risk with green chips than with blue chips but the benefit of taking the higher risk is that the potential returns can be higher.

Examples of green chips include shares in medium-sized companies that are operating profitably such as the smaller banks, smaller retailers and companies exploiting niche markets.

Fallen angel shares

A fallen angel is a company that was previously well regarded by investors (or was a blue chip), but has fallen on hard times and so the share price has dropped considerably from its former highs. The dilemma for investors is whether the shares will rise from the ashes and become blue chip again or whether the downturn will persist or perhaps even get worse.

Cyclical shares

These are shares in a company with profits (and share prices) that tend to cycle in phase with the market. That is, when the market is up cyclical shares do well, but when the market is down they do poorly. For example, shares issued by manufacturers and retailers of non-essential or luxury products generally fall into this category.

Defensive shares

Shares are considered to be defensive when they tend to be fairly immune from market fluctuations, generally because product demand isn't greatly affected by ups and downs in the economy (such as changes to interest rates or consumer demand). For example, a property trust generates its income from property rentals and these rentals tend to remain relatively stable even during periods of low economic growth.

Defensive stocks are usually of the blue-chip or green-chip type and may include major banks, infrastructure/utilities stocks, and suppliers/retailers of essential items such as food and energy. Also fixed-dividend preference shares and hybrid preference shares are considered to be defensive, because they tend not to closely follow market fluctuations.

Interestingly, alcohol and gambling stocks are usually considered to be defensive because consumers tend not to reduce spending on these products even when times are tough. Indeed, consumers may even increase spending in tough times.

Growth shares

Shares are considered to be in the growth category when investors perceive a high potential for growth in profitability and, therefore, in share price. That's to say, the business may not be particularly profitable at present but investors perceive blue sky potential because the business may be on the verge of a breakthrough in some new technology or may be expanding into significant new markets.

Growth shares usually have high price-to-earnings ratios (PEs), which means that they're expensive based on current profits. (I discuss PEs in detail in chapter 8.)

Volatile shares

Volatility in a share price (or in the market as a whole) is a measure of the extent of the fluctuations in price over a relatively short time period. This gives traders the potential to make significant short-term profits but there's also more risk and therefore a higher possibility of short-term losses.

Speculative shares

Speculative shares are regarded as the most risky because there's no established demand for the products of the business and, indeed, there may not be a saleable product at all. These shares are also known as *penny dreadfuls* because they're usually low in price (often in cents rather than dollars). Typically, the company operates at a loss and pays no dividend. Needless to say, the price often fluctuates considerably, so they're volatile and significant amounts may be made or lost by trading the shares. Trading is usually short-term for quick profits, rather than longer term investing as is more usual with blue chip, green chip or defensive types of shares.

Examples of speculative shares include small mining and resource shares, new technology shares, biotechs, and IPOs.

Note

The main reason you can make (or lose) significantly on speculative shares lies in simple mathematics. If you buy a share when the price is 10 cents and this rises by 10 cents, you make 100% profit on the trade. However, if a share price is $1, a price rise of 10 cents produces a profit margin of 10%, and if the share price is $10, a price rise of 10 cents gives a profit margin of only 1%. In other words, the higher a share price, the more the price must move in order to produce a significant gain (or loss).

Value shares

A share is considered to be good value when it's perceived to be trading at a discount to its true value. Perhaps the shares are unpopular or being overlooked by investors—usually because the potential for future profit growth seems low. Sometimes the business is seen as 'boring' and investors and traders are looking for more exciting prospects. Often value shares have a good dividend and are attractive to investors seeking dividend income. They usually have low PEs.

Liquid and illiquid shares

Liquidity is measured by the annual volume of shares traded as a percentage of the number of shares on issue, and it can be in the range of 20% to 100% or more annually. Liquid shares trade frequently (daily) with high trading volume. On the other hand, illiquid shares aren't traded frequently and turnover in share ownership is low—perhaps as low as 0.1% annually. Shares are usually illiquid when a high proportion of the shares are held by a small number of investors who don't trade them frequently. Illiquid shares are more risky because you may not be able to sell when you want to, and if you really want to sell you may have to accept a low price.

Note

More than one descriptor may apply to any particular share. For example, a fallen angel could also be a value share, a defensive share and a liquid share. A speculative share could also be a growth share, a cyclical share and a liquid share.

Trading shares and other securities

Trading is the act of buying or selling. For a trade to take place, both buyer and seller must agree exactly on the trade price and also the number of shares or securities that will change hands. If trading is active, the price may fluctuate from day to day and, indeed, within the course of a day while the exchange is open.

Notes

- Shares or other tradeable securities have no fixed value, since the price can fluctuate with each trade.

- I discuss trade prices and market forces driving prices in detail in chapter 5.

- Settlement for a transaction doesn't occur in real time (although this may be the case in the future). At the time of writing, settlement occurs after a two-working-day delay, or T+2. This means that when you trade, the transfer of ownership and cash automatically takes place two working days after the trade.

Theoretically you can trade shares or other securities in the same way as any other asset—that is, by direct negotiation with a willing buyer or seller. While some large value securities are traded in this way, it's generally difficult and inconvenient for most traders to direct trade and the most convenient and widely used method is to arrange the trade using a securities exchange. However, you need to be licensed to deal directly with the exchange and if you don't have this licence you need a licensed agent to act on your behalf and according to your instructions. These agents are known as *brokers*.

Notes

- You can transfer ownership of shares without trading them. If buyer and seller are known to one another, ownership transfer can occur by completing a transfer of ownership form obtainable from your broker. Most common ownership transfers occur in this way from one family member to another, or from a deceased estate to beneficiaries. Unless the transfer occurs as a result of a deceased estate, the transfer is regarded by the Australian Tax Office (ATO) as a capital gains tax event (discussed in detail in chapter 4).

- You can trade using a securities exchange facility only when the exchange is open for business.

Investors and traders

These descriptors are often used almost synonymously but an important distinction exists between investors and traders, which I discuss further in later chapters. Essentially, investors are looking for longer term wealth growth and invest for the longer haul, whereas traders aren't interested in longer term wealth growth but rather in making short-term trading profits by selling at a higher price than their original buy price.

Brokers and brokerage

By far the most common way shares (or other securities) are traded is by means of brokers, who are essentially agents acting on behalf of their clients. As well as transacting the trade, most brokers provide investing information and research. Naturally, brokers charge a fee for service according to a tiered fee structure and this fee is known as *brokerage*. Brokerage depends on the value of the trade and also on the level of service provided by the broker. The level of service can vary from trading only (no advice) to full advice and management of a client's portfolio.

Nowadays many brokers offer an internet service where no personal contact occurs and trades are conducted electronically without human intervention. This has several advantages including reduced brokerage and faster and easier order placement. If you want further information about online investing, please refer to my book *Online Investing on the Australian Sharemarket*.

Parcel and portfolio

A parcel is a distinct lot of shares. For example, you could decide to buy a parcel of 1000 shares in Woolworths. Later you might decide to sell 500 of them. In this case, you would be selling a parcel of 500 and still holding a parcel of 500 shares of Woolworths.

A portfolio is the total shareholding of an investor. It's a list of each stock owned and the number of shares in each that are held. The total value of a portfolio is obtained by multiplying the number of shares by the market price of each share and then adding all the values. Because share prices constantly change as trades transact, portfolio value is a 'snapshot' and is valid only at a certain point in time.

Securities exchanges

A securities exchange is essentially a business that is set up for trading securities that are listed with them. In order for a business enterprise to be listed, it needs to comply with the exchange's listing rules and pay a listing fee. To then remain listed, the business must continue complying with the rules and paying an ongoing fee.

Notes

- In this book, I might refer to 'market', 'stock market' or 'sharemarket', but each of these means the same and I'm not trying to make any distinction between them.

- Listed companies must comply with regulations at all times and if any doubts about breaches exist, the company can be suspended from listing. For serious breaches, a company can be delisted, either temporarily or permanently. Enforced delisting can also occur if a company fails to pay fees or becomes insolvent (bankrupt). Voluntary delisting for a short time period (one or two days) can also take place at the request of the directors—usually because some major change is about to be announced and the directors are trying to prevent speculative trading on rumours until the matter's official. Any type of trading suspension is also known as a *trading halt* because the stock can't be traded during this time, regardless of the reason for the suspension.

- For the ASX, trading hours at the time of writing are 10 am to 4 pm on business days.

- Not all public companies or investment products are listed on a securities exchange. In this case, the trading of shares and share-ownership arrangements are organised by the business itself.

The main securities exchanges operating in Australia at the time of writing are covered in the following sections.

Australian Securities Exchange (ASX)

This is by far the most popular securities exchange and it usually has the shares of about 2000 companies listed with it. The ASX operates in

Australia and has offices in Sydney, Melbourne and Perth. It facilitates trading in most types of securities, including shares, options, warrants and futures. The ASX is not just a trading facility but also provides a great deal of information in areas such as share prices, company information, company announcements and investor education, so it is a good source of financial information for investors (or potential investors). Interestingly, the ASX was originally a cooperative but is now a listed company, which means it's listed on its own stock exchange!

National Stock Exchange of Australia (NSX)

This exchange was set up to cater more specifically for smaller types of businesses. Not all brokers are licensed with this exchange so if you want to trade any securities listed with it you need to ensure the broker is licensed with the exchange. The exchange's website provides a list of securities listed and the brokers licensed to trade.

Chi-X Australia

This is the most recent exchange licensed in Australia which operates its own trading system independent to the ASX and provides trading in Australian equities, ETFs, indices, funds and warrants as well as global shares. Other brokers such as CommSec may (at their discretion) send orders to Chi-X for execution as they seek the best possible price obtainable for a trade.

Note

In some cases, a business may choose to list its shares on several exchanges. For example, some shares listed on the New Zealand exchange are also listed with the ASX. In this case, you can trade shares in a New Zealand business by placing orders with the Australian exchange.

Codes

In order to make the referencing and listing of securities easier, each share or investment instrument is designated with a unique code. This code can be a simple three-letter one—for example, WOW for Woolworths and CBA for Commonwealth Bank. For other financial instruments such as preference shares, options (company issued and ETOs) and warrants, the code may be up to six letters. In addition to letters, sometimes numbers are also used in the code.

Notes

- It is a good idea to keep a list of the codes for all shares or securities you own or are interested in.

- You can obtain these codes from many websites (including the ASX site), and your broker should also have them.

Trading method

In the past, trading securities occurred on a noisy trading floor as brokers negotiated prices and reached agreement on trades. Today, most exchanges use a fully computerised system that operates according to a program without human intervention but some countries still have exchanges where trading is conducted on a trading floor by brokers.

The use of a fully computerised transparent trading system presents a huge advantage for small investors with access to the internet. It provides a level playing field where anyone can obtain up-to-date share trading and investing information. A small investor working from home can obtain the same information and trade on an equal basis with a large broking firm in the city with a large number of expert staff and millions of dollars of investment capital!

Bulls and bears

A bull market occurs when the market as a whole is rising because more buyers than sellers are active. The buyers driving up the prices are known as *bulls*. Conversely a falling market is known as a *bear market* and the sellers driving prices down are known as *bears*. Incidentally, no-one is exactly sure how these terms came into use, but one explanation is that bulls strike up with their horns whereas bears hit down with their paws.

Volume

Volume is a measure of the trading activity for an individual share or for the market as a whole. It can be measured by the number of securities traded or the value of those securities. Volume is usually measured each day up to the current time but after trading for the day ceases. In this case, the volume is known as the *daily volume*. When a trade occurs, each buyer of a share requires a corresponding seller, so shares volume is the number of shares bought or the number of shares sold, because these two numbers must be exactly equal. Also, when there's a trade, the buy and sell price are the same for that trade, so a trade can't take place unless buyers and sellers agree on both price and volume for that parcel.

Note

Shares volume is not the sum of the shares bought and the shares sold.

Understanding other types of securities

Apart from the shares I've described, a large number of different types of securities (investment instruments) are accessible to investors.

These include:

- trusts
- managed funds
- stapled securities
- bonds
- derivatives
- contracts for difference (CFDs).

Note

Because this book is primarily about shares, I discuss only the most common types of securities closely allied to shares.

Trusts

Business trusts aren't companies (or corporations) in the sense that they don't have a separate legal identity (body corporate). They're set up by trust deed and are controlled by trustees on behalf of the beneficiaries. Rather than issuing shares, the assets of the trust are divided up into a certain number of units of equal value. Common types of business trusts include property trusts and cash management trusts. Under current Australian taxation law, trusts don't pay tax on profits distributed to unit holders, so the dividend from a trust is unfranked. (Franked and unfranked dividends are discussed in chapter 4.)

Some trusts are listed and traded on securities exchanges, so market forces determine the price of units for these trusts in the same way as for shares. From an investor's point of view, units in a listed trust are really no different from shares except for the different taxation implications on distributed profits. However, the majority of business trusts operating in Australia aren't listed, and in order to invest in one of these, you need to fill out an application form in the prospectus (as you would for an IPO). In this case, the buy and sell (cash in–out) price of the units is determined daily by the trust according to the value of its investments.

Note

Many family trusts are also set up in Australia but these are not business trusts because they involve personal relationships.

Managed funds

Managed funds are very similar to unit trusts. They're usually set up and controlled by large banks, insurance companies or investment companies. You usually have to invest a minimum amount first but after that you may be able to add to the amount on a regular basis. Some managed funds are listed but the majority aren't. In order to invest in an unlisted fund, you need to complete the application form in the prospectus.

When a managed fund is listed, it is known as an *exchange-traded fund* (ETF). Then you can buy or sell the units just like listed shares or trusts, with the buy and sell prices governed by market forces. When the fund is unlisted, the buy and sell price of units (cash in–out price) is based upon day-to-day valuations of the fund's assets.

The attraction of managed funds is that financial 'experts' manage the funds and your investment capital is spread among various securities, providing in-built diversification. Also you can invest in ventures not readily accessible otherwise, such as global resources or companies operating in developing economies. The downside is that you lose direct control of your investment and ongoing management fees reduce your investment return. These fees are usually calculated as an annual management expense ratio (MER). Entry or exit fees could also be charged for non-tradeable funds.

Stapled securities

In some cases, businesses are split into separate entities. For example, a property trust may be split into the holding company (which owns the properties) and the management company (which manages the business on a day-to-day basis and pursues development opportunities). However, for trading purposes, the separate entities are combined into a single tradeable instrument known as a *stapled security*. For an investor, the only difference between a stapled security and an ordinary share or unit is that the taxation treatment of each entity comprising the stapled security is usually different.

Bonds

Many governments throughout the world periodically issue bonds as a means of raising additional capital to fund government projects. Bonds pay a fixed interest that is a certain percentage of the face value of the bonds. The face value is the initial value of the bonds but is adjusted according to movements in the consumer price index (CPI). This means that if the CPI goes down, the bonds will be worth less but if it goes up, they will be worth more. In Australia, Commonwealth Government–issued bonds are guaranteed by the government and are therefore considered to be a very safe investment.

If you are interested in investing in government bonds, you can do so using the ASX trading facility to trade exchange-traded treasury bonds.

As well as government bonds, some companies issue corporate bonds. These are essentially a fixed-interest loan but, unlike government bonds, they are not government guaranteed and therefore carry more risk. The advantage is that their value doesn't fluctuate like the share price and so they provide a more stable investment. These bonds can be traded directly on the Australian Bond Exchange (ABX).

Derivatives

A derivative is a tradeable investment instrument that doesn't have an intrinsic value of its own but derives its value from some other underlying instrument or commodity. Apart from exchange-traded options (ETOs), the most common type of traded derivatives are warrants and futures contracts. These are rather similar in concept to ETOs but are available in many different types, tailored for many different investor requirements.

The many types of derivatives and the trading of them is outside the scope of this book, but bear in mind that they're considered high-risk and generally traded only by experienced investors. This is because derivatives provide leverage or gearing for a trade—meaning you can make or lose more by trading the derivative rather than the underlying instrument. In common parlance, this is called 'getting more bang for your trading buck'. In the past, the Sydney Futures Exchange (SFE) was the specific exchange for derivative trading, but this exchange was taken over by the ASX so many derivatives can be traded on the ASX.

Contracts for difference (CFDs)

Another popular way of gearing your trades is by trading CFDs rather than shares. When you trade a CFD, you don't actually buy or sell shares; rather, you enter (or open) a contract with a CFD provider to buy or sell the shares. The shares may or may not be physically traded by the CFD provider, depending on their trading model. Some time later, you close the contract with a contra-transaction, and the difference between the opening and closing value of the contract (less fees and charges) is your profit or loss on the deal—hence the term *contract for difference*.

A great advantage of CFD trading is that most CFD providers allow a high level of gearing—usually as high as 10:1 but possibly as high as 20:1. A 10:1 level of gearing allows you to trade shares with a value of up to $100000 with only $10000 of your own capital! Another significant advantage of CFD trading is that you can profit in falling markets because you can open a CFD contract to sell shares you haven't bought. Then you close the contract some time later with a contract to buy those shares. If the share price falls between the contract opening and closing periods, you make a profit from the fall.

While all this sounds like a great deal, you need to be aware that the risk is magnified by the same amount as the extent of your gearing. That's great if you get it right but not so good if you get it wrong! Also CFD providers charge interest daily on the full value of outstanding buy contracts and there may also be a significantly higher trading cost.

Notes

- Because of the higher costs and level of risk with CFD trading, it's usually not recommended for anyone other than experienced traders.

- Since this book is written at a basic level, I won't go into CFD trading in any further detail.

Looking at the practical aspects of share ownership in Australia

Share ownership is an example of Pareto's principle (also known as the 80/20 rule) because a small number of large investors own a large number of shares whereas a large number of small investors own a small number of shares. The large investors are typically institutions such as investment companies, trusts and superannuation companies, which invest the funds contributed by their members. Also, directors are usually major shareholders in their own companies and hold large parcels of shares. The small investors are often known as 'mum and dad' investors and may include ordinary Australians who dabble in shares, others who receive shares from a deceased estate and self-funded retirees who invest in shares. Also, some companies reward their employees with shares rather than cash so these employees become shareholders. In many cases, these shareholders may be 'passive' investors because they tend to hold onto their shares and seldom trade (if at all).

The following sections discuss some of the practical aspects of owning shares in Australia.

Share registry

A share registry maintains a record of shareholders in a stock, the number of shares held by them and personal information such as addresses and tax file numbers. These records are used when dividends and company information is distributed. A few of the larger companies maintain their own share registries, but in most cases listed companies contract the work out to a specialist share registry, such as Computershare, Link Market Services or Boardroom.

Note

If you have a query about your dividend or other shareholder information, you need to contact the share registry, not the company itself.

Issuer and dealer sponsorship

When you become a shareholder, your shareholding can be recorded in one of two ways: issuer or dealer sponsorship.

Issuer sponsorship

Issuer sponsorship was the original method, and while it's sometimes used today it is becoming increasingly rare. The share registry (issuer) allocates a shareholder reference number (SRN), which will be the same for all the shares you hold in that stock but different for each different stock you own. If you decide to sell any shares, you'll need to quote the SRN when you place your order.

Dealer sponsorship

This popular method uses the Clearing House Electronic Sub-register System (CHESS). Individual shareholders can't deal directly with CHESS (a subsidiary of the ASX) so you have to be sponsored. The sponsor (or dealer) is usually your broker and both online and offline brokers give you the option of using the CHESS system if you become a customer. You're then given a unique holder identification number (HIN), which will apply to all shares you hold under CHESS with that sponsor. Should your share holding change because you trade those shares or are issued additional shares by the company, you will be issued with a new CHESS statement (however, there may be some time delay).

CHESS has two main advantages. These are:

1. *Once you know your HIN, you can start to trade.* If you're not in CHESS, you can't sell shares you've bought until you know your SRN and it could take several weeks before the share registry advises you of your SRN. This is a great disadvantage if you're trading speculative shares or want to sell shares quickly after you've bought them.

2. *If you trade through the same broker, you've only one number to keep track of rather than having a different SRN for each stock.* You don't even have to quote this number when you sell, because your broker knows your HIN.

Notes

-   As the CHESS system is free, I suggest you join it.

-   If you hold any SRN registered shares, you can easily transfer them into CHESS by contacting your sponsoring broker. Usually no fee is involved and it's not considered a capital gains tax event.

-   If you're using the CHESS system, you can't sell shares using a different broker from the one you used to purchase the shares because your HIN will be different. However, you can easily transfer shares from one broker to another if you wish to do so. Again, you need to contact your sponsoring broker.

Board of directors

In public companies, it's clearly impossible to obtain a consensus of all shareholders on major decisions, so it's necessary to have a board of directors whose primary function is to look after the interests of the shareholders. The board meets regularly (usually once a month) and is made up mostly of part-time members who are often well-known and respected citizens. Often, part-time board members serve on various company boards. A board member may also be full-time manager—for example, the managing director and chief executive officer (CEO). The most senior executive of the board is the chairperson of the board, who chairs meetings and acts as the company's official spokesperson.

As well as making any major decisions, the board appoints the company's executives and other senior managers responsible for the day-to-day operation of the business.

Corporation laws and exchange regulations

All businesses in Australia must comply with corporation laws. These laws are designed to protect the public at large and shareholders from fraud and corruption, as well as ensuring there's fair competition and that all necessary records are kept by corporations. The law is administered by the Australian Securities and Investments Commission (ASIC), which will investigate any alleged fraud or breach of corporation law and prosecute if warranted.

Securities exchanges also have their own listing rules and regulations that aim to prevent unscrupulous business practices. For example, in order to avoid what's known as *insider trading*, the ASX requires that any information (other than commercially confidential information) must be announced to the ASX prior to being released to the press or made public. In theory, this should guarantee that everyone can access the same information at the same time, but in practice insider trading is notoriously difficult to stamp out completely.

The ASX oversees market activity and will query any trading that appears out of the ordinary or suspect—for example, when a share price suddenly rises or falls significantly without any obvious justification. The ASX also keeps tabs on brokers and any broker found to be in breach of ASX rules can be fined or stripped of their trading rights.

Company meetings

All companies are required by law to hold a meeting of all shareholders at least once a year, and this meeting is known as an annual general meeting (AGM). At this meeting the shareholders vote to elect the directors and to vote on any matters that require their approval—including directors' remuneration. In addition to the AGM, companies are required to hold shareholder meetings when any major change is proposed to the company structure or nature of its business.

At company shareholder meetings, the principle of one share, one vote applies, so majority shareholders have far more say and sway than small investors. Depending on where the company is located, company meetings could be held at venues and at times that are inconvenient to the majority of smaller investors, so company meetings are usually attended by only a small number of shareholders. However, shareholders can exercise a proxy vote by authorising someone else to vote on their behalf.

Note

The Australian Shareholders' Association acts to protect the rights of member shareholders, and will attend meetings and vote on behalf of members if given the authority to do so.

Company takeovers, mergers and splits

A *takeover* occurs when one company (the predator) acquires the majority of the shares (51% or more) in another company and thus obtains control of it.

A *merger* occurs when two companies merge—that is, join forces to form a single corporation rather than competing with one another.

A *split* occurs when a company decides to separate into separate corporations—usually because the directors feel that the nature of some of the enterprises within the business aren't sufficiently related and would be more profitable if they operated independently of one another.

Notes

- Often when a company is taken over, the original company name is abandoned. However, when there's good brand identification or customer loyalty, the same name may be used, even though the company may be a subsidiary of the predator.

- Generally speaking, when a takeover is in the offing, the share price of the company being taken over will usually rise, whereas the price of the predator may fall. The reason is that in order to obtain director approval for the takeover, the predator has to offer a higher price than the current market price.

- Takeovers are described as 'friendly' when the directors of each company negotiate the takeover and reach agreement. If no such agreement is in place, the takeover is 'unfriendly' or 'hostile'.

- Takeovers and mergers require shareholder approval and are overseen by ASIC, which tends to oppose them if they believe the result will be reduced competition and increased price for consumers. Also, unions may oppose them on the basis of likely job losses for their members.

- Often, the company code changes when a company takeover, merger or split occurs.

- Mergers and splits of the shares issued by a company can also occur and shouldn't be confused with company mergers and splits. I discuss these in some detail in chapter 7.

- Companies can legally own shares in other companies and, indeed, companies can also buy back their own shares either directly from shareholders or on the open market.

Before moving on ...

I strongly suggest that before moving on to the next chapter you attempt the learning exercises that follow. They'll enable you to assess your comprehension of what was covered in this chapter and will help to reinforce your knowledge. To obtain maximum benefit from the learning exercises, you should attempt to answer them without referring to the solutions provided at the end of this chapter, and so avoid the temptation to compare my solution with yours.

Learning exercises

1.1 Generally speaking, even in capitalistic economies, some business enterprises are government owned and not available for ownership by investors. Why is this so, and what type of business enterprises might you expect to be government owned? What benefits do you see from investor rather than government ownership?

1.2 What are the two main ways a business enterprise can obtain capital and what are the main advantages and disadvantages of each?

1.3 What is the difference between a share and a stock?

1.4 What do the following acronyms or abbreviations stand for?

AGM, ASIC, ASX, ATO, CEO, CFD, CHESS, ETF, ETO, FPO, HIN, IPO, LIC, LTD, NL, PTY LTD, MER, SRN

1.5 Why do you think the public cannot place orders directly with the ASX and why must all orders be placed through a broker?

1.6 When you become a shareholder in a company, what four important aspects of the business do you share with other shareholders?

1.7 I own 1674 shares in a listed company at a time when the number of shares on issue is 1058548613. What is my proportion of the ownership of the business?

1.8 If a listed company issues more shares, what effect should this have on the price? Conversely, if the company buys back shares and removes them from circulation, what effect should this have on the price?

1.9 The ASX uses a fully computerised and transparent trading system that ensures all information and announcements are accessible to everyone at the same time. What benefit does this provide to small investors?

1.10 What advantages and disadvantages do you see in a listed company issuing a large number of shares of low value rather than a small number of shares of large value?

1.11 What advantages and disadvantages are there of buying shares in a listed investment company or a managed fund rather than buying shares directly?

1.12 What are the two main advantages and disadvantages of trading CFDs rather than shares?

1.13 Why should a prudent investor consider IPOs generally as speculative?

1.14 Why can't you buy shares in Bunnings Warehouse? What is the only way you can share in the profits of Bunnings?

1.15 What circumstances do you think may cause directors of a listed company to seek temporary voluntary delisting?

1.16 Generally speaking, when a takeover is proposed the share price of the taken-over company will rise, whereas the price of the predator falls. Why is this so?

1.17 What's meant by 'insider trading' and how does the ASX try to stamp it out?

1.18 Complete the following table, showing how to invest in and how the price is determined for the four entities shown.

Trust/fund	How to invest in	Price
Unit trust (unlisted)		
Unit trust (listed)		
Managed fund (unlisted)		
Managed fund (listed)		

Learning exercises solutions

1.1　Generally speaking, large essential services deemed to be in the national interest are government owned and controlled. Examples include postal services, energy production, defence and water conservation. Usually, investor ownership produces benefits in the form of higher efficiency and reduced costs by eliminating bureaucracy and streamlining the management structure. Also because of the motivational aspects, investor ownership usually results in productivity gains and this is one of the main reasons socialism and government ownership has declined.

1.2　The two main ways of obtaining capital are loan capital and equity capital.

The advantages and disadvantages for loan capital are:

» *Advantages:* Doesn't require conformance with legal restrictions or set-up costs, and can be obtained quickly. Doesn't dilute shareholder returns.

» *Disadvantages:* Loans require asset backing (collateral) and regular interest payments. This places the business at risk if loan repayments cannot be met.

For equity capital:

» *Advantages:* No loan repayments are involved and there is no risk of not being able to meet interest obligations.

» *Disadvantages:* Lengthy set-up time is involved, many legal procedures need to be met and these are costly. Also, the more shares that are issued, the more each shareholder's return is diluted.

1.3　A share is the smallest unit of the division of ownership of a business enterprise. A stock is the total of all the shares issued by that enterprise and is also the total shareholding of an investor in that enterprise.

1.4   The acronyms or abbreviations stand for the following:

» *AGM:* annual general meeting

» *ASIC:* Australian Securities and Investments Commission

» *ASX:* Australian Securities Exchange

» *ATO:* Australian Tax Office

» *CEO:* chief executive officer

» *CFD:* contract for difference

» *CHESS:* Clearing House Electronic Sub-register System

» *ETF:* exchange-traded fund

» *ETO:* exchange-traded option

» *FPO:* fully paid ordinary (share)

» *HIN:* holder identification number

» *IPO:* initial public offering (float)

» *LIC:* listed investment company

» *LTD:* Limited (liability)

» *NL:* no liability

» *PTY LTD:* Proprietary Limited

» *MER:* management expense ratio

» *SRN:* shareholder reference number

1.5   Because there are so many small shareholders, it would be extremely difficult for the ASX to ensure the bona fides of each of them and to ensure that they had sufficient available funds to trade. Instead, orders are placed through a small number of licensed brokers and each broker deals directly with their own clients.

1.6   The four main aspects you share are:

» profits (and losses)

» risks

» ownership (assets and liabilities)

» management.

1.7 I own 0.00016% of the business.

1.8 If more shares are issued, the share price is likely to fall in proportion, whereas if shares are bought back, the share price is likely to rise.

1.9 This means small investors can compete with large investors on a level playing field. The computerised system ensures that no preference is given to large investors' orders.

1.10 Advantages:

» Greater flexibility for investors—investors can vary the extent of their equity by varying the number of shares held.

» More capital can be raised because small investors (with relatively small amounts of capital) can also invest.

» Greater flexibility of trading—large or small parcels can be traded.

Disadvantages:

» More difficult (and costly) to keep track of all shareholders and their holdings and to provide reports and other documents.

» More difficult to obtain consensus decisions from all shareholders.

1.11 Advantages are diversification and spreading of the risks by buying only one stock, and having 'experts' manage the investment.

Disadvantages are loss of control and payment of management expense and overhead costs that reduce investment returns.

1.12 The two main advantages are very high gearing is possible, and profits can be made when prices fall and not just when they rise. The two main disadvantages are high level of risk, and increased costs through high trading costs and interest payments being levied.

1.13   A prudent investor should consider most IPOs as speculative because if the venture is a new one there is no track record, and performance projections are based upon predictions, which can be overly optimistic. Even if the company has previously been trading successfully as a private company, there's no guarantee that it will continue to do so after floating. History shows that many companies have not made a success of the conversion from a private to a public company.

1.14   Bunnings Warehouse is not a publicly listed company so shares are not available to the general public. They are a fully owned subsidiary of Wesfarmers so the only way you can get a slice of the action at Bunnings is to become a Wesfarmers shareholder.

1.15   Voluntary delisting is usually requested when major changes are afoot and a lot of speculation and rumours are circulating about them. The board tries to prevent profiteering on the basis of these rumours and thus requests delisting until an official announcement has been released to the ASX.

1.16   The predator usually has to buy the shares at a higher price than the current market price in order to obtain director and shareholder approval for the takeover. Hence, the price of the company being taken over usually rises. The price of the predator usually falls because they need to fund the acquisition and pay a relatively high price for the acquisition. However, if the market takes the long-term view that the takeover will result in greater market share and rationalisation, the price may rise—if not immediately, then at some point after the takeover.

1.17   Insider trading occurs when someone tries to make profitable trades from information they have that's not available to the general market. The ASX attempts to stamp out the practice by ensuring that all information released by a listed company must first be given to the ASX and then released by them so that all investors have access to it at the same time. Also, the ASX monitors share prices and director trades and requires explanation of any sudden price jumps or falls that are not explainable by company announcements. In addition, in times of major changes that could affect share prices, trading is halted so no-one can benefit (or get hurt) by trading during this period.

1.18 See the following completed table.

Trust/fund	How to invest in	Price
Unit trust (unlisted)	By filling out the application form in the prospectus and making payment arrangements	Set by the trust based on the day-to-day valuation of its assets
Unit trust (listed)	By purchasing units using the ASX trading facility	Set by market forces of supply and demand
Managed fund (unlisted)	By filling out the application form in the prospectus and making payment arrangements	Set by the fund based on the day-to-day valuation of its assets
Managed fund (listed)	By purchasing units using the ASX trading facility	Set by market forces of supply and demand

Chapter 2

Understanding the basics of investing

In this chapter, I discuss the basics of investing that apply to investing in general. In later chapters, I focus on shares investing in particular.

Making a profit from your investment

You can profit from an investment in two ways:

1. capital gain

2. income.

Capital gain

Capital gain (or loss) is the difference in the value of your investment at a later point in time compared to the investment's initial value (after trading costs have been deducted). For example, if you buy 5000 shares for $1.00 each and sell them later when the price has risen to $1.20, you've made a capital gain of $0.20 per share or $1000 total capital gain profit (excluding trading costs). However, if the shares go down in price and you sell them for $0.80, you've made a capital loss of $0.20 per share or a total capital loss of $1000 (again, excluding trading costs).

It's important to note that capital gains (or losses) are unrealised or paper gains or losses until the selling transaction occurs. This is why some traders or investors hold onto losing investments for too long—because they do not have to come to terms with the loss until the sale occurs.

Income

In many cases, an investment will produce ongoing or recurring income that you receive on a regular basis. With an investment account, this income is interest on the balance of the account, with property it's rental income and with shares it's most commonly dividends.

Total profit

The total profit on your investment is the sum of the capital gain and the investment income. Not all investments produce both these types of profit. The three variations are:

1. income but no capital gain

2. capital gain but no income

3. capital gain and income.

Income but no capital gain

If you invest in a bank account or any other type of cash account, you receive investment income but no capital gain because at the end of the investment period you get back only what you originally put in.

Capital gain but no income

If you buy a block of land, you may make a capital gain but you receive no investment income (unless you're able to rent the land). In fact, your investment income is usually negative—that is, an outgoing cost because you have expenses you need to pay in order to keep the land. If you buy some non-dividend paying shares, you also have the possibility of capital gain but receive no income. However, unlike real estate no holding costs are associated with shares.

Capital gain and income

If you buy a rental property or dividend-paying shares, you receive regular income and also have the possibility of capital gain. In this case, you can get a double whammy profit on the investment.

Evaluating profitability of an investment

The profitability of an investment can be looked at (or evaluated) in two ways. These are:

1. cash profit

2. return on capital invested.

Cash profit

Cash profit is the dollar profit. Four different cash profit figures are actually used:

1. before-tax profit

2. after-tax profit

3. real (inflation-adjusted) profit before tax

4. real (inflation-adjusted) profit after tax.

When you are looking at profit statistics, it is important to ascertain which of these profit figures apply. The before-tax profit is the raw or gross profit, whereas the after-tax profit is the profit after any tax payable has been deducted. The real or inflation-adjusted profit is the profit adjusted for inflation, so (as the name suggests) it's the real profit in terms of purchasing power. (I'll go into these in somewhat greater depth shortly.)

Capital invested

Before discussing return on capital invested, it's important to understand the true meaning of capital invested. At first sight, it seems to be a relatively simple concept but, in fact, it's often misinterpreted. To clarify, consider the situation where you open a term deposit with a bank and deposit $100 000 in the account. You receive regular interest payments, which you spend. Some years later, you close the account and get your $100 000 back. Clearly, your invested capital was $100 000 and it didn't change over the term of the investment.

Suppose, however, that instead of a term investment, you invest $100 000 in shares. Some years later, the price has risen and those shares are now worth $200 000. How much capital do you have invested in those shares?

You could argue that you invested $100 000 in the shares and, since you didn't add to or reduce that amount, that's your capital invested. This would give you the return on initial capital invested. Although this is often calculated and stated in this way, this gives you a false picture. Your capital invested in those shares is now actually $200 000 because that's their current worth and what you would receive if you sold them. Therefore, when the value of an investment changes with time, the capital invested also changes.

Example

A friend tells you he bought an investment property 10 years ago and his rental return is currently averaging 8%. You query further and discover he calculates this the following way:

- My net rental income per year (after all costs are deducted) is $16 000

- The original purchase price of the property (including costs) was $200 000

- Therefore my rental return is: $\dfrac{16\,000}{200\,000} \times 100 = 8\%$

Can you spot any flaws in his calculation?

The flaw is that the 8% annual return your friend calculated is based on the original property value some years ago, whereas the rental income is the current rental income. He's dividing apples by oranges! In order to obtain the true current return, your friend needs to compare apples with apples and use the current property value.

When you query further, your friend tells you that the current property value is $400 000. Therefore his current rental return is 4%, because that figure is based on the current rental and the current property value.

So you can see that with any investment if the value of the investment changes (as it does with property and shares) it's misleading to calculate current return on capital using the original capital invested.

Average annual capital invested

When the value of an investment changes with time, it's clearly not correct to use the initial value of the capital invested. It's also not logical to use the final value because that doesn't truly represent the amount of capital that's been invested over the term of the investment. I think the best compromise is to use the average value, that is:

$$\frac{\left(\text{Initial value} + \text{final value}\right)}{2}$$

Return on capital invested

Imagine a friend tells you 'I've made $10000 profit on my shares this year'. You may think this sounds very good but, in fact, this figure doesn't give you the true picture of the profitability of their share investing. To get the full picture, you need to know the return on capital invested. This is the profit per annum divided by the capital invested and expressed as a percentage; that is:

$$\text{Return on capital invested} = \frac{\text{Annual profit}}{\text{Capital invested}} \times 100$$

So if the capital invested by your friend in shares is $50000, the return on capital for the year is an excellent 20%. However, if the capital invested is $250000, the same dollar profit represents a return of 4%, which isn't nearly as good.

Notes

- Return on capital invested is often shortened and referred to as 'return on capital' or even simply 'return'.
- An astute investor always thinks of profitability in terms of the percentage return on capital invested, not just dollar profit.

As profit can be stated in one of four ways, return on capital depends on what profit figure is used and can be:

- before-tax profit
- after-tax profit
- real (inflation-adjusted) profit before tax
- real (inflation-adjusted) profit after tax.

As previously discussed, because return on capital depends on which profit figure is used, it is important to know this when looking at statistics. Also, as I stated previously, capital invested can be interpreted in three ways:

- initial value of capital invested
- final value of capital invested
- average value of capital invested.

So you can see that return on capital invested has 12 possible interpretations, depending on which type of profit and which capital invested figures are used! I believe the most realistic capital invested value is the average annual return on capital.

Average annual return on capital

The average annual return on capital is the annual profit divided by the average capital invested and converted to a percentage; that is:

$$\text{Average annual return on capital} = \frac{\text{Annual profit}}{\text{Average capital invested}} \times 100$$

Note

Bear in mind that when calculating the average annual return on capital, you need to be clear on which type of profit is used.

Equivalent annual return on capital

In some cases, the time period of the investment may be less than one year. Because return on capital is calculated on an annual basis, you can use an equivalent annual return. You can calculate your profit over the term of the investment and then convert it to an equivalent annual return using the following formula:

$$\text{Equivalent return on capital} = \frac{\text{Profit} \times 52 \times 100}{\text{Average capital invested} \times \text{weeks held}}$$

Notes

- To get a more precise measure, you can base equivalent annual return on the number of days rather than weeks but it is usually sufficiently accurate to use the number of weeks or even the number of months.

- Another way of calculating the equivalent annual return is to calculate the percentage return and then adjust it for the length of time of the investment. This is illustrated in the example that follows.

Example

You buy some shares for a total cost (including brokerage) of $8430. You hold them for 32 weeks and then sell them for a net value of $9820. What was your equivalent annual return on this transaction?

$$\text{Your average capital invested} \quad = \quad \frac{(\$8430 + \$9820)}{2}$$

$$= \quad \$9125$$

$$\text{Your net profit} \quad = \quad \$9820 - \$8430$$

$$= \quad \$1390$$

$$\text{Your equivalent annual return} \quad = \quad \frac{\$1390 \times 52 \times 100}{\$9125 \times 32}$$

$$= \quad \textbf{24.75\%}$$

Note

Another way of calculating the equivalent annual return is as follows:

Raw return $= \left(\$1390 \div \$9125\right) \times 100 = 15.23\%$

Equivalent annual return $= 15.23 \times \left(52 \div 32\right) = \textbf{24.75}\%$

Growing your wealth

The basic principle of growing your wealth is this:

In order to grow your wealth, the after-tax return on your investment must be greater than the inflation rate.

It follows that if the after-tax return on your investment is lower than the inflation rate, your wealth is reducing.

Another way of stating this principle is:

In order to grow your wealth, the after-tax, inflation-adjusted return on your investment must be positive (greater than zero).

You need to consider four factors in any investment that can reduce profitability. They are:

1. in/out costs

2. holding costs

3. tax

4. inflation.

In/out costs

These are the costs associated with getting into the investment and getting out of it (if and when you decide to do so). With property, these costs are relatively high and include agent's fees and commission, stamp duty, legal costs and search costs. For this reason, property investing tends to be a longer term proposition.

With shares, the in/out costs are far lower and usually involve brokerage only. With online brokers, brokerage can be as low as 0.1% or 0.2% of the parcel value, and because buying and selling can be done so quickly, short-term trading in shares is very common.

Holding costs

Holding costs are ongoing or recurring costs associated with holding an investment. With property, these costs are usually very significant and include mortgage and interest charges, council rates and fees, insurance, property depreciation and maintenance, agent's fees and land taxes. These costs can reduce the income so much that the investment may become an outgoing expense rather than one producing an income. When this occurs it's known as *negative gearing*.

One of the great benefits of share investing is that there are usually no holding costs at all (unless you've taken out a loan of some type to buy shares), so negative gearing with shares is not nearly as common as it is with investment property.

Tax on profit

Tax payable on profit reduces the investment return because it's money that's taken out of profits at tax time and received by the ATO. The tax implications of share investing are detailed in chapter 4, so I won't discuss them further here.

Inflation

Cash has virtually no intrinsic value and has value only because of purchasing power. Inflation decreases the purchasing power of money and, therefore, reduces profitability in terms of what a cash profit will buy in goods and services. So when trying to grow your wealth, you need to consider how inflation will erode the after-tax return on your invested capital. As mentioned, the after-tax return on investment after inflation is known as the *real* return or sometimes the *inflation-adjusted* return. It's what you're really getting in terms of purchasing power.

For instance, suppose you're receiving an after-tax return of 3% on an investment at a time when the inflation rate is also 3%. This means that your real return is zero and your wealth isn't growing. Indeed, the capital you've invested is just marking time. However, if your return on capital is 3% before tax and you have to pay tax on the profits, then your real return after tax is negative and, in fact, your wealth is reducing rather than increasing.

Considering investment risks

It's important to consider the risks involved with any investment because risk and return are fundamentally related. Share investing risks are treated in detail in chapter 13 but I'll introduce the basics now.

Risk applies to both capital gains and income.

Capital gains risk

This is the risk that your investment may not increase in value and, rather, could reduce. The very worst-case scenario is that you could lose all the money you've invested; that is, you lose all your invested capital.

Income risk

This is the risk that your investment may not produce the expected income. For example, with an investment property, it's the risk that the tenant may default on rental payments; with shares, it's the risk that if company profits reduce, the directors may decide to reduce (or eliminate) the dividend.

Relationship between risk and return

A general principle that applies to all investments is that investors relate risk and return in the following way:

The higher the perceived risk, the greater the potential return.

Or expressed another way:

The lower the perceived risk, the lower the potential return.

I use the word *perceived* with risk because it depends on investors' perceptions of riskiness and this may not necessarily reflect the real risk. And I use the word *potential* with return because, like risk, it depends on investors' perceptions, which don't necessarily pan out in practice.

For example, speculative shares are often purchased on the basis of 'blue sky potential'—that is, the potential for high capital gains in the future. This doesn't always turn out to be the case, and often blue or green chip shares produce better capital gains than speculative ones.

All investors (including myself) would love to be able to invest in ventures that produce high returns with low risk but the inescapable relationship between risk and return means that:

If you want a higher return on your capital, you must be prepared to take more risk.

The whole point of taking more risk is that you have the opportunity (or potential) for greater return. However, the greater the risk, the less certain you can be that the high return will actually be achieved.

Note

Different investors have different attitudes towards risk and it's important to match your investment risk to your risk profile (this is covered in more detail in chapter 6).

Taking advantage of compound growth

If you have an interest-bearing investment where the interest rate doesn't change during the term of the investment, two scenarios are possible:

1. *As you receive income from the investment you spend it.* This means that the capital invested and your income won't change over the term of the investment. This is known as *simple interest* because the dollar amount of interest (income on the investment) remains the same.

2. *As you receive income from the investment you don't spend it but instead reinvest it so the income adds to the capital invested.* This means that your capital invested and income will both grow over the term of the investment. This is known as *compound interest* because the profit is re-invested and compounds the value of the investment.

Notes

- In the short term, compounding doesn't have much effect but in the long term it can make a huge difference.

- An interesting fact about compounding is that the higher the growth rate, the greater the effect of compounding. For example, over the long term, a 10% growth rate will generate far more than twice the growth in value that a growth rate of 5% will.

- If you are trying to build your wealth, the maths of compounding means that the sooner you jump on the bandwagon the better. The early years have a far greater effect than the later years.

- Compounding also works in reverse, so if you have a loan, the sooner you start to pay it off the better.

Example

Compare the profitability of an investment of $10 000 returning 10% pa over 10 years using simple and compound interest:

- *Simple interest:* With simple interest you take out the profit (and don't reinvest it), so your profit each year is $1000 and, after 10 years, you've received $10 000 total profit. Your capital of $10 000 has been returned to you but, in fact, because of inflation it's worth less in terms of today's purchasing power.

- *Compound interest:* You don't take out your profit each year but reinvest it. Now, your total profit is $15 930 so, because of compounding, you've made $5930 more profit. Furthermore your invested capital has risen from $10 000 to $25 930. This is a huge difference compared to the initial $10 000 invested!

The calculations behind these figures are shown in table 2.1 (rounded to the nearest whole number of dollars). You can verify these figures for yourself using a spreadsheet. You can see that your investment grows by $1000 in the first year, but by the tenth year, the growth has more than doubled to $2360. This increase is often referred to as 'the power of compound interest' but there is nothing magical about it, simply mathematical facts.

Table 2.1: Growth of an investment (at 10% compound return)

Year	Value start of year ($)	Annual growth ($)	Value end of year ($)
1	10 000	1000	11 000
2	11 000	1100	12 100
3	12 100	1210	13 310
4	13 310	1330	14 640
5	14 640	1460	16 100
6	16 100	1610	17 710
7	17 710	1770	19 480
8	19 480	1950	21 430
9	21 430	2140	23 570
10	23 570	2360	25 930

Compound growth formulas

You can use a spreadsheet to calculate compound interested (as I did to determine the figures in table 2.1) but you can also use mathematical formulas. These formulas can also be used to work backward when you want to calculate the rate of return if you know the initial and final values of the investment. The formulas are:

1. $G = P_2 / P_1$

2. $P_2 = G \times P_1$

3. $G = (1 + i)^n$

4. $i = G^{1/n} - 1$

In these formulas:

- G = compound growth factor (ratio between final and initial investment values)

- P_2 = investment value in n years' time

- P_1 = initial investment value (year 0)

- i = rate of return on the investment per annum (or interest) expressed as a decimal (for example, 10% = 0.1)

- n = number of years (or term) of the investment.

Note

To use formulas 3 and 4, you need to use the y^x function on a calculator.

Examples

Rather than calculating values each year, as in table 2.1, use the formulas to calculate the value of the investment in 10 years' time.

In this case:

- $P_1 = \$10\,000$

- $i = 10\% = 0.1$

- $n = 10$

Using formula 3:

$$
\begin{aligned}
G &= (1+i)^n \\
&= (1+0.1)^{10} \\
&= (1.1)^{10} \\
&= \textbf{2.594}
\end{aligned}
$$

Using formula 2:

$$
\begin{aligned}
P_2 &= G \times P_1 \\
&= 10\,000 \times 2.594 \\
&= \textbf{\$25\,940}
\end{aligned}
$$

Note

This is slightly different from the value of 25 930 shown in table 2.1 because of what's known as *rounding error*. The values in the table were rounded off, so they're not quite as accurate as the calculated value.

Here's another example to highlight the importance of compounding.

A friend tells you that he's just sold a block of land he bought 10 years ago. He's very pleased with his return on capital because he's averaged 20% and, over the same period, the stock market averaged 13%. This has reinforced his conviction that property is a better investment than shares.

You ask him how he worked out his return and he explains it this way:

'I bought the land for $100 000 and sold it for $300 000. So my profit was $200 000 over 10 years, which is an average of $20 000 per year. Because I invested $100 000, my average return on capital was 20%.'

What do you think of this? I hope you've spotted the error (which by the way is a very common one). Your friend has forgotten about compounding. In fact, had he received a 20% return on capital each year, after 10 years he would have sold the land for $619 200! I think you'll agree, that's a huge difference. In fact, his true return on capital was 11.6% per annum, and was less than the sharemarket return over the same period.

Notes

- I used the compound growth formulas to calculate these results and I'll show you how in the next example.
- Your friend has ignored purchasing and selling costs and also holding costs, which no doubt would have been considerable and reduced the real profitability considerably.

Consider the following:

1. Calculate the value of a block of land costing $100 000 in 10 years' time if the land value increases by 20% pa.

2. If the land was sold for $300 000, after 10 years, what was the rate of return?

For the first example:

- $P_1 = \$100\,000$

- $n = 10$

- $i = 0.2\,(20\%)$

Using formula 3:

$$
\begin{aligned}
G &= (1+0.2)^{10} \\
&= 1.2^{10} \\
&= \mathbf{6.192}
\end{aligned}
$$

Using formula 2:

$$
\begin{aligned}
P_2 &= G \times P_1 \\
&= 6.192 \times 10\,000 \\
&= \mathbf{\$619\,200}
\end{aligned}
$$

For the second example:

- $P_1 = \$100\,000$

- $P_2 = \$300\,000$

- $n = 10$

Using formula 1:

$$
\begin{aligned}
G &= P_2 \times P_1 \\
&= 300\,000/100\,000 \\
&= \mathbf{3}
\end{aligned}
$$

Using formula 4:

$$
\begin{aligned}
i &= G^{1/n} - 1 \\
&= 3^{0.1} - 1 \\
&= 1.116 - 1 \\
&= 0.116 \\
&= \mathbf{11.6\%}
\end{aligned}
$$

Compound growth table

In order to save you the number crunching on your calculator or the laborious process of constructing a compound growth table, I've done it for you. Please refer to table 2.2 overleaf. In this table, I've calculated the compound growth factor for time periods up to 40 years with annual growth rates from 3% to 16%.

Examples

Use table 2.2 to determine the value of $1000 invested for 10 years with 10% growth per annum.

Firstly, go down to the 10-year row and across to the 10% annual growth rate column. You can see that the compound growth factor is 2.59. Multiply 2.59 by the original value of the investment ($1000) and you get $2590. This is slightly different from the formula value I calculated previously of $2594 because the table has been rounded (the formula is more precise).

As another example, use table 2.2 to determine the return on capital invested when your friend sells the block he bought for $100000 for $300000 10 years later.

To do this, work backward in the table. Now:

- $P_2 = \$300\,000$

- $P_1 = \$100\,000$

So the compound growth factor is $300\,000/100\,000 = 3$.

The period of the investment is 10 years so go down to the 10-year row in the table. Now go across the columns and try to find a value of 3. There's no exact value of 3 but 11% is 2.84 and 12% is 3.11. So the growth rate is about halfway between 11% and 12%, so about 11.5% (in fact, it calculates out at 11.6%).

Note

You can obtain a more precise value by interpolating the differences but that's for the more mathematically minded readers and I won't explain the procedure here.

Table 2.2: Compound growth factor

Yrs	Annual growth rate %													
	3%	4%	5%	6%	7%	8%	9%	10%	11%	12%	13%	14%	15%	16%
1	1.03	1.04	1.05	1.06	1.07	1.08	1.09	1.10	1.11	1.12	1.13	1.142	1.15	1.16
2	1.06	1.08	1.10	1.12	1.14	1.17	1.19	1.21	1.23	1.25	1.28	1.30	1.32	1.35
3	1.09	1.13	1.16	1.19	1.23	1.26	1.30	1.33	1.37	1.40	1.44	1.48	1.52	1.56
4	1.13	1.17	1.22	1.26	1.31	1.36	1.41	1.46	1.52	1.57	1.63	1.68	1.75	1.81
5	1.16	1.22	1.28	1.34	1.40	1.47	1.54	1.61	1.69	1.76	1.84	1.92	2.01	2.10
6	1.19	1.27	1.34	1.42	1.50	1.59	1.68	1.77	1.87	1.97	2.08	2.19	2.31	2.44
7	1.23	1.32	1.41	1.50	1.61	1.71	1.83	1.95	2.08	2.21	2.35	2.50	2.66	2.83
8	1.27	1.37	1.48	1.59	1.72	1.85	1.99	2.14	2.30	2.48	2.66	2.85	3.06	3.28
9	1.30	1.42	1.55	1.69	1.84	2.00	2.17	2.36	2.56	2.77	3.00	3.25	3.52	3.80
10	1.34	1.48	1.63	1.79	1.97	2.16	2.37	2.59	2.84	3.11	3.39	3.71	4.05	4.41
11	1.38	1.54	1.71	1.90	2.10	2.33	2.58	2.85	3.15	3.48	3.84	4.23	4.65	5.12
12	1.43	1.60	1.80	2.01	2.25	2.52	2.81	3.14	3.50	3.90	4.33	4.82	5.35	5.94
13	1.44	1.67	1.89	2.13	2.41	2.72	3.07	3.45	3.88	4.36	4.90	5.49	6.15	6.89
14	1.51	1.73	1.98	2.26	2.58	2.94	3.34	3.80	4.31	4.89	5.53	6.26	7.08	7.99
15	1.56	1.80	2.08	2.40	2.76	3.17	3.64	4.18	4.78	5.47	6.25	7.14	8.14	9.27
16	1.60	1.88	2.18	2.54	2.95	3.43	3.97	4.59	5.31	6.13	7.07	8.14	9.36	10.70
17	1.65	1.95	2.29	2.69	3.16	3.70	4.33	5.05	5.90	6.87	7.99	9.28	10.80	12.50
18	1.70	2.03	2.41	2.85	3.38	4.00	4.72	5.56	6.54	7.69	9.02	10.58	12.40	14.50
19	1.75	2.11	2.53	3.03	3.62	4.32	5.14	6.12	7.26	8.61	10.20	12.06	14.20	16.80

Yrs	Annual growth rate %													
	3%	4%	5%	6%	7%	8%	9%	10%	11%	12%	13%	14%	15%	16%
20	1.81	2.19	2.65	3.21	3.87	4.66	5.60	6.73	8.06	9.65	11.50	13.74	16.40	19.50
21	1.86	2.28	2.79	3.40	4.14	5.03	6.11	7.40	8.95	10.80	13.00	15.67	18.80	22.60
22	1.92	2.37	2.93	3.60	4.43	5.44	6.66	8.14	9.93	12.10	14.70	17.86	21.60	26.20
23	1.97	2.47	3.07	3.82	4.74	5.87	7.26	8.95	11.00	13.60	16.60	20.36	24.90	30.40
24	2.03	2.57	3.23	4.05	5.07	6.34	7.91	9.85	12.20	15.20	18.80	23.21	28.60	35.20
25	2.09	2.67	3.39	4.29	5.43	6.85	8.62	10.80	13.60	17.00	21.20	26.43	2.90	40.90
26	2.16	2.78	3.56	4.55	5.81	7.40	9.40	11.90	15.10	19.00	24.00	30.17	37.90	47.40
27	2.22	2.89	3.73	4.82	6.21	7.99	10.20	13.10	16.70	21.30	27.10	34.39	43.50	55.00
28	2.29	3.00	3.92	5.11	6.65	8.63	11.20	14.40	18.60	23.90	30.60	39.20	50.10	63.80
29	2.36	3.12	4.12	5.42	7.11	9.32	12.20	15.90	20.60	26.70	34.60	44.69	57.60	74.00
30	2.43	3.25	4.32	5.74	7.61	10.10	13.30	17.40	22.90	30.00	39.10	50.95	66.20	85.80
31	2.50	3.38	4.54	6.09	8.15	10.90	14.50	19.20	25.40	33.60	44.20	58.08	76.10	99.60
32	2.58	3.51	4.76	6.45	8.72	11.70	15.80	21.10	28.20	37.60	49.90	66.21	87.60	116.00
33	2.65	3.65	5.00	6.84	9.33	12.70	17.20	23.20	31.30	42.10	56.40	75.48	101.00	134.00
34	2.73	3.80	5.25	7.25	9.98	13.70	18.70	25.50	34.80	47.10	63.80	86.05	116.00	155.00
35	2.81	3.95	5.52	7.69	10.70	14.80	20.40	28.10	38.60	52.80	72.10	98.10	133.00	180.00
36	2.90	4.11	5.79	8.15	11.40	16.00	22.30	30.90	42.80	59.10	81.40	111.80	153.00	209.00
37	2.99	4.27	6.08	8.64	12.20	17.20	24.30	34.00	47.50	66.20	92.00	127.50	176.00	243.00
38	3.07	4.44	6.39	9.15	13.10	18.60	26.40	37.40	52.80	74.20	104.00	145.30	203.00	281.00
39	3.17	4.62	6.70	9.70	14.00	20.10	28.80	41.10	58.60	83.10	118.00	165.70	233.00	326.00
40	3.26	4.81	7.04	10.30	15.00	21.70	31.40	45.30	65.00	93.10	133.00	188.90	268.00	379.00

Learning exercises

2.1 What are the two ways you can profit from an investment and how do you work out the total profit?

2.2 What's meant by the return on an investment and why is it more important than the dollar profit?

2.3 What's the basic principle of investing that applies if you wish to grow your wealth?

2.4 What are the four factors that can eat away at the real profitability of an investment?

2.5 In her book *From Strength to Strength*, Sara Henderson writes, 'From July 1986 to September 1987, I played the stock market...In the next 12 months Bullo River made $114000 in trading shares and a little less the following year'.

As an investor, what conclusion can you make about Sara's profitability?

2.6 Many listed shares pay dividends. Why would anyone buy shares that don't pay a dividend or in a business that is running at a loss, when so many shares are available in companies that are making a profit and paying a dividend?

2.7 Negative gearing means making an annual loss on an investment. Why would anyone want to do that?

2.8 Your share portfolio is worth $126540 at the start of the financial year. At the end of the year, your portfolio is worth $142350. That year inflation averaged 2.6%. What was your percentage capital gain on the average capital invested and your real (inflation-adjusted) capital gain?

2.9 You buy 10000 speculative shares for $0.46 each. You hold them for 127 days and then sell them for $0.54 each. If your trading cost on each trade is $20, what was your equivalent annual return on the transaction?

2.10 You buy a parcel of 5000 shares at a price of $1.06. Six months later, you sell them for $1.24. During the six months, you receive a dividend of 5¢ per share (unfranked). If your trading costs are $55.00 per transaction, what was your dollar profit and return on initial and average capital invested (before tax)?

2.11 How realistic do you think the following investor statements are?

Jack: 'I want a high return but I don't want to take much risk.'

Jill: 'I want a high return and I realise that sometimes I might make a loss.'

Jane: 'I don't want to take much risk and I realise that I'll not make a high return.'

2.12 Calculate the change in value of $1000 capital invested in each of the following four scenarios if the interest is re-invested. Comment on the result:

a. Invested for 10 years with 5% annual return

b. Invested for 20 years with 5% annual return

c. Invested for 10 years with 10% annual return

d. Invested for 20 years with 10% annual return

2.13 When Jack was born, his parents put aside $5000 on his behalf and invested in shares. They decide to re-invest the dividend. The shares grow in value by an average of 9% (capital gain and dividend).

Jill is the same age as Jack. Jill's parents meet Jack's parents when Jack is 10 years old and decide they'll make the same investment for Jill.

When Jack and Jill turn 21, each of their parents sell the shares and give the money to them.

How much money will Jack and Jill each receive? What does this example show you?

2.14 Referring to the previous question, say inflation averaged 4% over the 21 years of the total investment. What's the real increase in the value of the cash Jack and Jill receive on their 21st birthdays in terms of the purchasing power of the money originally invested?

What does this example show you with regard to the effect inflation can have on wealth creation?

2.15 I invested $80 000 in a managed fund. Four years later, I withdrew and received a payout of $92 321. What was my percentage return on the initial capital invested?

Learning exercises solutions

2.1 The two ways of making a profit are capital gain and income. The total profit is the sum of the two.

2.2 Return on investment is the dollar profit per annum divided by the capital invested and expressed as a percentage. It's more important than dollar profit because it's the true measure of profitability of an investment.

2.3 The basic principle of wealth growth is that, in order to grow your wealth, the after-tax return on your investment must be greater than the inflation rate.

2.4 The four factors to consider that can eat away at the real profitability in any investment are:

» in/out costs

» holding costs

» profit taxes

» inflation.

2.5 While the dollar profit seems very good, we're not told how much capital Sara invested for her share trading. So we don't really know what her true profitability was.

2.6 Investors buy shares that don't provide a dividend or are issued by a business not making a profit because they expect (or hope) to make capital gain in the future. Profitable companies that pay a reliable dividend don't usually have the large price swings of the more speculative shares and, therefore, are perceived to have less potential for high short-term capital gains.

2.7 Investors negatively gear because, under current taxation laws in Australia, the losses are tax-deductible and so reduce their tax payable. When they eventually sell, they hope to recoup all the accumulated annual losses and show a net profit by making a large capital gain on the investment.

2.8 Your capital gain $= \$142\,350 - \$126\,540$
$= \$15\,810$

Average capital invested $= (\$142\,350 + \$126\,540) \div 2$
$= \$134\,445$

Percentage return on capital invested $= (\$15\,810 \div \$134\,445) \times 100$

$= \mathbf{11.8\%}$

Real (inflation-adjusted) return $= 11.8 - 2.6$
$= \mathbf{9.2\%}$

2.9 Buy cost = \$4620 and sell value = \$5380

Average capital invested $= (\$4620 + \$5380) \div 2$
$= \$5000$

Profit $= \$5380 - \$4620$
$= \$760$

Raw return $= (\$760 \div 5000) \times 100$
$= 15.2\%$

Equivalent annual return $= 15.2 \times 365 \div 127$
$= \mathbf{43.7\%}$

2.10 Your dividend $= \$0.05 \times 5000$
$= \$250$

Capital gain $= 5000 \times (\$1.24 - \$1.06) - (2 \times \$55)$
$= \$790$

Total profit (before tax) $= \$250 + \$790$
$= \mathbf{\$1040}$

Initial capital invested $= 5000 \times \$1.06 + \$55$
$= \$5355$

Return on initial capital invested $= \$1040 \div \$5355$

$= 0.194$
$= 19.4\%$ in six months
$= \mathbf{38.8\%}$ per annum

Average capital invested $= 5000 \times (\$1.06 + \$1.24) \div 2$
$= \$5750$

Return on average capital invested
$$= \$1040 \div \$5750$$
$$= 0.1809$$
$$= 18.09\% \text{ in six months}$$
$$= \mathbf{36.2\%} \text{ per annum}$$

2.11 Jill and Jane are realistic and should be able to find investments that suit them. Jack is being unrealistic and has little chance of getting a high return unless he's prepared to take more risk.

2.12 The comparison is outlined in the following table. Note that in this table I used table 2.2 (refer to pages 52–53) to obtain the compound growth factor.

Scenario	Years	Annual growth rate	Compound growth factor	Final capital value	Increase in value
a.	10	5%	1.63	$1630	$630
b.	20	5%	2.65	$2650	$1650
c.	10	10%	2.59	$2590	$1590
d.	20	10%	6.73	$6730	$5730

Note: You see the 'power of compound interest' applies to both the term of the investment and to the annual growth rate.

2.13 Jack's investment time period is 21 years. From table 2.2, 9% growth over 21 years gives a compound growth factor of 6.11. Therefore, Jack will receive $5000 \times 6.11 = \mathbf{\$30\,550}$.

Note: The formula provides the more precise answer of **$30 544**.

Jill's investment time period is 11 years. From table 2.2, 9% growth over 11 years gives a compound growth factor of 2.58. Therefore, Jill will receive $5000 \times 2.58 = \mathbf{\$12\,900}$.

Note: The formula provides the more precise answer of **$12 902**.

This example again shows the 'power of compound interest': Jack receives a much larger amount than Jill because the money for him has been invested for a longer time period.

2.14 If the rate of inflation were 4%, the real return in terms of purchasing power was 5% (9% − 4%).

Jack's investment time period is 21 years. From table 2.2, 5% growth over 21 years gives a compound growth factor of 2.79. Therefore, Jack will receive $5000 × 2.79 = $13950. The real increase in value is $13950 − $5000 = **$8950**.

Note: The formula provides the more precise answer of $13930 for the cash Jack receives.

Jill's investment time period is 11 years. From table 2.2, 5% growth over 11 years gives a compound growth factor of 1.71. Therefore, Jill will receive $5000 × 1.71 = $8550 and the real increase in value is $8550 − $5000 = **$3550**.

Note: The formula provides the more precise answer of $8552 for the cash Jill receives.

This example shows that a relatively high rate of inflation can really eat into wealth in the long term and this is one reason the Australian government tries to keep inflation below 3%.

2.15 The compound growth factor is 92321 ÷ 80000 = 1.154. Going to table 2.2, for a four-year period, this annual growth rate lies about halfway between 3.00% and 4.00%, or about 3.50%. *Note:* If you're good at using a calculator, you'll find the precise answer is **3.65%**.

Chapter 3

Investing in shares

In this chapter, I consider the positives and negatives of share investing so you can get a balanced picture of the advantages and disadvantages involved. I compare shares with other asset classes and conclude by looking at what the future holds for share investors.

Understanding the positives of share investing

Investing in shares has many positives, including the following:

- high rate of return
- liquidity
- ease of trading
- low trading cost
- no holding costs or hassles

- flexibility of investment

- taxation benefits

- social security treatment

- wealth of information available

- interest and satisfaction

- providing capital for Australian businesses.

High rate of return

The Australian share market has an excellent history of long-term profitability. You can see this in figure 3.1, which charts the All Ordinaries index over the past 40 years. This index provides a measure of the value of the 500 largest shares on the Australian market and is the best measure of shares value because it represents over 99% of the Australian market.

You can clearly see that over this period, despite two severe downturns— namely, following the terrorist attacks in New York in 2001 and the global financial crisis (GFC, or sub-prime mortgage debacle) in 2007–8— the index recovered and rose again. As is a common feature of the sharemarket, other blips can be seen along the way but the overall trend has been upward. There is no reason to suspect that this won't continue in the future. The index was set at 500 points in 1980 and, after 40 years, it had risen to about 7000 points. Using compound growth formula 4, discussed in chapter 2, this means the average annual compound growth rate was 6.8%.

In addition to the growth in value (capital gain), many Australian shares pay a dividend. For the Australian market, dividend income traditionally averages around 4%. Very often, this dividend is fully franked, so the grossed-up dividend yield is about 5.7%. Adding this to the average growth rate of 6.8% gives a total return of 12.5%. This is a very respectable return and explains why shares are one of the major investment instruments used by investors from small 'mum and dad' investors to large financial institutions and superannuation providers.

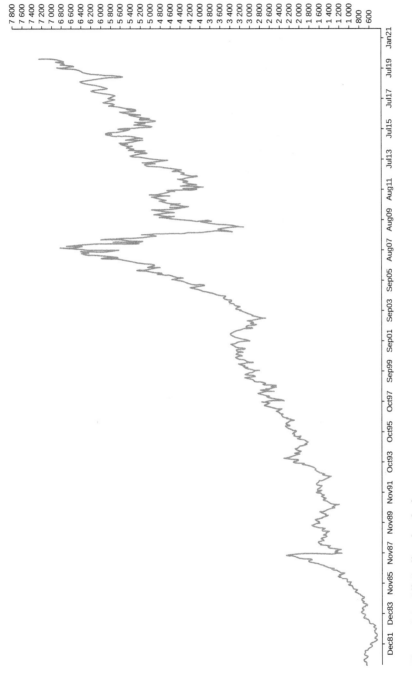

Figure 3.1: All Ordinaries index
Source: Incredible Charts

Notes

- For an astute investor, major downturns in the market present opportunities to make excellent profits. For example, the GFC and the terrorist attacks in New York caused severe downturns in financial markets, including Australian shares, but after they were over share prices rose steeply again.
- I discuss grossing-up of dividends in chapter 4.
- The All Ordinaries index measures the growth in value of the major listed shares, but any individual share can produce a much better, or worse, result.
- Many listed shares don't pay a dividend and, if you invest in these, you need a higher capital gain to compensate for the absence of a dividend.

Caution

You need to exercise caution when reading reports comparing the performance of various asset classes such as cash, fixed-interest securities, property, Australian shares and international shares. Because returns fluctuate and the various asset classes are usually out of step with one another, the time period chosen can greatly affect the comparison. You can prove almost any investment is better than any other simply by choosing the most favourable time period. I've shown this diagrammatically in figure 3.2.

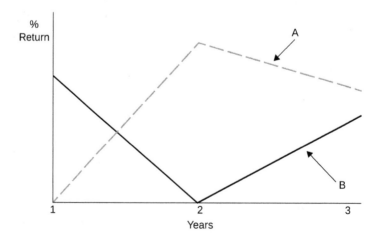

Figure 3.2: Comparison of two investments (A and B)

You can see that in the time period of year 1 to 3, A was a better investment than B, but over the shorter time period of year 2 to 3, B was a much better investment than A. This is a simplified example, but it illustrates my point.

Liquidity

An outstanding benefit of most shares is their liquidity, which means that you can trade them very easily and quickly. As I mentioned in chapter 1, a few listed shares are illiquid and don't trade very often. However, these are unusual and, in any case, you are well advised to stay away from them unless you have very good reasons. For the vast majority of listed shares, many trades transact each business day, so illiquidity is seldom a problem.

Ease of trading

As well as being able to trade shares quickly, another outstanding advantage of share investing is that you can trade them so easily. Once you've set up an account with a broker (online or offline), trading is a breeze. If you trade offline, all that's needed is a phone call. If you trade online, once you've logged on, you simply check the action and place your order. In either case, no fuss, no bother, it's that simple.

Notes

- Modern telecommunications technology allows you to access the internet or call your broker from a mobile phone or other electronic device. So you can arrange to trade shares whenever the exchange is open for trading.

- You can also place orders when the exchange is closed, but I don't recommend you do this.

Low trading cost

Another outstanding benefit of shares is that you can trade shares at very low cost. Using an online broker, you can trade a $10 000 parcel of shares for about $20 (including GST and all charges) and this equates to only 0.2%! Some online brokers are even cheaper and you may be able to trade a parcel of shares online for as low as $10. If you've ever been involved in the purchase or sale of a property, you'll appreciate how low this cost is in comparison to the costs and charges involved in buying or selling property.

No holding costs or hassles

Virtually no costs or hassles are associated with holding shares. No maintenance or insurance costs, fees or commissions, land taxes or any other costs are associated with holding shares. You'll be sent all relevant information or documents (such as shareholding statements, company reports and dividend statements) without it costing you a cent—regardless of the value of your shareholding! Nor are any hassles associated with holding shares—you don't have to worry about property maintenance, finding suitable tenants, collecting rents or paying bills or charges of any type. With shares, all you need to do is to keep track of them and include all capital gains and dividends in your income tax return. I'll show you how to do this in later chapters.

Nowadays many brokers (both online and offline) will keep your records so you really don't have any hassles at all. Also, the ATO will have a record of your dividend payments and will pre-fill the information for you if you use the online options.

Note

You can nominate to receive company reports and information via the internet rather than by mail.

Flexibility of investment

Shares are a very flexible form of investment. This flexibility applies in several ways, including:

- Amount of capital invested, because you can invest any amount from a few hundred dollars to many thousands of dollars. However, ASX regulations don't allow you to buy a parcel of shares valued at less than $500 if you don't already own some of the same shares. You can sell a parcel of any value but small parcels may not be economical because the trading cost may be a high proportion of the total value (or even exceed it).

- Diversifying your investment, because when you invest in shares you don't need to put 'all your eggs in one basket'. You can spread your investment very easily because many different types of shares in different market sectors are available. If you buy shares (or units) in a listed investment company or managed fund, you can automatically diversify with just one stock holding.

- Changing strategies quickly and without penalty, because with the low cost of trading shares you can easily and quickly change strategies. For example, if you buy shares on the expectation of a price rise and this doesn't occur, you can quickly and easily 'get out' and sell those shares. You're not locked into a share investment for any fixed term and there are no penalties if you change your mind (other than trading costs).

Taxation benefits

When it comes to tax time, share investing has the unique benefit that it's the only form of investing where you can receive a built-in tax rebate with your income. Franked dividends come with imputation credits (or franking credits) that you receive as a tax offset. At the time of writing, you'll get these as a cash payment even if you don't pay any income tax. I discuss this in detail in chapter 4.

Also, shares allow you to legally and conveniently split income simply by deciding in whose name the shares will be registered. This strategy can reduce the overall tax that needs to be paid by a partnership. Obviously, you need to make prior arrangements with the other partner and your broker if you wish to do this. However, generally speaking, the ATO frowns on any strategy that aims to reduce tax without some other valid reason for it. So if you want to income split, you need to be in a personal partnership or have some other justifiable reason for splitting the share ownership.

Notes

- If you share ownership, you need to be confident your partner is reliable and trustworthy.

- If you register shares in the name of someone under the age of 18, you need to be aware of the special tax provisions that apply to unearned income of minors.

- As I discussed in chapter 1, ownership of shares can be changed without necessarily selling and buying back the shares.

Social security treatment

If you're receiving a pension (full or part) or any other type of social security benefit, profit made from shares (either capital gain or dividends) doesn't count as income, regardless as to how much you received from your shares. However, a deeming rate is applied to the value of your share portfolio and it's used to calculate a notional income. You need to check this out if these conditions apply to you.

Wealth of information available

With shares, a huge amount of information is readily available that allows you to make informed decisions. Most of this information is free and accessible from your own home if you have access to the internet. (For specific details about this information, please refer to my book *Online Investing on the Australian Sharemarket*.) With many other asset classes you may be considering, you may find it very difficult to obtain the information you need to make an informed decision. For example, if you're thinking of investing in property, is it better to invest in a home unit, residential property, block of land or commercial property, and which location produces the highest returns? Answers to these types of questions may not be difficult to obtain.

Interest and satisfaction

Share investing can be a satisfying interest as well as a profitable one, and it's a good way of keeping you mentally active. You can develop your own trading system and test it by simulated trading with hypothetical portfolios. Experimenting with different trading systems allows you to develop the one most suited to your needs without committing any dollars.

Providing capital for Australian businesses

In the overall picture, Australian share investors contribute a great deal of the capital needed for Australian businesses. Without this, Australian businesses wouldn't have the capital needed to develop and grow and thus provide a better standard of living for all Australians. Instead, they would be owned and managed by overseas investors with the profits going offshore instead of staying in Australia and benefiting Australians.

Keeping in mind the downsides of share investing

Clearly, many people shy away from shares and, like most things in life, share investing isn't all good news. The negatives include:

- Shares prices can fall.

- Shares prices can be volatile.

- Factors beyond your control may intervene.

- Share investing can be stressful.

- You need some knowledge.

In order to give you a balanced picture, I discuss these negatives in the following sections.

Share prices can fall

Seldom (never?) does the price of a share rise all the time without ever falling. There is no way of mitigating this fact and so if you invest in shares, you have to accept that share prices can fall as well as rise. In addition, the dividend can also fall if the business becomes less profitable.

Note

Risk management strategies you can use with shares are provided in later chapters of this book and also in my online investing book.

Share prices can be volatile

Volatility is a measure of the extent of the variation over a relatively short time period. Without doubt, share prices can be volatile and rise and fall significantly from day to day or even in the course of a day's trading. Sometimes only a few share prices change significantly but other times the market as a whole is volatile. One reason shares are regarded as more volatile than other investments such as property is that share prices and market updates are publicised frequently and in far more detail than is the case with other forms of investment such as property.

Note

Because shares tend to be volatile, most financial advisers suggest that you should consider share investing (as opposed to trading) as a long-term investment of about seven years or more.

Factors beyond your control may intervene

Many factors can affect the shares in your portfolio or the market as a whole, over which you have no control and little forewarning. On occasions, I've researched a stock thoroughly and carefully timed my buy decision and the purchase price, only to have some unknown factor come to light a short time after buying that caused a sudden and unexpected drop in price. Generally, market reaction to bad news is so sudden that you simply cannot offload your shares in time to get a reasonable price. It's also disconcerting when the Australian market reacts because of factors in overseas economies (particularly the United States and China) that affect their economies but that have little obvious relevance to the Australian economy.

This problem has really no solution except to diversify and take a long-term view. As I discuss in later chapters, a diversified portfolio will usually have winners as well as losers and if you can limit your losses on the losers, you can still have a good result. For example, if you have 10 different shares in your portfolio about equally balanced in value, a sudden drop of 10% in the price of one will cause only a 1% drop in the value of your whole portfolio.

Note

Uncontrollable factors can also work in your favour and cause an unforeseen price rise. For example, unexpected good news (here or overseas) can cause a sudden upward jump in share price. However, generally speaking, bad news tends to have a more dramatic effect on price falls than good news has on price rises.

Share investing can be stressful

In bull markets, most share investors sleep well at night, secure in the knowledge that their wealth is increasing as time goes on. However, in bear markets or during a sudden and unexpected market drop, it's far more difficult to feel content with your share investment. While daily fluctuations are to be expected, it's difficult not to feel stressed when the market is trending down or bad news abounds and you can see the value of your shares falling.

You can mitigate this stress to some extent by having a diversified portfolio of good quality shares and by taking the view that share investing is a long-term proposition. You can also adopt a strategy called 'bottom drawer', which basically means that after you've bought good quality shares, you don't trade them often or worry about their day-to-day price fluctuations because you're confident that in the long term, they're going to produce good returns.

You need some knowledge

Unless you're going to pay an advisor to act on your behalf, share investing requires a certain amount of knowledge. It's not quite as simple as going to a bank and opening a term deposit. If you're not going to regard share investing as a form of gambling and rely mostly on luck, you need a certain amount of knowledge. As mentioned, a huge amount of information is available and being able to interpret it and make informed decisions can be a bit daunting if you're not an experienced investor.

However, the good news is that share investing isn't rocket science and if you continue reading this book and attempting the learning exercises, you're well on your way. I suggest when starting out, you research only a few shares (say, 10 or so) and practise with a hypothetical portfolio before you invest real dollars.

A stock market saying is also good to remember:

It's better to know a few stocks well rather than a well full of stocks.

Comparing shares and fixed-interest investments

Because of the perceived riskiness of shares, many people prefer to invest in other asset classes with negligible perceived risk such as bank accounts, term deposits or government guaranteed bonds. However, these types of investments involve several problems:

- *No capital growth.* That's to say, $100 000 invested in a term deposit or bond is still worth the same $100 000 at the end of the investment period, whether that be in months or years.

- *No inflation hedge.* With shares, the profits made by the business and the assets owned by it tend to match the inflation rate. For example, if the business owns the property it uses for the business, that property should increase in value as time goes on. Also a well-run business should re-invest part of its profits to counter the effect of depreciation and to ensure the business stays up to date with its assets. This also provides a hedge against inflation. A fixed-interest investment has no such inbuilt inflation hedge and, in fact, the value of the investment reduces in real terms due to the effect of inflation.

- *The interest on the investment is fully taxable.* This means that your after-tax income is considerably less than your before-tax income depending on your rate of tax.

On the other hand, with shares you have the prospect of capital growth, you have an inbuilt hedge against inflation and if your dividends are franked you pay less tax.

Example

Say I want to compare a capital investment of $10000 in fixed-interest securities with shares. I make the following assumptions:

- *Fixed-interest securities:* Interest rate 8% and investor tax rate 30%, giving an after-tax interest of 5.6%. All after-tax interest is reinvested.

- *Shares:* Capital growth rate 8% and dividend 4% fully franked. Investor tax works out to be 30% so the 4% dividend is tax-free. All after-tax dividend income is reinvested.

The value of both investments over the long term is shown in table 3.1.

Table 3.1: Fixed-interest securities and shares

Year	Fixed interest 8%		Shares 8%	
	$ Value	$ Interest	$ Value	$ Div
0	10000		10000	
1	10560	560	11200	400
2	11151	591	12544	448
3	11776	624	14049	502
4	12435	659	15735	562
5	13132	696	17623	629
6	13867	735	19738	705
7	14644	777	22107	790
8	15464	820	24760	884
9	16330	866	27731	990
10	17244	914	31058	1109
11	18210	966	34785	1242
12	19229	1020	38960	1391
13	20306	1077	43635	1558
14	21443	1137	48871	1745

(*continued*)

Table 3.1: Fixed-interest securities and shares (*cont'd*)

Year	Fixed interest 8%		Shares 8%	
	$ Value	$ Interest	$ Value	$ Div
15	22644	1201	54736	1955
16	23912	1268	61304	2189
17	25251	1339	68660	2452
18	26666	1414	76900	2746
19	28159	1493	86128	3076
20	29736	1577	96463	3445
21	31401	1665	108038	3859
22	33159	1758	121003	4322
23	35016	1857	135523	4840
24	36977	1961	151786	5421
25	39048	2071	170001	6071

In order to highlight the differences, the value of these two investments is charted in figure 3.3.

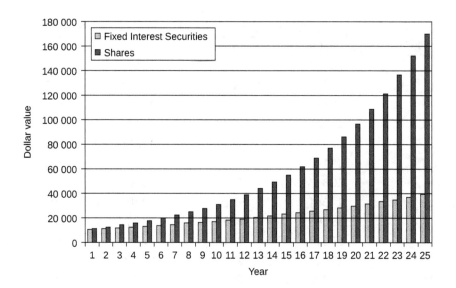

Figure 3.3: Long-term value of shares and fixed-interest securities

The same rate of return has been assumed for both investments but you can see the dramatic difference between them. At the end of the 25-year investment period, a fixed-interest investment of $10 000 has grown in value to a little over $39 000 and is earning $2071 in interest in the last year, whereas the shares would be worth about $170 000 and paying a dividend of over $6000. The difference is essentially because of the franking credits with the share dividends, which make them tax free.

What about the future?

What lies ahead for Australian share investors — can we expect continuing growth in the Australian market or could investing in Australian shares cease to be a good investment?

It's always difficult (impossible?) to predict the future, especially in financial matters but I'm optimistic that Australian shares will continue to be a longer term good investment well into the foreseeable future. My reasons for believing this are outlined in the following sections.

Benefits

I believe that some of the outstanding benefits of share investing will continue to attract investors in the foreseeable future. As I've outlined, some of the benefits such as liquidity, ease of trading, no holding hassles and flexibility are very attractive to all investors whether large or small. The taxation treatment of share profits and particularly the benefits of dividend franking are outstanding. However, that this will continue into the future is less certain, because governments have started tinkering with these benefits in order to increase revenue, so you need to keep close tabs on future developments.

History

Over a long period of time, the Australian market has essentially trended upward. Certainly, the market has gone down over certain periods or even over several years in a row but eventually it has recovered. I see no reason this should change in the foreseeable future.

Government and economy

Australia has a stable history of democratic government and is a free market, capitalistic economy with minimum government corruption. Arguably, Australia is the world's most successful multicultural nation and that is a very healthy sign. Businesses are generally free to conduct their affairs with minimum government interference. This environment encourages businesses to expand and for new businesses to spring up and this is all good for the economy.

While not all government decisions in the past have been good ones, for the most part we have been governed wisely with good economic management. This should continue into the future and ensure that economic disasters such as prolonged recessions or rampant inflation don't occur. There doesn't appear to be any reason this should change in the foreseeable future — except in previously unprecedented circumstances such as the global viral pandemic that occurred in early 2020 when preservation of health takes precedence over economic considerations. That's to say, when the whole world goes into shutdown in order to halt a viral spread, it is very difficult for Australia to avoid the subsequent economic downtrend regardless of any government action. Bear in mind that when one asset class (such as shares) is affected by a pandemic, almost all (if not all) other asset classes are similarly affected.

South-East Asia trading alliances

Australia has an enviable position among major world economies in that we have close proximity to South-East Asian markets, including China, Indonesia and Malaysia. These economies have been in a growth phase for some time and this growth is likely to continue into the future. These economies may expand at a slower rate in the future, but still provide a large and profitable market for Australian products.

Profit reinvestment

If company directors ensure that some of the profits are re-invested wisely back into their businesses, the profit of the company should continue to increase in the future as the business grows. Just like private industry, our government should invest taxation and other revenue into developments and infrastructure that will continue to provide opportunities for Australian businesses.

Technology

The trend in Australia is to embrace new technologies and also develop our own. By developing and investing in new technology, Australian companies should continue to prosper and become more productive in the future. I believe these technological developments will continue at an increased rate as Australia moves toward being more a 'clever country' than a 'lucky country'.

Rationalisation

Continuing takeovers, mergers and rationalisation should ensure that major Australian companies trim waste and improve efficiency and continue to prosper.

Population growth

Australia is one of the few nations in the world where we still have a substantial population growth. This is partly due to a birth rate slightly higher than other OECD countries and partly due to immigration. Continuing population growth provides growing markets for Australian businesses, and growing markets mean growing profits.

Resources

Australia has many saleable products that are in demand throughout the world. These include mined resources such as coal, iron, gas and uranium as well as grown resources such as wool and wheat. So far there is no indication that the well has run dry or that demand is decreasing for our exported products. True, coal exports have been under pressure because of global warming and the trend toward renewable energy sources but large demand still exists for coal for energy as well as steelmaking. The recent resources boom may diminish somewhat in the future but we have sufficient known resources and others that are undergoing development to ensure continuing prosperity.

Australia also has lots of sunlight and wind, and the development and growth of solar and wind power is continuing at an accelerating rate.

In addition, we are a well-respected educational nation and receive export earnings from overseas students studying in Australia, not to mention the Australian tourism industry, which is a continuing source of export earnings.

Before moving on ...

I have tried to present a factual and two-sided summary of the advantages and pitfalls associated with share investing. Only you can consider these and decide if share investing is for you. Because you are reading this book, I assume you hold shares already or want to 'get into' share investing. In either case, I believe your likelihood of success will improve if you study this book and attempt the learning exercises.

Learning exercises

3.1 What's meant by the liquidity of an investment and why is this a positive for share investors?

3.2 Why are shares a very flexible form of investing?

3.3 What are the two main tax benefits available with shares?

3.4 If you are on a social security pension, how does income made on shares affect your pension?

3.5 One investment advisor can prove that property produces better returns for investors than shares, whereas another can prove that shares are the better investment. What's the likely explanation?

3.6 What's meant by a 'bottom drawer' approach to share investing and what advantages and disadvantages do you see with this approach?

3.7 As a share investor, how can you reduce the stress you might feel in times of high market volatility?

3.8 If you're going to be a long-term share investor, what time period should you consider and why?

3.9 You would like to buy a small parcel of new shares that are trading at $0.57 per share. What's the minimum number of shares you can buy?

3.10 You have a well-paying full-time job while your wife works part-time and consequently earns considerably less. You are both starting to invest in shares and want to buy some speculative shares for quick capital gain profits and also some blue chip shares that pay a good dividend for the longer term. What is your best strategy to minimise your total tax for both of these types of shares?

3.11 You hold 2000 options in a mining company that are due to expire in six months. The options are currently trading for 1¢. Your trading cost is $20 for parcels in value up to $10 000.

What should you do in the following situations?

a. You think the options will go down in price.

b. You think the options will go up in price.

3.12 You have a diversified portfolio of 12 different shares in roughly equal values. One day when you check your portfolio, you're disturbed to find that bad news has caused one of your shares to drop in price by 16%.

a. What effect will that have on the overall value of your portfolio?

b. What percentage rise would be needed in your other shares to balance the drop in value of the one that has fallen?

c. What does this example show you?

3.13 Ten years ago, BAX Bank shares were trading for $8.26 and today they're trading for $27.28. Over the past 10 years the average dividend paid was 4%.

a. What was the capital gain growth rate?

b. What was the total investor return?

Note: For the purpose of simplifying this exercise you can ignore the effect of dividend imputation (franking).

3.14 Referring to BAX Bank shares in the previous question:

a. If you bought 10 000 shares 10 years ago and reinvested the dividends, what total value would the shares have today?

b. What would your total profit be?

c. If instead of buying the shares you'd invested the same amount in a term deposit with BAX Bank and received 8% interest that you re-invested at the same rate, how much profit would you have made?

Learning exercises solutions

3.1　Liquidity is the ease and speed at which you can convert an investment into cash. It's a positive for share investors because the vast majority of listed shares are highly liquid and can be traded very easily, so you can quickly convert shares to cash or cash to shares.

3.2　Shares are a very flexible form of investing because you can diversify very easily, you can vary the amount of your investment from several hundred dollars to any amount you like, and you can change strategies very easily if you change your mind.

3.3　The two main tax benefits of shares are the in-built tax rebate (offset) available with franked dividends and the fact that share ownership can easily be split and this makes income splitting legal (provided it can be justified).

3.4　Share income doesn't affect a social security pension. However, a deeming rate is applied and notional income is calculated on the value of the share investment.

3.5　The likely explanation is that each advisor is choosing a different time period. You can prove almost any investment is better than another if you carefully select the time period for the comparison.

3.6　A 'bottom drawer' approach to share investing is based on buying good quality stocks and holding them over a long period of time—you don't sell them due to a short-term price fall.

This approach has some advantages, including:

» you ignore short-term price fluctuations and avoid the stress associated with them

» in the long run, the method can produce good returns

» minimum trading costs are involved

» no capital gains tax liability (unless the shares are eventually sold)

» you don't need to spend a lot of time tweaking your portfolio.

The disadvantages of this approach include:

» you could be locked into a long-term price decline

» if you are an active trader and follow the market closely, you may be able to make higher returns if you are able to buy around the low point and sell around the high point.

3.7 A good way of reducing the stress you might feel in times of high market volatility is to invest in shares for the long term and not allow short-term price changes to worry you. You might even want to adopt a 'bottom drawer' approach. Another strategy is to have a diversified portfolio so price changes in a few shares won't have a significant effect on your total portfolio value.

3.8 It's generally considered that for long-term investing, you should think in terms of about seven years, essentially because that's the longest time the Australian market has taken to recover from a downturn.

3.9 Since the minimum order amount is $500 (for shares you don't own), you can buy a minimum of **878 shares**.

3.10 As you are on a higher marginal tax rate than your wife, your best strategy to minimise tax is to buy all the shares in both groups in her name. Whether the shares produce capital gains or dividends does make any difference, because both of these count as taxable income. Even if your wife pays little or no tax on her income, she will still receive the franking credits.

3.11 The solutions for each scenario are as follows:

a. You should hold the options, because they're not worth trading. The current value of the options is $20 if they are sold and the trading cost is $20, so you will not gain anything by selling them. If they go down in price, you will lose money.

b.   As your parcel is not worth trading at current prices, you could hold and hope the options go up in price before they expire. Alternatively, you could buy some more and get a parcel that would be more economical to trade.

3.12   For calculation purposes, suppose the parcel value of each of your shares is $1000 and the total portfolio value is $12 000.

a.   If one share drops by 16%, that is $160, meaning the portfolio will drop by **1.33%** $(\$160 \div 12\,000)$.

b.   The remaining 11 shares would have to gain $160 in total or $14.55 each, so they each need to rise by **1.46%**.

c.   This example demonstrates the importance of having a diversified portfolio because a significant drop in the value of one share can be balanced by a small increase in the value of the others.

3.13   The solutions for each scenario are as follows:

a.   Compound growth factor $= 27.28 \div 8.26$
$$= 3.303$$

Using formula 4 given in chapter 2:

$$
\begin{aligned}
i \;&=\; G^{1/n} - 1 \\
&=\; 3.303^{0.1} - 1 \\
&=\; 1.127 - 1 \\
&=\; 0.127 \\
&=\; \mathbf{12.7\%} \text{ (or use table 2.2 and interpolate)}
\end{aligned}
$$

b.   Total investor return $= 12.7 + 4 = \mathbf{16.7\%}$

3.14   The solutions for each scenario are as follows:

a.   Initial capital outlay $= 10\,000 \times \$8.26$
$$= \$82\,600$$

Using formula 3, $G = (1 + 0.167)^{10}$
$$= 4.68$$

So the shares would be worth $\$82\,600 \times 4.68 = \mathbf{\$386\,700}$.

b.   Total profit $= \$386\,700 - \$82\,600$
$$= \mathbf{\$304\,100}$$

c. At 8% interest, the investment would be worth

$$\$82\,600 \times (1+0.08)^{10} \quad = \quad \$82\,600 \times 2.16$$
$$= \quad \$178\,300$$

So the profit would be $\$178\,300 - \$82\,600 = \mathbf{\$95\,700}$.

Chapter 4

Profiting from shares

As we've seen, you can make a profit from shares in two ways—capital gains and dividends. In this chapter, I look more closely at each in turn and discuss how they're treated by the Australian Taxation Office (ATO). A quick general comment on taxation first.

Understanding taxation treatment of share profits

You may be wondering why you should be concerned about tax matters, particularly if you use an accountant to prepare your taxation return or perhaps don't pay tax anyway.

I believe you really need to understand the taxation implications of profits or losses made on shares because these may significantly affect the strategies you adopt when you are deciding whether to buy, sell or hold.

Notes

- Share income, whether in the form of capital gains or dividends, must be included in your income tax return.

- Income tax is based on financial year not calendar year.

- Any costs incurred are tax deductible. These include fees charged by financial advisors or managers, trading costs, or interest on loans used specifically for share investment (margin loans).

- You're not compelled by law to declare your tax file number when you invest in shares. However, if you don't submit your tax file number, withholding tax will be deducted from any dividends you receive and this tax will be calculated at the highest tax rate. Should withholding tax be deducted, this will be credited back to you when your tax for the financial year is calculated.

- If the ATO has your tax file number, they automatically compile your dividends and franking credits.

Making capital gains profits

If you sell a parcel of shares at a higher price than you originally paid for them after deducting trading or any other costs, you've made a capital gain. On the other hand, if you show a net loss after the sale, you've made a capital loss.

Actually, two types of capital gains are possible:

- *Real capital gain:* This is the actual profit you've made after selling shares.

- *Paper capital gain:* This is a theoretical profit that is not actually realised (converted into cash) because the shares haven't been sold.

An ordinary investor needs only to declare real profits when completing a taxation return, but it's still a good idea to keep regular tabs on your paper profits so you know how your portfolio is performing (I'll discuss this in detail in chapter 14). However, if you make share trading a business or derive most of your income from share trading, the ATO may classify you as a share trader. In this case, your taxable income will be based on paper profits (or losses) each financial year rather than realised profits.

Tax treatment of capital gains from shares

For taxation purposes, capital gains from share trading are income and taxed in the financial year that the sale occurred. Capital losses can't be offset against income, and can only be used as an offset against capital gains.

For example, if you make a $5000 taxable capital gain and a $3000 capital loss in one financial year, you have a net gain of $2000 and you need to include this as income in your tax return for that financial year. If, instead, you made a $3000 capital gain and a $5000 capital loss, you can't write off the net capital loss of $2000 against other income in that financial year. All you can do is carry losses forward until you make a capital gain some time in the future, and then reduce the gain in that financial year by the amount of the loss. The number of years the loss can be carried forward is not limited, and losses can be accumulated indefinitely until they can be written off against capital gain.

Notes

- Capital gains tax (CGT) was made law on 20 September 1985 so any shares (or other assets) acquired prior to this date are CGT exempt any time they are sold.
- When you die, any accumulated capital losses die with you and can't be passed on to your estate.

50% discount rule for capital gains

Capital loss isn't affected by the length of time you've held the shares. If you sell shares in one year and make a net loss, this loss can be written off against capital gains, no matter how long you held the shares—whether for one day or 10 years, it makes no difference.

However, the tax treatment of capital gain is very different. The full amount of the net capital gain is considered taxable income only if you've held the shares for less than 12 months. If you've held the shares for 12 months or more, only half the gain is taxable. Effectively, you get a 50% discount and this, of course, is very significant (particularly if you're a taxpayer on a high tax rate). For example, if your marginal tax rate is 37%, the 50% discount amounts to an 18.5% net gain for you.

However, the catch is if you sell shares for a profit that you've held for more than 12 months and other shares for a loss in the same financial year, you can't offset the loss against a 50% gain. You must apply full losses against full gains and only then apply the 50% rule if the remainder of the capital gain occurs with the shares you've held for 12 months or more. I'll show you how this works in the example that follows.

Note

Marginal tax rate is the rate of tax (or tax bracket you fall into) for every dollar of additional income you make.

Example

Determine your taxable capital gain in the following two scenarios:

1. You sell some shares you bought two years ago and, after deducting costs, you make a capital gain of $2000. In the same financial year, you also sell some speculative shares that you've held for only three months and you make a net loss of $800 on them.

2. You sell some shares you bought two years ago and you make a net capital gain of $800. In the same financial year, you also sell some speculative shares that you've held for only three months and you make a net loss of $2000 on them.

The capital gains for each scenario are as follows:

1. Your net capital gain is $2000 − $800 = $1200.

   Since the profitable shares have been owned for more than one year, only half this gain is taxable. So your taxable capital gain is

   $1200 ÷ 2 = $600

   This amount must be included as income in your tax return.

2. Your net capital gain is $800 − $2000 = −$1200 (loss)

   This loss can't be offset against income in your tax return but can be carried forward and offset against capital gains in future years.

Note

You can't calculate your taxable capital gain in the second scenario in this way:

Capital gain = $800

Because the shares were held for more than one year, only half the gain is taxable.

Therefore, taxable gain = $400.

Net loss = $400 − $2000 = −$1600 . This loss can be carried forward and offset against capital gain.

This is incorrect and you can't use the 50% discount rule if you make a net capital loss. You can carry forward a loss of $1200 not $1600.

Hold or sell?

If you've held some shares for less than one year and have made a good capital gain, you may be prompted to think of selling. However, you also need to consider the option of holding the shares until a year has elapsed so as to take advantage of the 50% discount.

This decision can be a difficult one if you're concerned that the price might drop while you're waiting for the year to elapse. You need to determine your break-even point, and how much your gain could be eroded should the price drop before the end of the year. In other words, would you be better off selling immediately or waiting?

To help you with this decision consider the following example.

Example

You've bought some shares that have risen in price and you're showing a net paper capital gain of $10 000. You'd like to sell the shares and bank the profit but you've held them for only 10 months. You'd like to take advantage of the 50% discount and wait until a year has elapsed. Suppose you decide to wait and the price does go down, how much could it fall before the break-even point? For the purpose of this example, I'll assume you're on a marginal tax rate of 32.5% + 2% Medicare levy.

The calculations are shown in table 4.1.

Table 4.1: Capital gains reduction to break even with CGT

Option	Net gain	Taxable gain	Tax payable	After-tax gain
Sell now	10000	10000	3450	6550
Wait two months with capital gain reduction %				
0	10000	5000	1725	8275
10	9000	4500	1552.50	7447.50
15	8500	4250	1466.25	7033.75
20	8000	4000	1380	6620

You can see from this table that the price would need to reduce by over 20% before you're better off selling the shares immediately and paying full tax on the capital gain rather than waiting and taking advantage of the 50% discount rule. Of course, if the price doesn't fall at all and remains steady, you're nearly $2000 better off by delaying the sale. Should the price rise instead of falling while you're waiting, you'll receive a double bonus!

Capital gain reduction and price drop formula

In order to quickly calculate the maximum capital gain reduction and price drop for any level of marginal tax, I've derived the following formulas:

$$Cd = T \div (2 - T/100)$$
$$Pd = (Ps - Pc) \times Cd/100$$

Where:

- Cd = Capital gain reduction $(\%)$
- T = Tax rate $(\%)$ (including Medicare levy)

- $Pd = \text{Price drop}(\$)$

- $Ps = \text{Current share price}(\$)$

- $Pc = \text{Cost price}(\$)$

Note

These formulas don't take into account trading costs. When these costs are included, the capital gain reduction and price drop will be a little less than that indicated by the formulas.

Example

You've bought some shares for $5 and the price has risen to $10. You've held the shares for nearly one year and you need to decide whether to sell now or wait until a year has elapsed. Determine by how much your capital gain could reduce and how much the price could fall in order for you to be worse off waiting rather than selling now. Do this for tax rates of 19%, 32.5%, 37% and 45% and include a 2% Medicare levy.

For a tax rate of 19%, $T = 21$.

Substituting in the formula, $Cd = 21 \div (2 - 21 \div 100) = 11.73\%$.

And $Pd = (10 - 5) \times 11.73 \div 100 = \$0.587$

Therefore, if the price doesn't drop to below $9.41, you're better off waiting before you sell.

Similarly, for tax rates of 32.5%, 37% and 45%, the capital gain reduction, price drop and break-even price calculates as shown in table 4.2.

Table 4.2: Profit reduction and break-even price with various levels of tax and 2% Medicare levy

Tax rate %	19	32.5	37	45
Capital gain reduction %	11.73	20.84	24.22	31.15
Price drop $	0.587	1.02	1.21	1.56
Break-even price $	9.41	8.98	8.79	8.44

You can see that as your tax rate increases, the break-even price falls and, at the highest rate of tax, the price would need to fall by about $1.56 before you're better off selling immediately. Also, you can see the importance of understanding CGT because it can have a significant impact on your trading decisions.

Deferring capital gains tax liability

The date of disposal (sale) is the critical factor in determining in which financial year the capital gain needs to be declared. For example, if you sell shares for profit on or before 30 June, the capital gain needs to be included in your taxation return for that financial year. If you sell them on 1 July, the gain occurs in the next financial year. In other words, keeping the shares for just one day longer defers the tax liability for a whole year! Of course, the reverse applies if you've made a loss on shares, where you're better off selling them before 30 June so you can include the loss in the current financial year if you have made capital gains on other shares in that year.

Note

Because the income tax financial year spans from July to June, the end of June and the beginning of July are usually high-volume trading periods as investors take advantage of the tax laws applying to capital gains.

Selling parcels of shares

If you have some shares you bought in a number of parcels, or received in different parcels over a period of time through a dividend investment plan, what are the tax implications if you want sell some (but not all) of them? According to tax law, when calculating your taxable capital gain for the year, you can nominate the shares you've sold in the manner that's most favourable to you. You don't have to use a FIFO (first in–first out) system and can instead use any method you wish—and you don't even have to justify your decision. The only requirement is that you keep track of which particular shares you sold and which you're still holding, so you know the cost price of each group.

Crystallising losses

If you have some shares that have gone down in price, you can't write off the paper capital loss (unless you are classified as a share trader). If you want to use the capital loss to reduce your tax you need to convert the paper loss to an actual loss. This is known as crystallising losses, and is a strategy you should consider if you're making good cash capital gains but only paper capital losses.

If you're reluctant to sell your loss shares because you think the price will likely rise again, you can consider selling the shares and buying them back later. This is an effective way of gaining an immediate benefit from your loss in the form of tax savings, but it has a few prickles:

- The ATO may view the combined transaction simply as tax avoidance and, if queried, you need to be able to justify why you sold and bought back some time later. The reason needs to be other than tax avoidance.

- You'll be up for two lots of transaction costs. However, if you trade on the internet, these may not be significant compared to the benefit of an immediate tax saving.

- If the share price rises after the sale, you have lost some potential profit. On the other hand, if the price drops after the sale, you're better off.

- You'll be treated as a new investor when you buy back, so you will need to re-activate your investor details such as tax file and bank account numbers.

- If the new parcel of shares is purchased at a lower price than originally, you will have a greater capital gains tax liability if you eventually sell.

Making profits from dividends

Profit made by a company is also known as *earnings*. When a company makes a profit, some of it will be used to pay interest on loans and some to pay company tax. The remaining after-tax profit can be used in some or all of the following ways:

- retained as reserves

- used to buy back shares

- distributed to shareholders.

The profit flow is shown in figure 4.1.

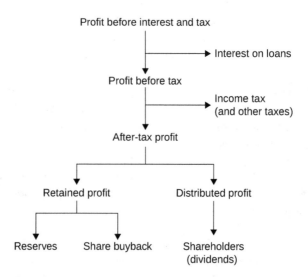

Figure 4.1 Profit flow in a company

When some of the profit is distributed to shareholders, it's usually in the form of dividends. A company can distribute profit to shareholders in other ways, such as special payments, but dividends are the most common. Dividends are a way of rewarding shareholders by returning some of the company's profits to them. After all, the shareholders own the company and are entitled to a share of the profits. Retained profit that goes into reserves can be used to purchase new plant or equipment, to make acquisitions, to enable the company to reduce its debts or for any other purpose deemed appropriate by the directors.

Notes

- Directors have direct control over how earnings will be used and, if they declare a dividend, what the dividend per share will be and when it will be paid.

- Not all listed companies pay dividends; in fact, the majority do not. Companies that don't pay a dividend are often operating at a loss or are making insufficient profit to enable a dividend to be paid.

- A company's financial year is divided into two six-monthly periods and accounts are published for each period. A dividend for the first six months is known as the *interim dividend* and for the last six months, as the *final dividend*. The total dividend is the sum of the two.

- In financial reports, the dividend per share or other dividend related ratios are always based on the total annual dividend.

- Most companies use the 1 July–30 June financial year, but they aren't compelled by law to do so and some companies use different financial periods for their accounts.

Understanding the importance of dividends

Dividends are important (particularly for a long-term investment portfolio) for the following reasons:

- Dividends are recurring income for investors and are usually a much safer form of income than capital gain. Even though the share price may fall, companies often retain (or even increase) the dividend.

- Recurring dividends are an indicator of financial stability and profitability (particularly if the dividend per share increases over time). Dividends are real dollars that are paid to investors and can't be massaged by creative accounting.

- Many companies maintain a good dividend even when their share price is trending down and this helps to offset paper capital losses.

- Consistent dividend payments are usually a sign of consistent profitability and directors who are concerned about the needs of shareholders.

I firmly believe that any long-term investor should weigh a portfolio with a good proportion of profitable companies that pay good dividends. You'll obtain further benefit from dividends if they're fully franked because you'll receive a substantial tax rebate. At the time of writing, even if you don't pay much tax (or any) you still receive the tax rebate as a cash payment from the ATO. In addition, shareholders who don't take the dividend in cash but participate in dividend reinvestment plans are automatically building up their investment in shares and so obtaining a 'double whammy' compounding effect because when future dividends are paid they're getting dividends on dividends.

Note

Not everyone agrees that companies should pay significant dividends. For example, US companies usually pay much lower dividends than Australian ones. The argument is that it is better to retain profits and re-invest the money back into the business for long-term benefit to shareholders. However, Australian investors are accustomed to receiving worthwhile dividends and often seek them when considering which companies to invest in.

Capital gain or dividend?

Many listed shares don't pay a dividend and, therefore, provide zero dividend yield. Clearly, investors buy these shares with the expectation (hope?) of high capital gain. Debate continues as to the value of dividends compared with capital gains. In bull markets, the argument for capital gain tends to be more prevalent because it may be easier to make higher profit. For example, if prices are generally trending upward, it may not be difficult to achieve a 10% profit in one year from price rises. On the other hand, a dividend yield as high as 10% is rare. In sideways trending or bear markets, the argument for dividend yield seems to gain ascendancy because of the reduced capital gains to be had and, indeed, most shares may be showing a capital loss. If these shares still pay a good dividend, investors perceive dividends as a source of profit in tough times.

Payout ratio

The profit paid out to investors compared to the total amount of profit is measured by a statistic called the *payout ratio* (PR). This is the amount paid out in dividends divided by the total profit or, alternatively, the dividend per share divided by earnings per share. It's usually expressed as a percentage and the formula is:

$$PR = \frac{DPS}{EPS} \times 100$$

Where:

- DPS = dividend per share (in cents)

- EPS = earnings per share (in cents)

In a profitable, stable and well-managed company, the payout ratio is usually in the region of 50 to 80%, meaning that 50 to 80% of the after-tax profit is returned to shareholders as dividends.

Dividend cover

The payout ratio can be inverted and then is known as the *dividend cover*. The formula is:

$$DC = \frac{EPS}{DPS} \times 100$$

The dividend cover is the extent to which the dividend is covered by after-tax profits. For example, if the dividend cover is 2, this means the company has made twice as much profit as it has paid out to shareholders. In this case, the payout ratio would be 50%.

Notes

- If the company makes a profit but doesn't pay a dividend, PR is zero and DC is theoretically infinity, but in share statistics this is shown as a blank—that is, dividend cover doesn't apply.

- It is possible for a company to pay out more in dividends than it makes in profit. It does this by drawing on reserves, but this is generally unhealthy and indicates the directors are trying to appease shareholders despite a profit downturn.

Dividend yield

One of the most important financial statistics used with dividends is the dividend yield (also known simply as *yield*). This is calculated in the following manner:

$$DY = \frac{\text{Dividend}}{\text{Share price}} \times 100$$

Notes

- The multiplication by 100 converts the fraction to a percentage because yield is always expressed as a percentage.

- The yield is the equivalent of interest obtained from an interest-bearing investment.

- In this formula, the dividend and share price must be in the same monetary units; that is, dollars or cents. However, a short cut for obtaining the dividend yield is to divide the dividend in cents by the share price in dollars. Then you don't need to multiply by 100 to get the yield as a percentage.

- The dividend per share used to calculate the yield is the total dividend, which is the sum of the interim and final dividends. That is, yield is always shown as a percentage annual yield.

- Even though the declared dividend changes only every six months, the dividend yield changes with each share transaction because the share price changes. If the price increases, the yield decreases and if the price decreases, the yield increases.

Reasonable yield

If you are attracted to dividends as a source of ongoing income, the question arises of what you should regard as a reasonable yield. You might think that the higher the yield the better, but you need to exercise caution with abnormally high yields for several reasons, namely:

- A very high yield indicates the company is paying out too much of its earnings and not retaining sufficient for the future.

- High yield may occur because the share price has fallen significantly and that is usually bad news.

- High yields cannot usually be sustained over the longer term and, if you buy shares because you are attracted to a high yield, you may find that in the future the dividend reduces significantly (or is even abandoned).

Therefore, I suggest you stay away from shares where the yield is significantly above the sharemarket average – which at the time of writing is about 5 or 6%. (Of course, this average can change—in 2020, many businesses looked at reducing dividends due to COVID-19.)

Tax rules applying to dividends

In the bad old days, companies paid tax on their profits and shareholders receiving dividends declared the dividend as income. This income was taxed at the shareholder's personal tax rate. This unfair double-taxation system was changed in 1987 with the introduction of dividend imputation. Now if a company pays tax on its profits and distributes some of the after-tax profit as dividends to shareholders, these dividends are known as *franked dividends* and carry an associated tax credit in the form of an imputation credit or franking credit. This credit can be claimed as a rebate (or offset) in your tax return and reduces your tax liability. If you don't pay tax (perhaps because your taxable income is below the threshold), at the time of writing you can still receive the franking credits in cash from the ATO. If the profit out of which the dividend is paid has been fully taxed by the ATO, the dividend is said to be fully franked or 100% franked. The company tax rate (for non–base rate companies—defined as those with a turnover of less than $50 million) at the time of writing is 30% and this means that if you fall into the 32.5% tax bracket (or below it) and you receive a fully franked dividend, you'll pay almost no tax on the dividend—it's almost tax-free earning, although the 2% Medicare levy still applies.

With the taxation system at the time of writing, if you don't need to pay income tax, after-tax dividend income can actually be greater than the before-tax income. This is because you receive the franking credits in cash from the ATO.

Note

Political parties in the past have dabbled with changing the franking credit system but so far any proposed changes have been unpopular with voters. It's also possible that the tax rate for corporations (30% for non–base rate companies) may also change in the future. If it does change, the amount of franking credits available to shareholders will also change. If the company tax rate falls, the franking credits will also fall because companies will pay less tax.

Example

To see how the system works, consider $1000 of company earnings before tax, distributed as a dividend. The company pays $300 tax and distributes $700 to shareholders. Shareholders receive a dividend of $700 carrying a franking (or imputation) credit of $300. When a shareholder declares the dividend in their tax return, the $300 franking credit is credited to them as a tax offset (or rebate).

Calculating the imputations (franking) credit

If an imputation credit is attached to a dividend, this will be shown on the dividend statement you receive. However, if the dividend is fully franked it's not hard to calculate. Divide the dividend by 0.7 to get the amount of profit before tax. Then multiply by 0.3 (30%) to get the amount of tax paid on the profit. This is the imputation credit. Let's break down the preceding example:

- the shareholder receives $700

- divide by 0.7 = $1000

- multiply by 0.3 = $300 (which is the tax paid by the company and the imputation credit the shareholder receives).

Note

Both the dividend and the imputation credit are included in your tax return as taxable income (even though you don't actually receive the imputation credit as income).

Franking level

The franking applied to dividends can vary from unfranked (zero franking) to 100% franking (fully franked). The level of franking can also change from time to time, although many companies maintain the same level of franking over long periods. It is also possible for companies to accumulate franking credits and so have a level of franking above 100%, but this is rare. Partial franking usually occurs when not all of the company profit is fully taxed. This can come about in a number of ways, including:

- If the corporation is set up as a trust (such as a property trust), no tax is payable on profits that are distributed to members. Therefore, dividends from trusts are unfranked (which means they carry zero franking credits).

- An Australian company may have offshore earnings that are not taxed by the ATO and, therefore, these earnings won't qualify for franking credits. Dividends from these companies could be partly franked (or unfranked).

Notes

- Sometimes the level of franking is indicated by the letter/s *f* meaning fully franked, *pf* meaning partly franked or no letter or *uf* meaning unfranked.
- With a partly franked dividend, you may need to research more thoroughly to find out the level of franking.

Dividend yields with different franking levels

Because the imputation credit is effectively a cash return from the ATO, franked dividends are more valuable than unfranked dividends. But how much more valuable? For example, which dividend is better in the following?

- Company A's 5% fully franked

- Company B's 7% unfranked

If you compare these yields as they seem at first sight, you're comparing apples with oranges. Unfortunately, many published financial statistics show raw yield only and so don't give you the full picture. You need some way of calculating the true equivalent value of a yield that takes into account the difference in franking.

You can do this by means of the grossing-up factor (G), which enables you to get a fair comparison between yields with different levels of franking.

The formula for G is:

$$G = 100 \div \left(100 - \left[\text{Company tax rate}\% \times \text{Franking}\% \div 100\right]\right)$$

For example, if the company tax rate is 30% and the level of franking is 60%:

$$
\begin{aligned}
G &= 100 \div \left(100 - \left[30 \times 60 \div 100\right]\right) \\
&= \mathbf{1.2195}
\end{aligned}
$$

To save you the calculation, I've included table 4.3, which is based on the current company tax rate of 30%.

Table 4.3: Grossing-up factor for various levels of franking

Franking (%)	Grossing-up factor	Franking (%)	Grossing-up factor
0	1.000	60	1.220
10	1.031	70	1.266
20	1.064	80	1.316
30	1.099	90	1.370
40	1.136	100	1.429
50	1.176		

You can now get a fair comparison of yields for any level of franking by multiplying the yield by the grossing-up factor and obtaining the grossed-up yield (GUY).

This means a fair comparison between a 7% unfranked and a 5% fully franked yield is as follows:

- 7% unfranked yield, GUY $= 7 \times 1.00 = 7.00\%$

- 5% fully franked yield, GUY $= 5 \times 1.429 = 7.15\%$

Now you're comparing apples with apples and you can see that a 5% fully franked yield is more valuable to you than a 7% unfranked yield.

Dividend dates

Four dates relate to dividends:

- *Announcement date:* This is the date when the dividend is announced so everyone knows what the next dividend will be and when it will be paid.

- *Ex-dividend date:* This is the cut-off trading date for payment of the dividend. Before this date, any shares purchased (and held past this date) are eligible for the current dividend. However, on and after this date, shares purchased don't qualify for the current dividend.

- *Record date (or books closing date):* This is the date at which the share ownership record is used by the share registry to determine eligibility for receipt of the dividend. As it takes a few days for share ownership changes to be recorded, the record date is usually four business days after the ex-dividend date.

- *Payment date:* This is the date when the dividend is actually paid (usually one to two months after the ex-dividend date).

Effect of dividend on the share price

Of the four dates mentioned in the preceding section, only two are likely to have any effect on share price. These are the announcement date and the ex-dividend date.

Announcement date

The announcement of the dividend usually doesn't have any significant effect on the price of the shares. This is because the market usually anticipates the dividend and so it is already built into the share price. The exception is if the company announces a dividend that is very different from market expectations. For example, an unexpected reduction in the dividend could cause the market to react unfavourably and the price will fall as a result. For this reason, directors are usually reluctant to decrease the expected dividend.

Ex-dividend date

This date almost always has a significant effect on the share price and on this date the price falls—usually by an amount equal to or close to the dividend (or sometimes by more for franked dividends because of the value of the franking credits). For example, if the last sale price today was $1.00 and tomorrow is the ex-dividend date for a dividend of $0.05, the opening trades tomorrow are likely to be about $0.95.

Notes

- Before you buy any dividend-paying shares, you should find out the next ex-dividend date. If the company hasn't announced the date, you can get a very good idea from past dividends because the date doesn't usually change by more than a day or two in each year.

- If you buy shares before the ex-dividend date and sell them when they go ex-dividend, you'll still receive the dividend even though you don't actually own the shares when the dividend is paid.

Dividend stripping

Even though shares almost always fall in price when they go ex-dividend, it's still often possible to make a profit by buying shares just prior to the ex-dividend date and then selling them a short time later. This practice is known as *dividend stripping* and can be profitable because the share price may not fall by the full value of the grossed-up dividend or, if it does, it may quickly recover all or most of the fall. Needless to say, dividend stripping is frowned on by the ATO, who try to limit its widespread use by using a rule known as the *45-day rule*. This rule states that you must hold the shares for at least 45 days in order to be able to claim the imputation credits. However, small shareholders are exempt from this rule if (at the time of writing) the total imputation credits claimed in any one year is less than $5000.

Dividend reinvestment plans

Some companies have what's known as a *dividend reinvestment plan* (DRP), which gives you the option of taking your dividend in shares instead of in cash.

You can find out if a DRP is in operation from financial statistics before you purchase shares but, in any case, if you buy shares where a DRP is in operation, you'll be asked by the share registry if you wish to participate in it. You're usually given one of the following choices:

- *No participation:* You'll receive the dividend in cash.

- *Full participation:* The full dividend is converted to shares. In this case, you'll receive no cash dividend but instead you'll be allocated additional shares.

- *Partial participation:* You nominate how many shares you want to participate in the DRP.

If a DRP is offered, you'll be advised how the plan works. Usually, the allocation price is based on the average share price over a stipulated number of trading days prior to the ex-dividend date. In some cases, an in-built bonus in the form of a discount factor (such as 2.5%) is applied to the price. Because you can't receive a fractional number of shares, the number you're allocated is rounded off to a whole number in accordance with the rules. Sometimes the number is rounded up (in which case, you receive an additional bonus), but more often the number is rounded down and a cash credit is carried forward and applied to the next dividend.

DRP tax implications

For income tax purposes, no distinction exists between cash dividends and dividends taken as shares under a DRP, and dividend income must be declared in either case. The tax calculation is exactly the same with a DRP and you receive the same rebate for any franking credits.

However, a complication with capital gains tax occurs if you subsequently sell any of the shares you received through a DRP—namely, that each parcel of shares has been acquired at a different time and at a different price and, therefore, the capital gains tax is different. If you sell any shares, you need to calculate the profit or loss on each parcel separately, so you need to keep accurate records of each one. Therefore, if you decide to participate in a DRP, you need to keep accurate records of each dividend.

Note

I find the most convenient way of keeping track of DRP dividends is to keep copies of dividend statements and file them in date order sequence. I also keep a master summary with each share that I update every time I receive a dividend.

Deciding whether to participate in a DRP

To help you decide whether to participate in a DRP, I've listed the advantages and disadvantages.

The advantages of a DRP are:

- Over a period of time, the number of shares you hold will increase and this increase will be at a compound rate. For example, if you hold 1000 shares that pay a consistent dividend of 5%, after 10 years your shareholding increases to 1630 shares and after 20 years to 2653 shares (please refer to the compound interest formula or table given in chapter 2).

- If a discount factor is applied to the allocation of shares under the DRP, you do even better. For example, a 2.5% discount increases your shareholding after 10 years to 1649 shares and after 20 years to 2719 shares.

- It's an effective long-term investing strategy because the dividend automatically accumulates as shares and you're not tempted to spend it.

- Shares accumulate at an average price over time. Averaging the cost price of shares is known as *cost averaging*, and this is a good way of smoothing out short-term volatility of the stock market.

Disadvantages of DRP include:

- You don't receive the cash. If you rely on dividends to boost your income, you may not be able to afford to forgo the income.

- The dividend must be declared as income in your tax return whether or not it's received in cash or shares. So if your marginal tax rate is greater that the company tax rate (30%), you have some tax to pay on the dividend even though you didn't receive any income to help you pay the tax. For example, if you're on the top tax rate of 45% and receive a fully franked dividend, the tax payable would be 17% (45% − 30% + 2% Medicare levy).

- If you decide to sell some or all of your shares, the capital gains tax calculation is more complex because you receive each parcel of shares at a different time and price. I use a spreadsheet to take the pain out of this calculation. If you use an accountant to prepare your tax return, the calculation won't worry you. But remember, you must keep good records.

Bonus share plan

In some cases, companies offer their shareholders a choice of a bonus share plan as well as a dividend reinvestment plan as another way they can receive their dividend in shares rather than cash. This plan is also known as a *dividend substitution share plan* (DSSP).

The difference is that if you elect to join this plan, you receive your dividend as new shares and they aren't regarded as income. This means that no franking credits are associated with these shares and you don't need to include them as income in your tax return. The catch is that these shares are regarded by the ATO as having a zero cost base, so much higher capital gains tax will be payable if you eventually sell. If a plan like this is available, I suggest you read the fine print and make the decision according to your own circumstances but, in most cases, I believe a DRP will prove to be the better plan if you want to forgo your cash dividend and take it in shares instead.

Selling shares while participating in a DRP

If you are in a DRP and decide to sell your entire holding of shares in a company, you need to be aware of a possible trap. There is a period after shares are allocated to you through the DRP before your shareholding in the new shares is registered. If you are not alert to this and sell the shares without checking your new dividend entitlement, you can find that you receive the new entitlement after the sale has been completed. In this case, you can be left holding a small parcel of shares with more nuisance value than anything else. So always check your entitlement of new shares before you decide to sell, so you know exactly how many shares you own and are entitled to.

Cash residue

If you are in a DRP that rounds down, the cash residue goes into your account and is added to your next dividend amount. So you don't lose the cash credited to your account when you sell (or die), this cash will be refunded to you (or your estate). If the share price is fairly low, this cash will be a small amount but if the share price is substantial, this amount could be more significant.

Real and apparent capital profit

When you receive shares issued in the DRP plan, theoretically (and legally and as far as the ATO is concerned), you purchased those shares at the DRP issue price. In fact, you didn't purchase them at all but received them free of charge to you. So over a period of time, your records will show that the shares you are holding cost you more than they actually did. If you eventually sell the shares (or pass them on to beneficiaries) the additional benefit is that the capital gains tax liability will be less than is apparent from your records.

If you wish to know your true profit, you can keep two records: one showing the book cost (or accounting cost) and the other showing the actual cost. This allows you to calculate and compare the book profit and the actual profit. This is illustrated in learning exercise 4.15.

Learning exercises

4.1 It's June. From a taxation point of view, when is the best time to sell the following shares?

    a. Shares that are showing an appreciable capital loss

    b. Shares that are showing an appreciable capital gain

4.2 On the day when shares are quoted ex-dividend, what would you expect to happen to the opening share price compared to the closing share price the day before? Explain your answer.

4.3 What are the four important dates for dividends and on which of these dates do you think a significant change in share price could occur and why?

4.4 When might you look for capital gains rather than dividends and when might you consider dividends to be more valuable?

4.5 Is it possible for the payout ratio to be zero, or greater than 100%? Explain your answer.

4.6 What would you consider to be a suitable payout ratio and dividend cover and why?

4.7 What is the range of franking applicable to dividends and which is best?

4.8 Which of the following yields is better?

    a. 3% ff

    b. 4% uf

4.9 Why should you always consider grossed-up yield rather than raw yield?

4.10 You buy some shares that currently have a yield of 4.5% and are 55% franked. What is the true value of this yield to you?

4.11 Briefly outline the benefits and disadvantages of joining a dividend reinvestment plan (if there is one) when you buy shares.

4.12 A listed company with 96 million shares on issue makes an after-tax profit of $12.4 million. The directors decide to distribute $7.68 million in dividends. What are the earnings per share, dividend per share, payout ratio and dividend cover?

4.13 What is the grossed-up yield of the following shares?

    a. NOP when the share price is $10.05 and the dividend is 63¢ per share, fully franked.

    b. QRS when the share price is $1.31 and the dividend is 8¢ per share, with 75% franking.

4.14 You own 554 TUV Bank shares and the final dividend is 75¢ per share. How many shares will you be allocated if you are participating fully in the DRP and the average price of TUV shares prior to the dividend is $32.42?

Note: Under the rules of the TUV plan, shares issued under the DRP are rounded up to the nearest whole number of shares.

4.15 You buy 2000 shares at a price of $8.64 and join the DRP plan. Some months later the company announces an interim dividend of $0.31 per share fully franked. Your dividend statement shows that your total dividend was $620 and you received 73 shares at an issue price of $8.49, so you now hold 2073 shares. If your trading cost was $50, work out the book cost of the shares you hold. You then sell the shares soon after for $8.93. Work out your taxable capital gain and your actual capital gain.

4.16 You hold 1000 shares that you bought 10 months ago for $5.00 and that are now trading at $10.00. Your marginal tax rate is 37% (+2% Medicare levy). For the purpose of this exercise, neglect trading costs.

    a. If you sell the shares now, what is your after-tax profit?

    b. If you decide to wait until you've held the shares for 12 months, how much could they drop in price in order for you to break even with after-tax profit?

    c. Prove the answer you obtained in part (b) by calculating the after-tax profit and show that it is the same as the amount you calculated in part (a).

4.17 You hold 1000 shares that you purchased for $3.26 and that you've held for nearly a year. You could sell them now for $5.43 but you'd like to wait until you've held them for 12 months. You're concerned that they might drop in price but you've identified a support level of $5.00 — that is, if the price does drop, you don't think it will go below $5.00. You're on a 37% marginal tax rate (+2% Medicare levy).

What is your best strategy — sell now or wait?

Learning exercises solutions

4.1 The solutions for each scenario are as follows:

    a. The best time to sell shares showing a loss is in June so you can write the capital loss off in the current financial year.

    b. The best time to sell profitable shares is in July so you can defer the capital gains tax liability for a year.

4.2 On the ex-dividend day, the opening share price is likely to fall by the amount of the dividend. The reason for this is that investors purchasing the shares will not receive the current dividend and so the shares are less valuable by the amount of the dividend. When the dividend is fully franked, the share price may fall by more than the dividend to take into account the value of the franking credits.

4.3 The four important dates are:

    » announcement date

    » ex-dividend date

    » record date

    » payment date.

    Of these dates, the one that has the most predictable influence on the share price is the ex-dividend date, when the price falls – usually by the amount of the dividend. The announcement date usually has little impact on the share price unless the directors announce a dividend appreciably different from market expectations.

4.4 In times of bull markets, capital gains are usually a more fruitful source of income than dividends because high short-term capital gains may be available on many shares. However, in times of sideways-trending or bear markets, dividends are more useful because capital gains may be difficult (or impossible) to obtain with most shares.

4.5 Yes, both these values are possible. Zero means that the company is not paying any dividend. A PR greater than 100% indicates that the company is using reserves to bolster the dividend.

4.6   I would regard a suitable payout ratio to be in the range of about 30 to 80%, meaning a dividend cover between 1.25 and 3.33. This indicates that the company is comfortably able to cover dividends from profits. A payout ratio above 100% (dividend cover less than 1) is generally unhealthy and means that the company is dipping into reserves to pay dividends. The directors may do this to appease shareholders and you should regard this with caution.

4.7   Dividends can be unfranked (zero franking) or fully franked (100% franking) or any level in between. It is also possible for the franking to be above 100% but this is very rare. For an investor, a fully franked dividend is better than an unfranked or partly franked one because this provides the best sustainable taxation benefit.

4.8   To get a fair comparison, calculate the grossed-up yield. If the dividend is fully franked the grossing-up factor is 1.429 and the grossed-up yield is $3 \times 1.429 = 4.29\%$. The unfranked yield is 4% so the 3% fully franked yield is better.

4.9   You should always consider grossed-up yield rather than raw yield because it gives you a true measure of the value of the yield and allows fair comparison when the franking level of shares is different.

4.10   Using the formula, GUF = 1.198 (or interpolate between 50 (1.176) and 60 (1.220) in table 4.3). So the true value of this yield to you is $4.5 \times 1.198 = \mathbf{5.39\%}$.

4.11   The advantages of a DRP are as follows:

» Over a period of time the number of shares you hold will increase and this increase will be at a compound rate.

» If a discount factor is applied to the allocation of shares under the DRP, you make extra profit.

» It's an effective long-term investing strategy because the dividend automatically accumulates as shares and you're not tempted to spend it.

» Shares accumulate at an average price over time and this is a good way of smoothing out short-term volatility of the stock market.

The disadvantages are:

» You don't receive the cash.

» The dividend must be declared as income in your tax return even though you haven't actually received the cash.

» If you decide to sell some or all of your shares, the capital gains tax calculation is more complex.

4.12 EPS $= 12.4 \div 96 = \$0.129 =$ **12.9¢**

DPS $= 7.68 \div 96 = \$0.08 =$ **8.0¢**

PR $= 7.68 \div 12.4 =$ **0.62** $(\text{or } 8.0 \div 12.9)$

DC $= 12.4 \div 7.68 =$ **1.61** $(\text{or } 12.9 \div 8.0)$

4.13 The solutions for each scenario are as follows:

a. NOP yield $= 63 \div 10.05 = 6.27\%$

From table 4.3, $G = 1.429$ (fully franked)

Therefore, GUY $= 6.27 \times 1.429 =$ **8.96%**

b. QRS yield $= 8 \div 1.31 = 6.11\%$

From table 4.3, $G = 1.29$ (75% franked)

Note: No figure is given for 75% so you can interpolate (that is, take the average) between 70 and 80%, which is $(1.266 + 1.316) \div 2 = 1.29\%$ (or use the formula to get the same result).

Therefore, GUY $= 6.11 \times 1.29 =$ **7.88%**

4.14 Cash dividend $= 0.75 \times 554 = \$415.50$

Shares allocated $= 415.50 \div 32.42 = 12.8$

Rounding up, you will receive **13 shares**.

4.15 The buy cost of your shares is $2000 \times \$8.64 + \$50 = \$17\,330$.

After the dividend, your book cost is $\$17\,330 + \$620 =$ **\$17 950**.

Your sales revenue is $2073 \times \$8.93 - \$50 = \$18\,462$.

Your taxable capital gain is $\$18\,462 - \$17\,950 =$ **\$512**.

Your actual capital gain is $\$18\,462 - \$17\,330 =$ **\$1132**.

You can see that a considerable difference exists between accounting profit and actual profit.

4.16 The solutions for each scenario are as follows:

    a.   Capital gain per share = $5.00

          Total capital gain   = $5 \times 1000 = \$5000$

          Tax   = $0.39 \times \$5000 = \$1950$

          After-tax profit   = $\$5000 - \$1950 = \textbf{\$3050}$

    b.   From table 4.2, for a tax rate of 37%, the capital gain reduction $Cd = 24.2\%$

        Therefore, price drop = $5 \times 0.242 = \textbf{\$1.21}$

        Current price = $10.00; therefore, price could drop to $10.00 - $1.21 = **$8.79**.

    c.   Wait until shares have been held 12 months, and sell for $8.79.

        Capital gain   = $(\$8.79 - 5) \times 1000 = \$3790$

        Taxable gain = $\$3790 \div 2 = \$1895$

        Tax   = $0.39 \times \$1895 = \$739$

        After-tax gain = $3790 – $739 = **$3051**, which is the same after-tax gain as obtained by selling now for $10.00 as calculated in part (a) (allowing for small rounding-off difference).

4.17 From table 4.2, for a tax rate of 37%, $Cd = 24.2\%$

    Price drop = $0.242 \times (\$5.43 - \$3.26) = \$0.525$

    Break-even price = $5.43 – $0.525 = $4.91

    Since you don't think the price will drop below $5.00, your best strategy is **to hold**.

Chapter 5

Understanding movements in share prices

Share prices are influenced by a number of factors and in this chapter I discuss the relevant factors in play and how they affect prices. This will give you a better understanding of share price movements and hopefully you will be able to use this knowledge to improve your share investing profitability.

Considering the influencing factors

Some of the factors that influence share prices include issue and market price, market and investor psychology and even herd instinct and momentum.

Issue price

When a company decides to float and issue shares, the price of those shares is the issue price. For example, if the company issues 100 million shares and the issue price of each share is $1.00 the company will raise $100 million in equity capital.

Share trading

When the shares are listed on an exchange and trading commences, the price is determined by market forces of supply and demand. The sharemarket is a free-enterprise market, where buyers and sellers compete. In Australia, no intervention comes from the government or any other authority (except to maintain fair competition and prevent corruption). Share trading is very much like an auction being carried out continually.

Bids and offers

The price buyers are prepared to pay for a parcel of shares is called the *bid*, and the price sellers are prepared to sell for is called the *offer*. A transaction occurs only when a bid and offer match exactly. The price at which this occurs is the current market price (or last sale price).

Changes in the market price

If more buyers want to buy shares at a price around the last sale price than sellers wanting to sell them, the price will rise. This is because buyers need to raise their bid price to get the number of shares they want. On the other hand, if sellers outnumber buyers, the sellers need to drop their offer price in order to be able to sell the desired number of shares. If for the majority of listed shares there's an excess of buyers, the market as a whole will rise, while an excess of sellers will cause a market fall.

Random and significant price variations

As shares are traded, the market price can vary from sale to sale and these variations are usually non-significant or random price variations. In more precise mathematical terms, they are non-statistically significant variations. However, at times, significant price changes can occur in a way that's not simply due to normal random variations.

I'll explain the difference between the two types of variation with an analogy. Suppose you travel to a certain destination at around the same time during each week day. If you record the daily journey times, what differences might you find from day to day? Perhaps one day the journey takes 30 minutes, and the next day 27 minutes and the day after 32 minutes. Variations like these are normal random variations and they're due to non-significant factors. After a while, you work out the average time and you find it's 30 minutes. But suppose one day the journey takes you 45 minutes — is this still a non-significant variation? I think you'll agree that this looks like a significant variation. It's probably due to some significant change — perhaps roadwork, trackwork, an accident or a breakdown that caused the extra travel time on this day.

In the sharemarket, random variations occur all the time in the normal course of trading as buyers and sellers compete. However, significant changes can occur to either an individual share or the market as a whole due to some major change. To determine whether the change is significant or not, you need to look at the degree of the change above or below the normal trend. The best way of doing this is to examine a price chart and identify trends and variations from the trend. I discuss this method in detail in chapter 9.

Market psychology

Competition between buyers and sellers explains why share prices tend to change with each transaction, but it doesn't explain why a particular investor (or number of investors) wants to buy at times when others want to sell. No doubt, a percentage of buy transactions occur because investors have accumulated cash they wish to invest, and a percentage of sell transactions occur because investors need cash. However, many trades occur for reasons other than these and are triggered by changes in investor sentiment, because psychology plays a big role in the sharemarket.

With all the technology available today, you might think that share investing is a scientific business; that is, that buy and sell decisions involving large sums of money are made by experts who spend all day honing their skills with the aid of sophisticated computer programs. It's certainly true that many scientific tools and computer programs can identify buying and selling opportunities and some may even initiate trades, but in the vast majority of cases people drive the market and humans are strongly influenced by moods and emotions. In many cases, significant market changes are triggered by anticipation of an event and often the triggering event does not take place at all. The time of year can also have a significant impact on share prices and certain months tend to be consistently better or worse than others. For example, the saying, 'Sell in May and go away' has arisen because June tends to be a down month for shares—probably because of the juggling that takes place prior to the end of the financial year. Expressions such as 'Santa Claus rally' have also emerged because around Christmas time share prices often rise as the festive mood flows on to the market.

Investor psychology

As I've said, humans with emotions make most investment decisions. Four important emotions affect investors, namely:

- *Optimism:* The belief that a share price (or overall market) will rise.

- *Pessimism:* The belief that a share price (or overall market) will fall.

- *Profit motive:* The desire to make profits and grow wealth. This is also described as FOMO (fear of missing out).

- *Loss aversion:* The fear of losing and diminishing wealth.

For most investors, a continual tug of war occurs between these emotions. Sometimes an investor can remain in one state or another for a prolonged period or, at other times, their emotions may change from one day to another or even within the course of a day. A change in emotion can be triggered by a number of factors and for an individual investor it may be as simple as feeling happy one day or down the next. Weather is well known to affect human moods and on bright, sunny days we tend to feel happier and more optimistic and on gloomy days our mood tends to be gloomier and more pessimistic.

In general, buyers are optimistic and believe prices will rise whereas sellers are pessimistic and believe prices will fall. Every share trade has both a buyer and a seller, so someone's right and someone's wrong. Viewing this objectively brings you to the conclusion that you have a 50% chance of being right when you trade shares on the expectation of future price movements.

Example

A long established company has fallen on hard times and is making less profit now than formerly. Investors may view this in the following ways:

- *Buyer:* 'The company is well established and has a good product. I know they have fallen on hard times but I believe they will overcome their difficulties and the share price will reflect this in the future. Therefore, I will buy now while the price is low and ride the upward trend when the price recovers.'

- *Seller:* 'The company is in trouble and the shares are falling. If I hold them any longer my profit will be eroded (or my losses will magnify). I had better get out while I can. I can always buy the shares back later if the company overcomes its difficulties. Therefore, I will sell now and get out of the downtrend.'

You can see that both views are perfectly justified from each investor's standpoint. The sad fact of the matter is that both cannot be right at the same time.

Note

You have to accept that you will not be right all the time when you make share trading decisions. The sharemarket has an element of unpredictability and no computer program and no human being can accurately predict how share prices will move. You are doing well if you can be right more often than you are wrong. Actually, you can still make an overall profit even when you make more losing trades than winning ones. You can do this by having good money management strategies in place, and I discuss this in chapter 13.

Economic cycles

Economies tend to cycle through periods of growth and prosperity, followed by stagnation or negative growth (known colloquially as *boom or bust*). The period of the cycle has historically been between 8 and 11 years. The sequence of events constituting the economic cycle is often depicted as a clock, as shown in figure 5.1 (overleaf).

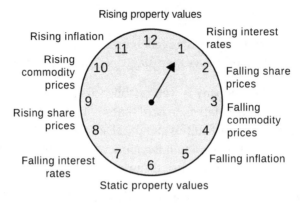

Figure 5.1: The economic clock

The various economic factors depicted on the clock don't cycle in unison, as depicted by their different positions around the clock face. In particular, share prices and property prices tend to be well out of phase with each other because share prices are very sensitive and react quickly to changing economic circumstances whereas property prices react more slowly and lag behind shares. For example, a change in interest rates generally has an immediate effect on equities whereas it may take a prolonged series of interest rate changes before the property market reacts.

Note

The economic clock provides a useful pictorial representation of economic cycling but shouldn't be taken too literally because many factors not depicted on the clock can affect an economy (or sectors of it) and the time period can vary considerably.

Herd instinct

Herd instinct has been part of human survival strategy since humans first walked the earth. Humans have survived through the ages because they formed tribes and did not try to exist on their own. This favoured survival because cooperation was mutually beneficial and there was safety in numbers when danger threatened. It may seem strange to say, but the herd instinct also applies to share traders who don't operate in a vacuum but know how prices are moving. This results in the tendency to follow the market and trade with the herd on the principle that the majority knows best. There's also the temptation to think that others may know something I don't. So most traders and investors trade with the trend and don't have the courage to go against it.

Note

Share investors and traders who go against the trend are known as *contrarians*.

Momentum

Because of the tendency to follow the herd and trade with a trend, once a trend starts it often continues (or even accelerates) without any real justification — everyone is just following everyone else. This is known as *momentum* and momentum often leads to irrational optimism or pessimism. The result is that if prices move upward, momentum often causes an overshoot so prices rise to irrational highs. Conversely, downward momentum often causes prices to undershoot to irrational lows.

Momentum causing overshoot and undershoot is illustrated in figure 5.2.

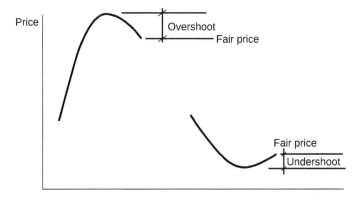

Figure 5.2: Momentum causing overshoot and undershoot

Momentum can affect a single share or the market as a whole. A dramatic example of momentum and irrational optimism occurred in Australia in 1969 with a mining stock—Poseidon. The company announced a promising nickel discovery during a world shortage of the metal. Within four months, amid much hype and publicity, momentum gathered pace and the share price soared from below a dollar to $280! There seemed no end in sight until the bubble eventually burst and the price quickly dropped. Seven years later, the company was placed in receivership without ever making a profit from nickel!

While this is an extreme example and unlikely to be repeated in modern times, nevertheless irrational (unjustified) price moves still occur in today's markets. Being able to recognise these will help you to avoid disasters and make profits by selling in an overshoot and buying in an undershoot. This requires you to exercise a 'contrarian' mentality, ignoring the 'hype' and not simply following the herd, but basing your trading/investing decisions on rational considerations.

Understanding how significant factors affect share price movements

Myriad factors can cause share prices to move significantly. They can be grouped into one of two groups, namely macroeconomic and microeconomic factors. Macroeconomic factors are those that affect the whole economy and flow on to the market and, therefore, have an impact on most shares, whereas microeconomic factors are significant factors that affect only one company (or sometimes a group of similar companies).

The following sections outline some of the important macroeconomic factors and microeconomic factors that affect Australian shares.

Significant events

Significant events both at home and abroad (particularly in the United States and China) are macroeconomic factors that affect the psychology of the entire Australian market (or world markets). For example, the terrorist attack in New York on 11 September 2001 caused a sudden drop in the US share market and had a flow-on effect to the Australian market, which dropped about 10% within a few days. More recently, the GFC (global financial crisis) and the COVID-19 pandemic affected the global economy and had a dramatic influence on Australian share prices, which tumbled in response.

Note

Australian market reaction to world events isn't necessarily sudden and can occur more slowly and over a longer period of time.

Government intervention

In a free economy, the laws of supply and demand act on the economy as a whole. If total demand exceeds supply, the economy grows and the price of goods and services tends to increase, causing inflation. On the other hand, when supply exceeds demand, the economy stagnates or even shrinks into negative growth — that is, a reduction in GDP (gross domestic product).

As well as the reduction in GDP, other undesirable effects of negative growth include a reduction in company profitability as demand shrinks and consumer and corporate spending reduces. This can then cause an increase in corporate failures, which result in job losses and an increase in unemployment. In turn, this reduces government income as revenue from income tax reduces but at the same time increases the government spending as more people (and even corporations) seek government assistance. Prolonged negative growth of two or more consecutive quarters is technically known as a *recession*.

Even though we enjoy a free economy, our government can exert control over the Australian economy to dampen the swings and thus prevent rampant inflation or recession. The government can stimulate the economy by increasing the level of government spending, introducing financial incentives (such as a home buyer's grant), reducing taxation or reducing interest rates or even direct financial assistance to individuals or businesses. Naturally, some opposite measures can be applied to dampen the economy. However, exact balancing of an economy is very difficult to achieve because, as we've seen, factors affecting an economy don't all react at the same time and in the same way. Given a choice, most governments (and certainly the Australian government) prefer a moderate level of inflation to the alternative of stagnation or negative growth. Generally, our government attempts to control inflation to a target level of between 2 and 3%.

Although in the past we've experienced periods of high inflation, high interest rates and some recessions, I believe our government has learned from the mistakes that have been made in the past and now generally practises more restrained government spending and sensible economic management. So it appears unlikely that rampant inflation or prolonged recessions will occur in the future.

Note

Inflation increases the price of goods and services and also results in an increase in company profits. In other words, inflation tends to cause share prices to increase according to the level of inflation. This is demonstrated in a numerical example in learning exercise 5.2.

Interest rates

One of the most significant macroeconomic events affecting shares is a change in interest rates. An increase in interest rates almost always causes a drop in share prices and it's not hard to see why. Most companies use loan capital to a greater or lesser extent and if their loan interest payments increase, profitability suffers proportionally and this reflects in the share price. As well as this, most consumers have mortgages and use personal loans and credit cards, so an increase in interest rates reduces their disposable income and affects companies and shares as follows:

Increasing interest rates → higher loan payments → lower disposable income → lower spending → lower product sales → lower company profits → falling share prices → falling share market.

Exports

Without doubt, economy of scale plays a very important role in company profitability. Simply stated this means that the higher the volume, the cheaper the production cost and the more competitive a company can be.

In comparison with other major economies throughout the world, Australia has a relatively small population and, therefore, a relatively small domestic market for Australian goods and services. Many Australian companies rely on exports to boost sales volume so they can achieve reasonable economies of scale. Therefore, if demand for Australian products falls on the world market, the profitability of many Australian companies will fall.

Technology

Technology changes over the years have resulted in higher productivity for companies and better utilisation of assets. You need only to reflect on the changes that have taken place in the banking and retailing sectors over the past few decades to see how technology has resulted in improved productivity. If companies are able to improve productivity, earnings grow and share prices rise in about the same proportion as the growth in productivity.

The interesting question is whether technology improvements can continue indefinitely or whether at some time a limit will be reached where no further gains can be achieved. I'm confident that the march of technology will progress into the foreseeable future, with Australian companies being able to reap benefits from improved technology.

Company announcements

Any significant new information about a company that's released to the market can affect investor sentiment and, therefore, the share price. However, in some cases a microeconomic factor can result in a flow-on effect to other companies in the same sector or even to the market as a whole. For example, if a major retailer announces a fall in sales, this may affect other retailers and may even drag the entire market down by invoking a general mood of pessimism.

Director trades

In Australia, directors are allowed to trade shares (or options) in their own company provided they don't use insider knowledge to profit from the trade. A director trading a significant number of shares can affect the share price. If the director sells, the share price is likely to fall because investors see this as indicative of negative sentiment and if the director buys, the share price is likely to rise because this is seen as indicative of confidence and positive sentiment.

Rumours

Investors focus primarily on the future and the market often anticipates changes and reacts to these prior to any official release. That is, trades can be based on rumours or predictions rather than facts. Consequently, when an announcement is made the market often reacts in an apparently illogical manner. For example, a favourable announcement may result in a price fall on the day it's made and vice versa! This effect is summed up in a stock market saying:

Traders buy on rumour and sell on news.

Notes

- Market rumours often turn out to be false—for example, when takeover speculation or anticipated interest rate changes don't eventuate.

- In a minority of cases, an announcement takes the market completely by surprise, with no prior rumours. Even though strict bans on insider trading are in place, it's very difficult to stamp out rumours and speculation based on those rumours.

Example

A company announces an increase in earnings and an increase in the dividend from 40 to 45 cents per share but the share price falls. What is the likely explanation?

The likely explanation is that analysts have noticed the increase in earnings and predicted that the company will increase the payout to shareholders by increasing the dividend. Their figures indicate the dividend will increase to 50 cents per share and this prediction spreads through the market. When the actual announcement is made, the increase in dividend is below market expectation and so the share price falls.

Change in earnings

One of the most critical microeconomic factors affecting investor sentiment about a company and hence its share price is the earnings or profit. Past earnings provide a guide but investors look to the future and are far more concerned about likely future earnings than past profitability. This is summed up by the market saying:

Today's investors cannot profit from yesterday's earnings.

When you think about it, this is clearly true—past earnings don't guarantee future profitability and a company that's been profitable in the past isn't necessarily going to be so in the future. However, when a change occurs or an announcement is made that investors perceive could affect future earnings, there's always a price reaction. The direction and severity of the price movement (in other words, whether the share price goes up or down and by how much), depends on the extent to which the change is viewed as having a favourable or unfavourable impact on earnings. In the same way, the overall market will react if an event occurs that is seen as being likely to affect future earnings of many of the larger listed companies.

So a vital principle underpinning share price movements is:

The price of a share (or the market as a whole) changes when an event occurs that investors perceive will affect future companies earnings (or the market as a whole). A perceived increase in future earnings tends to cause a price increase, while a decrease in earnings has the opposite effect.

Notes

- While investors focus primarily on future earnings rather than past earnings, it's true that historical earnings may provide a guide to the future and underpin investors' valuation of a share. For example, a company that's been profitable over some past years is less likely to suddenly become unprofitable than it is to continue being profitable.

- While today's investors cannot directly profit from yesterday's earnings, it's also true that if some of yesterday's profit has been reinvested in new equipment or technology, this could be of future benefit.

Change in net assets

Another fundamental microeconomic factor underpinning a share price is the net assets of the company—that is, assets minus liabilities. For example, imagine you are considering buying a business and two businesses, A and B, are available. Both produce the same amount of profit; however, business A owns the land, buildings, plant and equipment it uses while business B leases all of these. No doubt you'd be prepared to pay a lot more for business A, because you'd be getting a lot more 'bang for your buck' in the form of tangible assets that have a value regardless of the profitability of the business.

If the net assets change, the share price will usually respond, going up if net assets increase and down if they decrease. However, with most companies, net assets seldom change significantly unless a revaluation of assets or a takeover occurs. This is because for most companies, a large slice of their assets are *fixed assets*, such as land, buildings, plant and equipment, with a value that doesn't change significantly in the short term.

Notes

- Listed investment companies (LICs) have few assets other than their investments, so their net assets change frequently as the value of their investments goes up or down with market trends. The change in net assets will usually be reflected in the share price.

- Net assets indicate the 'bottom line' worth of a business; that is, what the business would really be worth if it folded.

- Occasionally a company will revalue assets (usually down) and this usually causes a drop in share price.

Dividends

As discussed in chapter 4, dividend payments affect the share price of companies that pay dividends. Prior to the ex-dividend date, the price usually rises in anticipation of the dividend because the expected dividend gets factored into the share price. On the ex-dividend date, the price falls—usually by the amount of the dividend, but sometimes by more for fully franked dividends to take into account the value of the imputations credits. Therefore, if you're watching a share price closely and you see a sudden drop when the shares open for trading, you need to check whether this drop is due to the shares going ex-dividend rather than a sudden change in investor sentiment.

Learning exercises

5.1   What's the difference between the following?

   a.   Random and significant price changes, and the
        cause of each.

   b.   Macroeconomic and microeconomic factors that affect
        share prices.

5.2   Complete the following table, in which the current situation
      of a company is compared to its situation some years later
      when an accumulated inflation of 50% has occurred. Assume
      a company tax rate of 30% and that inflation drives up the
      cost and selling price proportionately. However, the number of
      units produced, the number of shares on issue and the PE do
      not change. Draw conclusions from the figures calculated.

      Note: PE is the price-to-earnings ratio and is obtained
      by dividing the share price by the EPS (please refer to
      chapter 8).

	Current	**After 50% inflation**
Cost per unit	$1.00	
Selling price per unit	$1.50	
Profit per unit		
Units produced per annum	2 million	2 million
Earnings (before tax)		
Earnings (after tax)		
Shares on issue	10 million	10 million
Earnings per share		
PE	10	10
Share price		

5.3   What factors do you think may cause some months of
      the year to be significantly better than others on the stock
      market?

5.4   A company announces an increase in profitability yet on the
      day of the announcement the share price falls. What is the
      most likely reason for this?

5.5 How are share prices determined on the stock market and why do they fluctuate during the course of a single trading session?

5.6 Complete the following table, indicating the likely reason for the share price reacting the way it did in each case on the day of the announcement.

Case	Change in profit from previous period	Share price change on the day	Likely reason for price reaction
A	Increase	Rise	
B	Increase	Steady	
C	Increase	Fall	
D	Decrease	Rise	
E	Decrease	Steady	
F	Decrease	Fall	

5.7 Explain how you might be able to benefit from recognising the effect momentum has on share prices. Also, outline what cautions you should apply when attempting to benefit from the momentum effect.

5.8 Would you consider a significant increase in the price of crude oil to be a microeconomic or macroeconomic factor affecting the stock market? Explain.

5.9 What effect do interest rate changes usually have on share prices and why?

5.10 What is meant by 'real growth' and what is the most common way companies can achieve real growth over a prolonged period?

5.11 Outline some of the technological changes that have taken place in (a) banking and (b) retailing that have enabled companies in these industries to improve productivity and reduce costs.

5.12 When trading commences one morning, you notice the opening share price is considerably lower than the closing price the night before. What might be a likely explanation for this?

5.13 What's meant by a 'contrarian' and when might you consider being one?

5.14 What is the difference between earnings and profit?

5.15 What's meant by earning and net assets and why are they important factors underpinning a share price?

5.16 Why do investors look to the future earnings rather than current or past earnings when valuing shares?

5.17 When might you expect a significant change in the assets of a company? What listed companies report a continual change in assets and why?

Learning exercises solutions

5.1   The solutions for each scenario are as follows:

a. A random price change is due to a non-statistically significant variation and is to be expected in a free market. A significant price change is outside the range of normal variation and is due to some significant variation.

b. Macroeconomic factors are those that affect the whole economy and flow on to the share market and, therefore, have an impact on many shares. Microeconomic factors are local factors that affect just one company or perhaps a group of similar companies.

5.2   See the following completed table.

	Current	After 50% inflation
Cost per unit	$1.00	$1.50
Selling price per unit	$1.50	$2.25
Profit per unit	50¢	75¢
Units produced per annum	2 million	2 million
Earnings (before tax)	$1 million	$1.5 million
Earnings (after tax)	$0.7 million	$1.05 million
Shares on issue	10 million	10 million
Earnings per share	70¢	$1.05
PE	10	10
Share price	$7.00	$10.50

Conclusion: The share price has increased by 50%, which exactly matches the accumulated inflation rate.

5.3   Some of the factors that affect monthly share price variations include:

» seasonality of weather and its effect on product demand

» the close of one financial year and the start of another

» traditional school vacation and holiday periods

» traditional high consumer spending periods such as Christmas.

5.4 The most likely reason for the fall is that the market has anticipated the change in profitability and already factored this into the share price. On the day of the announcement, the price may drop if the announced increase in profitability is not in line with market expectations.

5.5 Share prices are determined by the interaction between demand and supply. If demand exceeds supply (at around the last trade price), the price will generally rise and vice versa.

5.6 See the following completed table.

Case	Change in profit from previous period	Share price change on the day	Likely reason for price reaction
A	Increase	Rise	Profit increase exceeds market expectation
B	Increase	Steady	Profit increase is in line with market expectation
C	Increase	Fall	Profit increase is below market expectation
D	Decrease	Rise	Profit decrease is below market expectation
E	Decrease	Steady	Profit decrease is in line with market expectation
F	Decrease	Fall	Profit decrease exceeds market expectation

5.7 The momentum effect can be used to your advantage if you recognise it. Undershoot may present an opportunity to buy at a bargain price because the market has downgraded the price below a fair level. Therefore, the price should correct in the future as more investors realise that the shares have been oversold and so you can profit from the price rise. Conversely, if you hold a share that has risen significantly in price, be alert to detect a downward movement and a time to sell as investors come to the realisation that the share is overpriced to above fair value.

The cautions that you should consider are:

» Beware of buying because a share looks cheap compared to historical prices. Wait until you are reasonably confident that the downward momentum is faltering. This means surrendering part of your profit, but it is a much safer strategy. Conversely, do not sell just because the price looks high until you are sure the uptrend momentum has faltered.

» Beware of steep trends (particularly uptrends) and remember the saying 'what goes up must come down'. Rapid increases in a share price are seldom maintained because short-term traders move in and take profits and an equally rapid downtrend correction in share price usually occurs soon after.

5.8   On the face of it, the price of crude oil appears to be a microeconomic factor affecting companies in the oil exploration or production business only. However, the fuel derivatives of crude are used so widely that a significant increase in the price of crude is likely to have a wide impact on many businesses. So really the price of crude can be regarded as a macroeconomic factor as much as a microeconomic factor.

5.9   Increasing interest rates usually cause share prices to fall and vice versa. The main reasons for this are:

» most companies use loan capital and an increase in loan payments reduces their profitability

» most consumers have mortgages or use credit of one form or another and an increase in interest rates reduces their disposable income and impacts on consumer demand.

5.10 Real growth is growth above inflation. A common way of achieving real growth is to re-invest some profit back into the business and so achieve higher productivity.

5.11 Some of the technological changes to improve productivity and reduce costs are:

a.   In the banking industry, changes include account computerisation, ATMs to reduce labour costs and number of branches needed, plastic account cards to reduce paperwork with banking transactions, internet banking and e-payments, and automated account services.

b.   In the retailing industry, the major changes include self-service checkouts, bar coding, automated transactions, automated warehouses and goods handling systems, computerised stock control and the introduction of generic products.

5.12 A likely explanation is that the shares went ex-dividend. In any case, you should check this out first before you delve further.

5.13 A contrarian doesn't 'follow the herd' but trades against the trend. Consider being a contrarian when you recognise irrational exuberance or pessimism in the stock market.

5.14 There is no difference and both terms mean exactly the same thing.

5.15 Earnings (profit) are total revenue minus total expenses. Net assets are total assets minus total liabilities.

Earnings are the major factor underpinning share prices because a business has to make a profit in order to survive. Net assets are an important factor because they indicate the bottom line worth of a business.

5.16 The stock market is forward thinking and investors look toward future earnings rather than present or past earnings. High profits in the past are no guarantee of future profitability and an investor cannot profit in the future from past earnings.

5.17 Most company's assets change only when a revaluation of assets or takeover occurs, because the value of most company assets doesn't change significantly in the short term. The exception is LICs because they don't own many assets other than their investments and the value of these does change from day to day in accordance with market price changes of their shares.

Chapter 6

Planning your investment in shares

In this chapter, I discuss the planning I believe you should undertake before you invest in shares. I look at why you need to plan, and what you should consider in your planning.

Understanding the benefits of planning

An old saying is worth repeating here because it applies to share investing as much as to any other human endeavour:

If you fail to plan, you plan to fail.

When I first started investing in shares, the idea of planning didn't even enter my mind. A good friend of mine 'played the market', so I asked him the contact details of his broker. I contacted the broker and started buying and selling shares based on the broker's recommendation and my 'gut feeling', peppered with a few tips here and there.

Many years later, and after making many mistakes, I've come to realise that this wasn't a good approach. Share investing should be planned and your planning should be done before—not after—you set up a share portfolio. Not only do you need a plan but, even more importantly, you also need to follow your plan. On most occasions when one of my share investments has resulted in a loss, it's been because I haven't followed my plan. We're all human and our emotions can override logic or rational considerations. It's most important not to divert from your plan on a whim or because of a mood swing. In fact, the less emotional and the more rational you are, the greater your likelihood of being a profitable share investor.

I hope by now I've convinced you that you need a plan and you need to follow it. I recommend that you write down your plan and keep it in a prominent place near your computer or on your desk and that you refer to it before contemplating a share trade. While the plan should be written, it shouldn't be set in concrete but should be reviewed periodically (I suggest every six months) because conditions change. I'll go into this aspect in greater detail in chapter 14.

Establishing your risk profile

Before you can formulate a suitable share investing plan, you need to know your risk profile because, as we've seen in previous chapters, risk and return are closely related. It's a good idea to match your share investments to your risk profile; for example, it's generally not a good idea to try to make fast profits by adopting high-risk strategies if they don't sit comfortably with you. This is known as applying 'the sleep test', which simply means that if you lose sleep worrying about your shares they aren't right for you.

Buying shares is really no different from buying anything else—you wouldn't buy clothes if they didn't fit you or if you didn't like their colour or style, would you? In the same way, it's not a good idea to invest in companies that you're not comfortable with. After all, once you've bought the shares, you're a part owner of the company.

Risk profiles

Traders and investors can be classed into common groups according to their motives and risk profiles. I describe these here.

Investor

An investor has accumulated capital that's not required for day-to-day living expenses but is used for the purpose of growing wealth.

Trader

A share trader makes frequent trades (buys and sells) and often buys and sells the same parcel of shares in one day.

Typical risk and return profiles for these are shown in table 6.1.

Table 6.1 Typical risk and return profiles for investors and traders

	Time frame	Risk	Potential return	Nature of the return
Investor	Medium – long	Low – medium	Medium	Interest + cap. gain
Trader	Short	High	High	Cap. gain only

You probably have a fair idea of your own profile and how much risk you're comfortable with. If not, several online quizzes on various websites are available to help you establish your risk profile.

Knowing what factors to consider in your plan

In your plan, you should consider a number of factors, including:

- your investment capital
- in whose name the shares will be registered
- the time you will devote to share investing
- your investment goals
- your investment mix
- your trading method
- your trading strategy

- frequency of review

- estate planning.

The following sections discuss these in greater detail.

Your investment capital

Your first step is to decide how much you'll invest in shares. Remember, the minimum buy order is $500 (for any shares you don't already own) but, practically, you need a total investment capital of several thousand dollars so you can obtain reasonable diversification. It's sometimes said that the amount you invest in shares should be no more than what you can afford to lose. I think that's a rather negative attitude; however, the important point is that it's dangerous to invest money in shares that you need for other essential purposes. In other words, your shares should be purchased using investment capital as opposed to essential capital. Also, it's a very good idea to keep a proportionate amount of your available capital in cash and not invest every single dollar into shares. It is very frustrating to come across a great investment opportunity but not to have the capital available to take advantage of it. Indeed, keeping some spare capital is an essential part of good risk management, as discussed in chapter 13.

Once you've planned how much you'll invest in shares, you also need to consider the following aspects:

- Will you invest a single lump sum, or will you build up your share portfolio over time by adding to it?

- Will you reinvest dividends or take them as cash? If a dividend reinvestment plan is offered, will you join it and receive additional shares instead of cash? (You may wish to refer back to chapter 4, where DRPs are discussed.)

- Will you gear your share investment by taking out a loan or by trading CFDs or derivatives? If you're starting out, doing so is probably not a good idea because of the higher risk. However, if you're a high-risk investor, you might consider this option.

In whose name the shares will be registered

Before you trade shares with any broker (online or offline), you need to set up a trading account (or accounts). When you do so, you need to state in whose name purchased shares will be registered. In many cases, investors make arrangements to register shares in names other than their own—for example, if they're in a personal partnership or when they're setting aside growth assets on behalf of minors (usually their children or grandchildren). If you want to do this, you need to check out the taxation implications of income splitting and unearned income of minors.

Another option is an investment partnership or club, which is a partnership set up specifically for the purpose of share investing. The benefits are that you spread the risk and have more capital available than if you go it alone. Also, you can bounce ideas around with others. However, you lose complete control, the set-up procedure is rather complex (because you need a partnership agreement) and you'll also need to submit a partnership tax return (in addition to your own personal tax return). If you're interested in setting up or joining a share investing partnership, I suggest you research further (for example, on the internet or by reading a dedicated book about it).

Note

Even if you don't get involved in a share investing partnership, it's a very good idea not to operate entirely in a vacuum and have someone you can bounce ideas around with. This could be a partner, family member or just a good friend who's also interested in shares.

The time you'll devote to share investing

You've probably heard the story (supposedly true) about the commentator who remarked to Gary Player after he'd won a golf tournament that luck had played an important part in his win. Player agreed but added, 'Yes, but I've noticed that the more I practice, the luckier I get'. The same principle applies to share investing and the more time and effort you devote to it, the more likely you are to be successful.

Some people make share trading a full-time activity, while others employ a bottom drawer approach and do very little other than purchase some blue chip shares and then sit on them. You'll probably fit in somewhere between these two extremes. As part of your plan, you need to consider how much time you're prepared to devote to share investing. You need time for research and to monitor your investments and the market.

The amount of time you need to devote to share investing is related to the number of shares you own or are tracking. With a reasonably large portfolio, you'll probably need up to one or two hours a week just to keep track of your shares and to keep your records up to date. With share research, the sky's virtually the limit and you could spend all day, every day on your computer, accessing the amount of information that's available.

Your investment goals

An essential (but often neglected) part of your share investment planning is to define your investment goals (also known as *objectives* or *targets*). Unless you set yourself goals, how do you know whether your investments are performing to your expectations? More importantly, how can you make decisions about your investments unless you have defined your requirements?

Consider the following dialogue from *Alice in Wonderland*:

Alice: Which way do I go from here?

Cat: It depends on where you want to go.

Alice: I don't much care where I go.

Cat: Then it doesn't much matter which way you go.

I've adapted this dialogue so that it reflects the share-investing environment:

Investor: Which shares should I buy?

Adviser: It depends on your investment goals.

Investor: I don't have investment goals.

Adviser: Then it doesn't much matter which shares you buy.

When defining your investment goals, consider the following questions:

- What's the term of my investment? Am I interested in long-term profitability (perhaps in my own superannuation fund) or am I hoping for a high short-term capital gain?

- What's my targeted profit?

- What's the preferred nature of my profit? Am I more interested in capital gains, dividends or a combination of both?

- Are there any special taxation considerations? Do I have any accrued capital losses that I can use to write off against capital gains?

- Do I need to consider social security implications?

Notes

- You don't need to define a single investment term—you can do some short-term trading as well as long-term investing. Indeed, it's an approach I use.

- You can express desired profit as a dollar amount. However, as I discuss in previous chapters, a better measure of financial profitability is the percentage return on the capital you've invested and that's what you should target.

- Your targeted profit should match your risk profile. If you want high security with low risk, you need to plan a lower return than if you're prepared to take more risk with less security.

- It's best to set realistic goals and not ones based upon spectacular returns, because history shows that these are unsustainable. I suggest a reasonable long-term goal is a capital growth about 3% above the inflation rate, with about a 3.5% yield. If you achieve this (or exceed it) over the long term, you're doing well and your real wealth is increasing.

- Another possibility is not just setting a goal that's a fixed percentage return on capital but also setting one relative to a market index (such as the All Ords index). The logic behind this idea is that it's unreasonable to expect your portfolio to grow at a rate of, say, 6% in a year when the general market has been flat or returned a negative result. Fund managers use this strategy by targeting their performance relative to a suitable index. If you're a medium-risk investor, setting a growth rate matching the All Ords is reasonable. If you're a higher risk investor, you might set a goal of capital growth at some percentage above the All Ords growth rate.

Your investment mix

You can now plan your investment mix. Conventional wisdom says you should avoid putting all your eggs in one basket and instead spread your investment cash pool around—that is, you should diversify. There's no reason why all your investments need to be in the same sectors or at the same level of risk. Rather, what's important is that your investment mix matches your profile. If you take a look at table 6.2, you'll see what I mean. In this table I show a hypothetical investment mix for various investor risk profiles.

Table 6.2: Hypothetical investment mix for various risk profiles

	Low-risk shares	Medium-risk shares	High-risk shares
Low-risk investor	90%	10%	0
Low- to medium-risk investor	70%	30%	0
Medium-risk investor	40%	40%	20%
Medium- to high-risk investor	20%	40%	40%
High-risk investor	10%	30%	60%

This table shows an investment strategy doesn't necessarily involve only one type of risk category. The proportionate amount of your investment capital in each type of risk category can vary, but should match your risk profile.

Notes

- If your goal is to beat the market—that is, get a substantially better return than the average investor—you need to take more risk. This means concentrating your investment on just a few shares rather than having a diversified portfolio with a number of shares. If you do this, you will be more of a trader than an investor.

- I discuss diversification in greater detail in chapter 13.

Investment choices

As I outlined in chapter 1, many investment choices are available. Even assuming you want to stick to Australian shares, you still have a bewildering choice, with over 2000 to choose from. I suggest you diversify by choosing shares in different sectors, so it's a good idea to hold off making any decisions about which sectors you want to invest in until you've read chapter 12.

Notes

- If you have only a small amount of investment capital, your range of choices will be restricted because you can't diversify greatly without leaving impractically small amounts in each basket. In this case, your best bet is a listed investment company or listed managed investment, which provides in-built sector diversification.

- Don't forget keeping some spare cash is a good idea—I suggest at least 10%.

Your trading method

As part of your planning, you'll need to consider how you'll trade; that is, how you'll place buy and sell orders. As I've previously said, it's possible to transfer share ownership directly but the vast majority of transactions are made through a broker. The two main types of broker are:

- offline broker

- online broker.

Within each of these major types are three different types of broker:

- full-service broker

- broker who gives advice

- no-advice broker.

Offline and online broker

Before the widespread use of the internet, all brokers operated offline. Most worked in an office and relied on personal contact or phone or fax to communicate with customers. Their overhead costs were high so the brokerage fee was substantial. As internet use grew, online trading mushroomed in popularity. Trading online has many advantages, including a low brokerage rate of around $20 or even less per order. This low brokerage makes trading in small parcels feasible and enables small investors to diversify to a greater extent than previously. Another great advantage of online trading is that most online sites contain a huge amount of information that their clients can access free of charge. This typically includes general information about the company, comprehensive financial statistics, charting facilities and technical indicators. Also, you can generally set up free watch lists and an alert service may be available (at additional cost—although some websites provide this service for free).

However, online trading requires some knowledge, internet expertise and confidence. Some additional risks are also involved, including a greater chance of making mistakes. So online trading may not be suitable for all investors. One way of getting into online trading is to initially use an offline broker who provides advice and ease into the online trading situation gradually. You can do this by setting up an online trading account and trading relatively small parcels of shares until you build up your expertise and confidence. As you do so, you can ease out of offline trading and more into online trading until eventually you can be trading exclusively online if the method suits you.

Full-service broker

As the name implies, a full-service broker provides a full financial service for clients, which can include:

- risk profile assessment

- investment advice, including how to best distribute your capital between the various types of investment instruments

- reviewing and reporting on your investments on a regular basis

- providing share research and recommendations of when to buy or sell

- trading on your behalf

- alerting you (usually by phone or email) when the price of a share reaches a pre-set level

- providing a trading summary at regular intervals, detailing your trades and the profit and/or loss on each trade

- total investment management, where you set up a managed discretionary account and allow the broker to manage your investment capital without any need for input from you.

Note

Many of the services provided by full-service brokers can be obtained free of charge using the internet. Please refer to my book *Online Investing on the Australian Sharemarket* for details.

Broker who gives advice

If you don't require all the services provided by a full-service broker but would still like someone to trade on your behalf and give advice when you want it, you can make arrangements with a broker who provides this type of service.

No-advice broker

Many offline brokers offer a no-frills, low-cost service, in order to try to win back some of the business they have lost to internet brokers. No-advice brokers execute your orders but don't give any advice regarding the merits or demerits of your proposed trades. You'll need to check the types of orders you can place with them, as the full range of order types may not be available with all discount brokers. The main advantage of using a no-advice broker rather than trading on the internet is that you're talking to a person rather than communicating with a computer. You'll be able to ask questions and seek clarification as long as this doesn't constitute investing advice.

Notes

- It's really a good idea to research and study before trading online and my online investing book is about the only one specifically written for the Australian online investor. Naturally I recommend it!

- You don't have to trade exclusively using one method or one broker. Using several broking services is not a problem provided you keep track of your HIN for each broker in the CHESS system. Also, you can readily transfer from one to another without any cost.

Your trading strategy

A most important part of your financial planning with shares is to decide on your trading strategy. If you use a full-service offline broker, it's no problem, because the broker will make trading decisions for you. If you decide to take control of your finances, however, you need to decide on your trading strategy — that is, the criteria you'll use to decide what shares to buy and sell and when to do so. Really experienced investors may be able to trade profitably using a 'gut feeling' approach, but most of us need to set out and follow a trading strategy. A strategy is so important that I suggest you have a written strategy before you place any trading orders.

Many trading strategies are available and some of the most important ones are described throughout this book (particularly in chapter 10). So I suggest you don't formulate your trading plan at this stage but leave it open until you've finished this book.

Frequency of review

An important aspect of your plan is how you will review your portfolio and the frequency of this review. Two types of review are actually required:

- reviewing your portfolio

- reviewing your plan.

Reviewing your portfolio

You should plan your minimum review period based on your temperament and type of shares held. For example, if you are very keen (or edgy) or if you own some speculative shares or the market is very volatile, you may wish to review your portfolio daily or even several times a day. The frequency of review is also highly dependent on your frequency of trading — if you are an active trader and trade each day (or several times a week) you need to review frequently. If you are a less active share investor, you don't really need to review all that frequently. In this case, I suggest you plan a detailed review on a weekly basis. You could even plan a convenient day and time when you will conduct your review. Clearly, this depends on when you have some time free from any commitments or distractions. Some time on a weekend may be the best option because the market is closed and you can get a picture of the weekly action.

Reviewing your plan

You need to consider reviewing your plan regularly but this doesn't need to be done frequently — in fact, it is better if you don't do it too often because having a plan is pointless if you chop and change it frequently. You need to stick to your plan and give it a fair trial before you consider changing it. I suggest an appropriate time interval for you reviewing your plan would be six months, but it could also be longer if you are happy with it.

Note

How you can perform these reviews is discussed in detail in chapter 14.

Estate planning

Although we often don't like to think about estate planning, it's prudent (and fair to your beneficiaries) to plan your estate properly and to set out your plan in the form of a legal will. Of course, as you get older, estate planning becomes increasingly important, and you may wish to obtain specialist advice about it.

As far as your share portfolio is concerned, the first thing to remember is that if you've bought shares and registered them in someone else's name, they legally own the shares so your death won't affect this in any way. However, shares held by you at the time of your death become part of your estate and will be inherited by your nominated beneficiaries. Under taxation law at the time of writing, death doesn't constitute a capital gains event and beneficiaries acquire inherited shares at their cost to you. So if a share portfolio is part of your estate, it's important to maintain accurate records of all shares in it. These records need to show the acquisition price and date of each parcel of shares and must go right back to the original acquisition date, even though this may have been in the distant past. This is especially important if you hold shares acquired through a DRP.

If your beneficiaries decide to keep their shares, the executors of your estate need to arrange ownership transfer through the sponsoring broker (for broker-sponsored shares held in CHESS) or the share registry (for issuer-sponsored shares held with an SRN). Your beneficiaries will pay no capital gains tax until such time as they sell some or all of their shares, when they'll pay tax at their marginal tax rate in the financial year of sale. So if you're on a lower tax rate than your beneficiaries, selling shares prior to your death could be financially beneficial. Needless to say, estate planning becomes a lot easier if you know just when you're going to die!

Notes

- Accrued capital losses can't be transferred to beneficiaries and can be offset against capital gains only if this is done prior to your death. So if you have any accrued capital losses, you can take advantage of them only by selling shares prior to your death.

- If your portfolio contains any shares acquired prior to the introduction of CGT (20 September 1985), these shares are CGT exempt if sold any time before you die. After that, the capital gains tax clock starts ticking for your beneficiaries, so they need to have these shares valued at the date of your death.

Learning exercises

6.1 When should you plan your investment in shares?

6.2 Why is it a good idea to have a written plan?

6.3 What's the most important thing to remember after completing your plan?

6.4 When should you consider changing your plan?

6.5 Why should you have a good idea of your risk profile before you plan your share investment?

6.6
    a. If you lose money on a share trade but followed your plan, what should you do?

    b. If you lose money on a share trade because you didn't follow your plan, what should you do?

6.7
    a. What funds might you consider suitable for investing in shares?

    b. Why is it a good idea to keep some spare cash and not invest all your investment capital?

    c. What's an easy way of increasing your investment capital in shares?

6.8 What are the advantages and disadvantages of setting up (or joining) an investment partnership?

6.9
    a. A share investor states their goal is to make as much profit as possible as quickly as possible. Do you think this is a suitable share investment goal?

    b. What five questions should you ask yourself when setting your goals?

6.10 A share investor states their goal is to double their share investment capital in the next two years. What do you think of this? What might be a better goal?

6.11 What's meant by diversification and why is it generally considered to be a good idea? What's the usual way of diversifying with shares?

6.12 How can you diversify your investment in shares with just one share?

6.13 Do your beneficiaries need to pay capital gains tax on acquisition of shares through your estate? If not, when do they pay CGT? What cost base is used for calculating the cost of their inherited shares?

Please note that no solutions are provided for this chapter's learning exercises from this point onward because the responses will differ for each person.

6.14 Complete the following table, outlining the cash and time you have available for share investing.

My cash and time available for share investing

Available cash I'd like to invest in shares:

Monthly savings I'd like to put aside for share investing:

Amount of loan capital (if any) I will use for share investing:

Proportion of dividends received I will reinvest in shares:

Name the shares will be registered in:

Average time in hours per week I am prepared to devote to share investing:

6.15 Complete the following table, outlining your investment goals.

Notes: Line 3 + Line 4 = Line 2.
Line 5 = Line 2 × (100 − your marginal tax rate) ÷ 100.

For example, if Line 2 is 10% and your marginal tax rate is 32.5%, then Line 5 would be 10% × (100 − 32.5) ÷ 100 = 6.75%.

My share investment goals

1. The proposed term of my share investment in years is:

2. My targeted percentage return on capital invested (before tax) is:

3. My targeted percentage return from capital gains (before tax) is:

4. My targeted percentage return from dividends (before tax) is:

My share investment goals

5. My targeted percentage return on capital invested (after tax) is:

6. Are there any special taxation considerations? If so, what are they?

7. Are there any social security implications? If so, what are they?

8. Have I made provision for my share investment portfolio in my will? How will my beneficiaries know the acquisition cost of inherited shares?

6.16 Decide on how you'll trade shares. If you decide to use an offline broker, decide what type you'd prefer. Obtain a list of brokers (for example, via the ASX website). Contact some brokers to ascertain the level of service they offer and the cost involved. Make your decision and set the wheels in motion. If you decide to trade online, find a site that provides a list of online brokers and compares service and cost so you can decide on one or two online brokers you'll use.

6.17 Taking into account your risk profile, complete the following investment mix table, outlining the amount of your available capital you'll allocate to the various share investing categories.

Note: Some of the answers you give may be zero dollars; your total investment capital (line 6) is the sum of lines 1 to 5.

My investment mix

Investment category	Dollars
Amount I'll hold as cash:	
Amount I'll invest in blue chip shares:	
Amount I'll invest in green chip shares:	
Amount I'll invest in speculative shares:	
Amount I'll invest in managed funds or LICs:	
My total investment capital:	

Learning exercises solutions

6.1   You should plan your investment in shares before you trade any shares; that is, before you place orders to buy or sell.

6.2   A written plan is a good idea because it encourages you to consider exactly what you are trying to achieve with your share investment and how you will achieve it. Also, you can refer to it each time you trade and this encourages you to stick to your plan.

6.3   After completing your plan, the most important thing is to stick to it.

6.4   You shouldn't change your plan on a whim or because you've made a bad trade. You should revisit your plan at regular intervals and evaluate its success and modify it only if this review indicates your plan can be improved.

6.5   Your planned investment strategy depends very much on your risk profile. Because risk and potential return are directly related, you really need to know your risk profile before you can properly plan.

6.6

    a.   Congratulate yourself! Well done!

    b.   Try to establish why you deviated from your plan and resolve not to make the same mistake next time.

6.7

    a.   The funds you invest in shares should be obtained from your investment cash pool and not include any funds needed for essential living purposes.

    b.   It's a good idea to keep some cash at all times. It's part of good risk management and allows you to take advantage of investing opportunities in the future.

    c.   An easy way of building up your investment in shares is to join the DRP (if one is available). In this way, your dividends are automatically re-invested in shares.

6.8   The advantages of an investment partnership are:

» more investment funds available

» sharing of risk

» sharing of ideas and strategies.

The disadvantages are:

» more complex set-up and dissolving procedure

» additional tax return required

» loss of complete control

» possible conflict with other members.

6.9

a.   The goal of 'making as much money as possible and as quickly as possible' is too vague to be a satisfactory goal for a share investment plan, even though it's something we all hope to do.

b.   For the purpose of a share-investing plan, the goal needs to be more specific and measurable (quantifiable) and should include the following five considerations:

» What's the term of my investment? Am I interested in long-term profitability (perhaps in my own superannuation fund) or am I hoping for a high short-term capital gain?

» What's my targeted profit?

» What's the preferred nature of my profit? Am I more interested in capital gains, dividends or a combination of both?

» Are there any special taxation considerations? For example, do I have any accrued capital losses that I can use to write off against capital gains?

» Do I need to consider social security implications?

6.10   Although this goal is one we'd all aspire to, the problem is that it's unrealistic (unlikely to be achieved). Goals that are unachievable are pointless. A better goal is more realistic; for example, a long-term return on capital of about 10% per year.

6.11 Diversification means essentially 'not putting all your eggs in the one basket'. The obvious advantage is that you spread risk. Usually, you diversify in shares by establishing a portfolio with different shares in different sectors.

6.12 You can diversify with shares by buying just one share in an LIC (listed investment company). These companies invest in other companies and so you are effectively diversifying by buying just one share.

6.13 No, your beneficiaries don't pay CGT unless they sell the shares they inherit. The cost base that will be used is your acquisition cost (for each parcel).

Note: No solutions are provided for 6.14 onward, because the responses will be different for each person.

Chapter 7

Taking advantage of share issues

The number of shares issued by a company is an important consideration for shareholders because it underpins the basic value of each share. As a share investor, it's important to understand how the number of shares can change and how any changes might affect you. In this chapter, I consider these aspects.

Understanding how the number of shares affects the share price

If the number of shares on issue is changed without any change in profit or output, the share price will be inversely proportional to the number of shares on issue—that is, if the number of shares doubles, the price will halve and if the number of shares halves, the price will double. For example, if a company valued at $200 million issues 100 million shares, each share has an intrinsic value of $2.00. However, if 200 million shares are issued, the intrinsic value of each share reduces to $1.00.

On the sharemarket, other factors often come into play and muddy the waters somewhat. For example, suppose a listed company issues 20% more shares at a price around the current market price. Investors anticipate that the additional equity capital the company receives will be put to good use by the directors and result in an increase in profitability of 30%. In this case, rather than the share price falling after the issue, it could well rise. However, if it's anticipated that the expected earnings won't increase in step with the additional equity capital obtained, the earnings per share will fall. The market won't like this and the share price will be downgraded.

Changing the number of shares

Essentially, two changes to the number shares on issue can occur:

- increasing the number of shares

- decreasing the number of shares.

These are completely different directions that the directors may decide to take, yet both are common. I discuss them in greater detail in the following sections.

Increasing the number of shares

After first listing, companies may issue additional shares. They usually do so in order to obtain more equity capital. They may need the additional capital for a number of reasons, such as:

- to reduce debt (reduce loan capital)

- to fund an acquisition or takeover

- to purchase new premises or major plant and equipment

- to fund a major restructuring of the business.

Another way a company can increase the shares on issue is by means of a split. In this case, the number of shares increases dramatically but the company obtains no additional equity capital. Shareholder approval is required for a split. (See the section 'Splits and consolidations', later in this chapter, for more information.)

Companies can't issue more shares willy-nilly and to protect investors, company law and ASX listing rules restrict the number of additional shares that can be issued without shareholder approval. As a general rule, a listed company can increase its issued capital by 15% per annum without requiring shareholder approval. Any increase in capital above this level must be approved by shareholders at a general meeting.

Decreasing number of shares

Listed companies sometimes reduce the number of shares on issue for various reasons, such as:

- *To increase the market value (price) of each share.* As already discussed, the share price is inversely proportional to the number of shares on issue. Therefore, if the company decreases the number of shares on issue, the price will rise. This can be desirable if the price is getting too low and the shares are being regarded as 'penny dreadfuls' or 'cheap and nasty'.

- *To increase the earnings per share and dividend per share.* The lower the number of shares over which to distribute profits, the higher the profit per share and the greater the dividend per share. This tends to keep shareholders happy as each share is being allocated a larger 'slice of the pie'.

Changing the number of shares on issue

A company can change the number of shares on issue in several ways. These include:

- bonus issue

- rights

- company-issued options

- splits and consolidations

- share buybacks

- dividend reinvestment plans

- share investment plans.

I discuss each of these in turn, and examine the likely effect on share price and benefits or downsides for shareholders.

Bonus issue

In the past, profitable companies often issued bonus shares from time to time as a kind of reward for loyal shareholders. For example, in a 1 for 10 bonus issue, for every 10 shares you hold, you receive one free share. As a shareholder, this may seem like a good deal because your shareholding increases by 10% and at no cost to you. In fact, bonus issues were no benefit to shareholders, simply because the share price fell proportionally after the issue. So you ended up holding 10% more shares, but each share was worth 10% less so you were no better off. In fact, you would have been somewhat worse off because of the cost to the company associated with the issue (in registry and postage costs), which reduced company profitability. Nowadays, companies rarely issue bonus shares—even when they're making good profits.

Rights

If you hold shares in a company that announces a rights issue, this enables you to obtain more shares at a certain price at any time prior to a cut-off date (expiry date). However, you're under no obligation to do so. Rights are usually issued free of charge, with your rights entitlement being calculated as a percentage of the number of shares you hold—although sometimes a maximum or minimum number is stipulated. If you exercise (or take up) your rights, they'll be converted some time later to fully paid ordinary shares but if you don't exercise your rights they'll lapse and become worthless.

The amount you'll have to pay is known as the *exercise price* and the cut-off date is known as the *expiry date*. The exercise price is usually at an attractive discount to the market price at the time of issue and the expiry date is usually a month or two after the issue is announced. Often the exercise price is given as a certain percentage below the average weighted closing price for a certain number of days prior to the expiry date or a certain maximum price. For example, the rights issue may specify 'the exercise price will be 2.5% below the average weighted closing price for five trading days prior to the expiry date or $14.00, whichever is the lowest'.

Like an IPO, some form of prospectus accompanies the issue and you can exercise your rights by filling out the application form (or completing it online). You are often given several options about the maximum number of shares (or maximum capital) you are entitled to obtain. No trading cost (brokerage or GST) is charged if you take up your rights. If the issue is over-subscribed, you may not be able to get all the shares you want and in this case you will be informed about the number of shares you were allocated and the excess cash will be refunded to you.

Rights issues come in two main flavours—namely, renounceable and non-renounceable. In a renounceable rights issue, the rights will be listed on an exchange and can be freely traded using its trading facility at any time up to the expiry date. In a non-renounceable rights issue, the rights won't be listed and can't be traded. The decision whether to make a rights issue renounceable or non-renounceable is made by the directors.

If shares you own offer a rights issue, you have the following alternatives depending on whether the issue is renounceable or non-renounceable.

Your options for a renounceable issue are:

- take up all the rights you're entitled to
- sell all your rights
- take up some of the rights and sell the remainder
- don't do anything (let your rights lapse).

For a non-renounceable issue, your options are:

- take up all the rights you're entitled to
- take up some of the rights and let the remainder lapse
- don't do anything (let all your rights lapse).

Notes

- If the rights issue is renounceable, letting any of your rights lapse without selling them would be foolish, unless the cost of selling them exceeds the amount you'd receive for them.

- If the issue is renounceable, once the rights are listed, anyone (including existing shareholders) can purchase rights on the sharemarket in the same way as if they were ordinary shares. After purchasing rights, the purchaser can convert the rights to fully paid shares if they want to by paying the exercise price to the company. The purchaser can also sell them again at any time prior to expiry.

Investor considerations

Exercising your right is usually of immediate benefit to you because you should be able to receive additional shares at a discount to the market price, without brokerage or GST. Because more shares are issued at a lower price than the current market price, the price of the shares will generally fall after the issue closes; however, prices usually don't fall sufficiently to offset the gain to shareholders.

In the longer term, if the directors use the additional equity capital to increase profitability, the issue should produce sustainable benefits for all shareholders. So if you can afford to do so, it's generally wise to take up your rights because you'll lose out if you don't. However, if the company's making a loss and running out of capital, a rights issue can leave you caught between a rock and a hard place. While you mightn't want to invest more money in a loss-making enterprise, if you (and other investors) don't do so, the company could run out of money, go into liquidation and then all shares could become virtually worthless.

Intrinsic value

Usually the exercise price is below the current market price, so you can receive additional shares at a discount. The intrinsic value of the rights is the difference between the share price and the exercise price. For example, if the exercise price is $12.00 and the shares are currently trading for $12.85, the intrinsic value is $0.85. In some cases, after the rights issue is announced and before the rights issue closes, the shares fall in value so the exercise price is above the current market price. In this case, the intrinsic value would be negative and taking up the rights would be pointless because buying the shares on the open market would be cheaper.

Note

Beware of a rights issue where the intrinsic value is negative—it's not a good sign.

Effect of a rights issue on the share price

As I've said, when rights are taken up by investors, the share price generally drops slightly after the closing date because additional shares have been issued at a lower price than the former market price. The theoretical effect on the share price can be calculated using the following formula:

$$Ps = (Pb \times N + Pe) \div (N + 1)$$

Where:

- Ps = theoretical price of the shares after the issue

- Pb= price of the shares before the issue

- Pe = exercise price of the rights

- N = number of shares needed to qualify for one right

Note

This formula can also be used with a bonus issue. In this case Pe = 0 because the additional shares are free.

Example

ABC shares are trading for $1.44. They announce a 1 for 10 rights issue at an exercise price of $1.00. What is the theoretical trading price of the shares after the issue?

In this case:

- Pb = $1.44

- Pe = $1.00

- N = 10

Substituting in the formula:

$$
\begin{aligned}
Ps &= (Pb \times N + Pe) \div (N + 1) \\
Ps &= (1.44 \times 10 + 1.00) \div (10 + 1) \\
&= 15.4 \div 11 \\
&= \mathbf{1.40}
\end{aligned}
$$

Therefore, the shares can be expected to trade for $1.40 after the issue (the share price will drop by 4¢).

Market price of rights

Rights usually have an intrinsic value because the issue price is lower than the share price. The intrinsic value (P) is:

$$P = Ps - Pe$$

Generally speaking, if the rights issue is renounceable, the rights will trade on the market at around the intrinsic value.

> ## Note
>
> As mentioned, occasionally the share price might fall to below the exercise price before expiry. If this happens, the intrinsic value will be negative and there'd be no reason to buy the rights.

Example

What is the intrinsic value of the rights in the previous example?

In this case:

$$
\begin{aligned}
P &= Ps - Pe \\
&= 1.40 - 1.00 \\
&= \mathbf{0.40}
\end{aligned}
$$

That is, the rights have an intrinsic value of 40¢ and if the issue is renounceable, the rights should trade at around this price. This makes sense because a rights purchaser pays 40¢ to the seller and then $1.00 to the company and thus obtains a fully paid share for $1.40. This is the same price as a fully paid share purchased on the sharemarket.

Trading rights

For traders or investors with a higher risk tolerance, trading rights rather than fully paid shares can produce higher profits. This is because the exercise price of rights doesn't change as the share price changes, so the market price of rights generally fluctuates by about the same dollar amount as the share price. For example, with the ABC shares previously discussed, if the share price were to rise by 5¢, the rights should also rise by about 5¢ and so trade at around 45¢. But because the rights are cheaper than the shares, trading the rights rather than the shares will produce a higher return on capital invested. However, should the share price fall, losses will also be magnified. So trading rights is more risky than trading shares.

Let's see the difference with a hypothetical example.

Example

Investor A buys 5000 ABC shares for $1.40. Some time afterward, the share price rises to $1.45. Investor B spends the same amount as investor A but buys ABC rights for 40¢.

When the share price rises to $1.45, the rights rise to 45¢.

What is the profit and percentage return on capital for both investors?

Investor A spends $5000 \times \$1.40 = \$7000$

When the share price rises to $1.45, the profit made is $5000 \times \$0.05 = \textbf{\$250}$.

The return on capital invested is $250 \div 7000 = 0.0357 = \textbf{3.57\%}$.

Investor B spends $7000 and so is able to buy $7000 \div 0.4 = 17500$ rights.

When the price of the rights rises by 5¢, the profit is $17500 \times \$0.05 = \textbf{\$875}$.

The return on capital is $\$875 \div \$7000 = 0.125 = \textbf{12.5\%}$.

This means investor B has made 3.5 times more profit than investor A by trading the rights rather than the shares.

Company-issued options

Company-issued options are very similar to a renounceable rights issue, except that the time period to expiry is usually much longer than that of a rights issue. For example, a typical rights issue may have an expiry date of only a month or two, whereas options may have an expiry date of several years forward from the time of issue.

Like rights, company-issued options are usually issued free of charge to existing shareholders. They are usually listed with the ASX and are tradeable. Often options are issued to related parties such as directors, senior executives or employees as part of their salary package. This is a form of bonus or incentive because the more profit the company makes, the higher the future share price and the more valuable the options. As a general rule, shareholder approval is required for options to be issued in this way to related parties.

Notes

- Company-issued options should not be confused with exchange-traded options (ETOs). A major difference is that companies only can issue company options whereas ordinary investors can write ETOs (subject to certain requirements). Writing an ETO is effectively offering the ETO for sale on the open market. When ETOs are exercised, this does not increase the number of shares on issue or the equity capital. Rather, it causes a transfer of ownership of the underlying shares from one party to another.

- Writing or trading ETOs is a specialised form of investing and not suitable for inexperienced investors. However, if you are interested in knowing more, the ASX produces brochures on the topic and provides information on their website. Also, you can refer to many excellent books.

Splits and consolidations

As we've seen, investor perceptions influence share prices. When the share price is high, investors tend to regard the shares as expensive and so may be reluctant to buy them. For example, say bank A's share price is $50 whereas bank B's price is $20. If both banks appear to be sound investments, investors will probably prefer bank B rather than A simply because they'll be able to buy more shares for the same amount of investment capital they have available. An investor spending, say, $10 000 would be able to buy only 200 shares in bank A but 500 shares in bank B. Now, as you and I both know, what's most important for investors is the percentage return on capital invested, and this doesn't depend upon the number of shares held. Nevertheless, investors (and particularly small investors) tend to shy away from shares they consider expensive.

To counter this perception, when a share price rises to high levels, the directors may propose a split. If shareholders approve of it, existing shares will be cancelled and new shares issued. So, with a 2:1 split, two new shares will be issued for each old share and the price of the new shares will be half that of the old shares. For example, a 2:1 split would bring bank A's share price down to $25 and thus more in parity with bank B's at $20.

On the other hand, when the share price is low, investors tend to perceive the stock as cheap (and nasty) and, therefore, speculative and risky, and so may tend to shy away from it. The shares will generally be traded by short-term traders only, who buy them with the intention of selling them a short time later for quick profit, and they won't be regarded by investors as suitable for long-term investment. So, if the share price is too low, directors may propose a consolidation. This will reduce the number of shares on issue and the share price will rise proportionally. For example, if a 10¢ share is consolidated at 10:1, the new shares will trade for $1.00.

Notes

- Splits and consolidations have a dramatic impact on the number of issued shares, but don't affect equity capital or reserves in any way other than that the additional administration expense may cause a small reduction in profitability.

- If you notice a sudden significant jump or fall in a share price in the published statistics, it's most likely due to a split or consolidation. However, the software used to produce share price charts often automatically adjust for splits or consolidations, meaning no significant change may be evident on the chart.

- Sometimes a spit or consolidation can also mean a change in name and code of the shares, but usually an issue of new shares simply replaces the old ones. In either case, a shareholder will receive a new holding statement showing the number of shares held after the split or consolidation.

Share buyback

When a company is making a profit, the directors decide how much of this profit (if any) should be distributed to shareholders as a dividend and how much will be retained. (You may wish to refer to chapter 4, figure 4.1, where profit flow was outlined.) Retained profits go into reserves and may be used for purposes such as to fund business expansion, buy new equipment or to reduce debt. If the company has accumulated reserves and has no immediate need to use them for the uses already mentioned, the directors may decide to use some reserve capital to buy back its own shares. In this case, the directors are effectively deciding that the best use for some of the retained profit is to purchase more shares in their own company.

A share buyback can be done off market (by means of an offer document to existing shareholders only), or on market (by buying the shares on the open market in the same way as any other buyer). Either way, when the shares are bought back by the company, they must be cancelled and this reduces the number of shares on issue and also the issued capital.

Investor considerations

A share buyback is essentially a win/win situation for the company and its shareholders. The company wins because fewer shares are on issue after the buyback and so future profits and dividends can be distributed over a smaller number of shares. Shareholders who decide to retain their shares will appreciate this because the earnings per share and the dividend per share will increase and this will make the shares more valuable. Shareholders who participate in the buyback will also usually win because the company needs to offer a good price in order to get significant shareholder participation. No transaction costs are involved so effectively shareholders are selling their shares without brokerage at a good price.

In an on-market buyback, all shareholders win because the share price should rise, making their shares more valuable. This is because the additional demand resulting from the company buying large parcels of shares will naturally tend to drive the price higher.

Dividend reinvestment plan

As outlined in chapter 4, a dividend reinvestment plan (DRP) allows shareholders to take their dividend in shares rather than cash. The company obtains additional capital because less of its profit is distributed to shareholders.

Whether or not a company has a DRP in operation is entirely at the discretion of the directors. From a director's point of view, a DRP reduces the dividend cash payout to investors and so frees up capital that may be used to reduce debt or to fund capital expenditure. The disadvantage is that, as time goes on, increasingly more shares are on issue, so profits and dividends have to be distributed over a greater number of shares. Also, administration costs are associated with the operation of a plan. Offering a DRP is not set in concrete and can be changed by the board, who can decide to suspend an existing plan or introduce one at any time. Naturally, an announcement must be made prior to the change so all share investors are informed.

Because shareholder participation is voluntary, it's difficult to know how many shareholders participate in a DRP and, therefore, to determine the long-term effect on the share price. Generally speaking, there's no significant difference to the share price whether the dividend is distributed as cash or shares. In either case, when the shares are quoted ex-dividend, the price will usually fall by the same amount.

Share investment plans

In some cases a company may offer a share plan in addition to the DRP known by some other name such as Dividend Substitution Share Plan (DSSP) or Bonus Share Plan (BSP). The idea is basically the same – the shareholder forgoes the dividend in cash in favour of receiving additional shares. As no dividend is received, these shareholders will not receive any franking credits and will usually not be subject to income tax on the dividend. However on disposal of these shares, a higher capital gains tax will apply, because from a legal viewpoint, these shares were received at zero cost. Therefore this type of plan is usually suitable only for investors on a high marginal rate of tax and for most investors participation in the DRP will be a better option.

Learning exercises

7.1   When a company first lists (floats), what effect will the number of shares issued have on the offer price?

7.2   Provide four reasons a listed company may wish to obtain additional equity capital.

7.3   Why do shareholders rarely profit from a bonus issue?

7.4   Complete the following table, outlining the effect on company equity capital and the likely effect on the share price resulting from the changes to the number of issued shares.

	Effect on equity capital	Effect on share price
Bonus issue		
Rights issue		
Options issue		
Dividend reinvestment plan		
Split		
Consolidation		
Share buyback		

7.5   Outline the four strategies available to you when a company in which you hold shares has a renounceable rights issue, or the three strategies when it is non-renounceable.

7.6   What is meant by the intrinsic value of rights or company-issued options? When will the intrinsic value be negative?

7.7   What are the main differences between company-issued rights and options?

7.8   What are the advantages and disadvantages of trading rights and company-issued options rather than the fully paid shares?

7.9   Investor A buys 3000 PQR shares for $1.86. Investor B spends the same amount as investor A but buys PQR company-issued options for 83¢. When the share price rises by 7¢, the rights rise by 5¢.

Calculate the profit and percentage return on capital for both investors (ignoring any trading costs).

7.10   Under what circumstances might directors propose a split or a consolidation?

7.11   What are the two ways a share buyback can occur, and what are the likely benefits to shareholders after a buyback?

7.12   A company has a renounceable rights issue. You don't want to invest any more money in the company but you decide not to sell your rights. Why might you choose to do this?

7.13   Shares in a company are trading at $5.20. The company announces a 2 for 5 non-renounceable rights issue at $4.50. Determine the likely effect of this issue on:

a. the share price

b. a shareholder holding 1000 shares taking up the rights

c. a shareholder holding 1000 shares not taking up the rights.

7.14   Suppose that for the company in learning exercise 7.13, the rights issue had been renounceable. Determine the theoretical market price of the rights and the financial effect on a shareholder with 1000 shares selling the rights.

7.15   You hold 6300 shares in a company that announces a renounceable 1 for 10 rights issue at $1.05. The shares are trading at $1.25 at the time of the issue.

a. What is the theoretical price of the shares after the issue?

b. What is the theoretical price of the rights?

c. How much will you have to pay to take up your rights?

d. How much will you receive if you sell your rights at the theoretical market price using an online broker with a trading cost of $20?

7.16 A company's shares are trading for $20 when a 2:1 share split is announced. What will be the price of the shares after the split?

7.17 A listed company's shares are trading for $1.08 when a 5:1 consolidation is announced. If you hold 1400 shares, how many new shares will you hold after the consolidation and what is the likely market price? Also compare your capital invested before and after the consolidation.

Learning exercises solutions

7.1 The offer price will be inversely proportional to the number of shares issued; that is, the more shares, the lower the price.

7.2 Some reasons a listed company may wish to obtain more equity capital are:

» to reduce debt (reduce loan capital)

» to fund an acquisition (takeover)

» to purchase new premises or major plant and equipment

» to fund a major restructuring of the business.

7.3 Shareholders rarely profit from a bonus issue because after the issue, the price of the shares drops in proportion to the number of additional shares received, so the value of the shareholding remains the same.

7.4 See the following completed table

	Effect on equity capital	Effect on share price
Bonus issue	None	Reduces in proportion
Rights issue	Increases	Reduces slightly
Options issue	Increases	Reduces slightly
Dividend reinvestment plan	Increases	Little
Split	None	Reduces in proportion
Consolidation	None	Increases in proportion
Share buyback	Reduces	Increases in proportion

7.5 During a rights issue, you have the following strategies available to you.

For a renounceable issue, you can:

» take up all the rights you're entitled to

» sell all your rights

» take up some of the rights and sell the remainder

» not do anything (let all your rights lapse).

Your options during a non-renounceable issue are:

» take up all the rights you're entitled to

» take up some of the rights and let the remainder lapse

» not to do anything (let all your rights lapse).

7.6 The intrinsic value is the difference between the share price and the exercise price. The intrinsic value will be negative when the exercise price is higher than the share price.

7.7 The main differences between company-issued rights and options are:

» Options usually have a much longer time period to expiry.

» Rights are often non-renounceable whereas options are almost always listed.

» Options often have a negative intrinsic value whereas this is unusual with rights.

» Options are usually priced on the market with a time value built into the price whereas this is not usual with rights.

» The market price of rights usually changes by the same amount as the share price but with options it does not usually change by the same amount as the share price but less than it.

7.8 The main advantage of trading rights and company-issued options is that a higher return on capital is possible should the share price rise. The main disadvantage is that there is a higher downside potential and so rights and options trading is more risky.

7.9 Investor A spends $3000 \times \$1.86 = \$5580$.

When the share price rises by 7¢, the profit made is $3000 \times \$0.07 = \textbf{\$210}$.

The return on capital invested is $210 \div 5580 = 0.0357 = \textbf{3.76\%}$.

Investor B spends $5580 and so is able to buy $5580 \div 0.83 = 6723$ options.

When the price of the options rises by 5¢, the profit is
$6723 \times \$0.05 = $ **\$336**.

The return on capital is $\$336 \div \$5580 = 0.0602 = $ **6.02%**.

7.10 Splits usually occur when the share price rises to a high level that directors feel might deter some investors. Consolidations usually occur when the share price is too low and the shares are perceived as having a 'penny dreadful' status.

7.11 A company can buy back its own shares either off market (from existing shareholders only) or on market. The likely benefit to shareholders is that after the buyback the shares will become more valuable so the price should rise and the dividend per share should also rise.

7.12 The most likely reason you might choose to do this is because the cost of selling your rights (brokerage and GST) will be more than the amount you will receive from the sale.

7.13 The solutions for each scenario are as follows:
a. Using the formula:

» $Pb = 5.20$

» $Pe = 4.50$

» $N = 2.5$ (a 2 for 5 rights issue means that 5 shares qualify for 2 rights, so 2.5 shares qualify for 1 right)

Substituting in the formula:

$$Ps = (5.2 \times 2.5 + 4.5) \div 3.5$$
$$= \textbf{\$5.00}$$

Therefore, the theoretical price of the shares after the issue will be **\$5.00** and the share price will have dropped by **20¢**.

b. A shareholder with 1000 shares would have a value of \$5200 before the issue. Taking up the rights, the shareholder will receive 400 shares at a cost of $\$1800(400 \times \$4.50)$. Therefore, the shareholder's total cost is $\$7000(\$5200 + \$1800)$.

After the issue, the shareholder holds 1400 shares worth $5.00 each; that is, the total value of the shares is $7000 $(1400 \times \$5.00)$ and the shareholder has made neither a profit nor a loss by taking up the rights.

c. After the rights issue the shares would be worth $5000 $(1000 \times \$5.00)$ and a loss of $200 will occur by not taking up the rights.

7.14 The theoretical market price of the rights is the intrinsic value, and this is:

$$
\begin{aligned}
P &= \$5.00 - \$4.50 \\
&= \$0.5 \\
&= \textbf{50¢}
\end{aligned}
$$

A shareholder holding 1000 shares would receive 400 rights and would be able to sell them for $200 $(400 \times \$0.50)$. This will balance the $200 capital loss resulting from the rights issue and the shareholder will break even except for the cost involved with selling the rights.

7.15 The solutions for each scenario are as follows:
   a. The theoretical price of the shares after the issue is $(10 \times \$1.25 + 1 \times \$1.05) \div 11 = \textbf{\$1.23}$.

   b. The theoretical price of the rights is $\$1.23 - \$1.05 = \$0.18$ or **18¢**.

   c. If you take up the rights, you will receive 630 rights and will have to pay $630 \times \$1.05 = \textbf{\$661.50}$.

   d. If you sell your rights, you will receive $630 \times \$0.18 - \$20 = \textbf{\$93.40}$

7.16 The price of the shares will be **$10** after the split.

7.17 You would receive **280** shares and the price would most likely change to **$5.40**.

Capital invested before the consolidation = $1400 \times \$1.08 = \textbf{\$1512}$.

Capital invested after the consolidation = $280 \times \$5.40 = \textbf{\$1512}$.

Chapter 8

Using fundamental analysis to guide your investing decisions

In this chapter, I discuss an approach to share investing known as *fundamental analysis*. This is a 'bottom-up' approach where you look at the basic factors of relevance to shares and use them to compare different shares. It's based on the principle that if the basics of the business are sound, its shares are basically sound because the company is built on a firm foundation. Therefore, its shares should prove to be a good long-term investment, even though there might be some short-term fluctuations in the company's fortunes. This means fundamental analysis is a valuable tool for you if you are investing for the long term, but may also provide useful guidance when you are considering any purchase or sell decisions. If you want to make short-term profits from share price volatility in the market this kind of analysis is not really relevant for you and traders generally do not use it. (Traders focus more on technical analysis, which I cover in the next chapter.)

Understanding financial periods

Each business uses a 12-month period for calculating and releasing financial results and this is known as the *financial year* (or fiscal year) as distinct from the calendar year. The most common financial year in Australia is from 1 July in one year to 30 June the following year, but this is not always the case. The financial year is broken up into two six-monthly periods, the first six months being known as the *interim period* and the last six months as the *final period*.

Note

Sometimes in financial reports or reviews, terms such as 'results for last year' are actually based on the last calendar year. So you need to exercise some caution and make sure you're clear about what period of time is being used.

How do you decide if a share has sound fundamentals? For some listed companies, you might already have some idea of the nature and value of their business. I think most Australians would have some knowledge about well-known listed companies such as BHP, Rio Tinto, Commonwealth Bank (and other major banks), Qantas, Woodside Petroleum, Woolworths or Coles. One way of obtaining more detailed information would be to conduct an on-location site inspection, talk to the management, customers, staff and suppliers and examine the books and financial accounts. Clearly this approach isn't feasible for the average investor (although large stockbrokers or managed fund executives may be able to do some of these things). So most investors must rely on the information about a company that's published and accessible to them. Their stockbroker, financial advisor or analyst should have detailed information but most investors use the internet, which is a wonderful tool for obtaining this information, available across many websites. If you trade using an online broker, your online broker's site should also have most (if not all) of the information you seek.

Understanding the various types of fundamentals

Essentially, two types of fundamentals are used:

* general fundamentals
* financial fundamentals.

General fundamentals

General fundamentals relate to the overall business and include factors such as:

* the size of the business in terms of dollar turnover, number of employees or market valuation
* the length of time the business has been in operation
* what the business does—for example, does it produce a physical product such as petroleum, clothing or pet food, or is the business essentially one that provides customers services, such as retailing, health care or funeral services?
* brand identification and market acceptance of the business and its products
* trends in product demand—is market share increasing or decreasing? Are any possible changes in competition or consumer or governmental attitudes on the horizon that could affect product demand?
* patent rights, trademarks or special marketing arrangements for the products of the business
* the markets for the products—for example, do they cater for the domestic market only or are their products exported?

- whether demand for their products is likely to increase or decrease in the future and whether any new markets could be exploited

- the directors on the board and the company's management executives. The important considerations are their expertise, experience and track record

- the availability and stability of the workforce with the skills needed to keep the company operating profitably

- the likelihood of further improvements in profitability by technological advances or rationalisation

- the stability and availability of supply of the raw materials or goods needed by the business

- the ethics of the business — for example, are the products or services needed or produced by the company ethically sourced? Are the employees and customers treated fairly and ethically?

Of course, this is not necessarily a complete list and other factors may be of relevance.

Evaluating general fundamentals

It's difficult to evaluate most general fundamentals in a quantitative (numerical) fashion, so you need to apply a more subjective (qualitative) approach by learning as much as you can about the business and considering the opinions of 'expert' analysts and financial institutions. Then you can make your own assessment of the factors I've listed and decide whether or not you think the business is one you'd like to invest your hard-earned dollars in.

Financial fundamentals

These fundamentals concern the financial statistics relevant to the business. They include such factors as:

- sales turnover (revenue)

- margin of profit on sales

- capital invested in the business

- profit (earnings)

- return on capital invested

- amount of debt.

Again, this is not necessarily a complete list of the financial fundamentals of importance to a company.

Evaluating financial fundamentals

Financial fundamentals can essentially be evaluated using two different approaches and I suggest you try both. The two approaches are:

1. snapshot

2. trends over time.

In the snapshot approach, you look at the statistics of the company at a given point in time and compare them to the statistics of other companies and so obtain a comparison. You need to realise that the statistics and the comparison are valid only for this single point in time, and before or after this time the comparison may be entirely different. The usual point in time chosen is the most recent for which valid statistics are available.

In the trends-over-time approach, you look at how the statistics have changed over a time period. This allows you to identify any trends and see whether the business has been growing and improving in profitability, or shrinking and declining in profitability. The time period you choose is entirely up to you—a typical time period for a long-term investor is 10 years. If future projections are available, you can also estimate likely future trends and then come to your own conclusions as to whether or not you think an established trend will continue into the future.

A few notes of caution are appropriate here:

- Projections into the future are always uncertain because the future is notoriously difficult to predict.

- Often, no universal method of calculating key statistics is available, and various different sources may give different values for the same statistic. If you are using a statistic to compare different companies, you need to ensure you use the same source for comparison purposes.

- Errors can occur, so if any statistic appears suspect it's a good idea to try to obtain confirmation about it from another source.

- Financial statistics are based on available information and this is usually updated and published only every six months. A lot can change in a six-month period and the average investor will not be privy to these changes.

- Mark Twain once said, 'There are lies, damn lies and statistics'. In other words, you can prove almost anything with statistics by selectively choosing the way you calculate them. Despite regulatory requirements, clever accountants may be able to 'massage the figures' or 'cook the books' and when a company collapses without any obvious external causes, it's clear that the published financial accounts weren't revealing the true picture. Unfortunately, you can't do much about this except to exercise extreme caution when a business seems to be financially healthy according to the published accounts and the directors are optimistic and pumping it up, yet the share price is going down.

Using key statistics to your advantage

A great deal of financial information is available about listed shares, and you may think you need to be an accountant to clearly understand and interpret the masses of figures. The good news is that this information can be summarised as key statistics in a way that's understandable without the need for particular accounting expertise. Once you can understand the key statistics, you can evaluate financial fundamentals in an objective (rational) manner rather than in a subjective one (gut feeling).

Financial ratios

Financial statistics are often calculated as ratios because a single value on its own may not be very meaningful. For example, you may think that dollar profit (earnings) is a good measure of profitability, until you consider that the larger the business, the more profit it should be making. So in order to use profit as a measure of financial performance, you need to be able to put the profit into perspective in accordance with the size of the business.

To illustrate this, let's compare two companies: A and B. Their profits last year were:

- *A:* $300 000

- *B:* $1.4 million.

Does this mean that B was much more profitable than A? In dollar terms, the answer is 'yes'—B made much more profit than A. But suppose the capital invested in A is $1 million and in B, $10 million. Let's calculate the return on capital invested, which is:

- *A:* 30%

- *B:* 14%.

Now it's clear that A is far more profitable than B because it shows a higher return on capital invested. That is, company A uses the available capital more profitably than company B. So you can see that the ratio of profit to capital invested is a far more meaningful statistic than profit alone and allows you to compare the profitability of two businesses of different sizes on an 'apples to apples' basis.

Notes

- Decimal ratios are often converted to percentages but each expresses exactly the same proportionality. The only difference is that the percentage scale is from 0 to 100 whereas the decimal ratio scale is from 0 to 1. To convert a decimal ratio to a percentage, simply multiply by 100. For example, the decimal ratio 0.2 expressed as a percentage is 20%.

- There's no universally agreed symbol for each statistic and the ones I use may not be the same as the ones used in other websites or publications.

Market capitalisation

Market capitalisation (market cap or MC) is a widely quoted statistic that gives an indication of the size of a business in terms of market value—that is, the total monetary value shareholders place on the business. It's calculated using the following formula:

$$MC = \text{Number of ordinary shares} \times \text{Share price}$$

Because market cap is based on the share price, it fluctuates as the share price changes. In a market report, you might hear something like, 'investors wiped $10 million off the value of the stock today'. This means that the share price fell to the extent that the market cap for the stock dropped by $10 million that day. It is also possible to determine the total market cap of the major listed companies on the Australian market and so quote overall market direction—for example, in a major bear market, '$10 billion dollars was wiped off the market'.

Note

Market cap depends on share price, which in turn depends on investor perceptions and so doesn't reflect the capital of the business in any way. So if MC increases, the business has no more capital available and when MC goes down, it has no less.

Interpreting the market cap statistic

The largest listed companies in Australia have market caps of above $10 billion. Smaller companies have market caps below $100 million and the smallest 'micro' ones have market caps below $10 million. As a general rule, blue chips have a high market cap, green chips a medium market cap and speculative shares a low market cap.

I suggest that for core shares in your portfolio, you avoid the low market cap ones (with market caps below about $100 million) because they're the most volatile and risky. However, if you're interested in short-term trading profit, you might want to trade smaller market cap shares because their inherent volatility provides a greater potential for significant short-term price movements.

Earnings

Earnings is another name for profit and it's the difference between revenue (or sales value) and the cost incurred in producing that revenue. If revenue is less than cost, the business is running at a loss.

Three profit-related statistics are often calculated:

1. *Profit before interest and tax:* This is the gross profit before tax and interest on loans is paid.

2. *Profit before tax:* The gross profit before tax is paid.

3. *After-tax profit:* The net profit after tax and all expenses have been paid. If any preference shares were issued, the dividends paid on these is also usually deducted because these are like a loan.

Notes

- Profit statistics usually exclude extraordinary profits/losses (those not related to normal business activities). For example, the sale of a subsidiary or acquisition of another will not be included, because these are considered as one-off events and unlikely to be repeated.

- Because three profit-related figures are possible, you need to check which one is being used. You can assume that 'earnings' (unqualified) means after-tax profit.

- In addition to historical earnings, you may be able to obtain analysts' estimates of projected earnings—usually for one or two years forward.

Interpreting the earnings statistic

As I've already pointed out, earnings alone is not a true indication of profitability. However, it's more meaningful when used with a trends-over-time approach. All investors or shareholders like to see that earnings increased in the past and, more importantly, earnings are forecast to increase in the future.

Earnings per share

When total earnings is divided by the number of issued ordinary shares, the resultant statistic is the earnings per share (EPS). It's usually expressed as cents per share and measures the amount of profit attributable to each ordinary share.

EPS is calculated as:

$$EPS = \frac{\text{After-tax profit}}{\text{Number of ordinary shares}}$$

Note

In published statistics, if EPS is negative (loss) it's often shown simply as a blank.

Interpreting the EPS statistic

EPS is a more widely quoted statistic than earnings because it's more meaningful. As we've seen in the previous chapter, the more shares over which profit is distributed, the less each shareholder receives, so EPS is more important from a shareholder's viewpoint than total earnings. Past earnings can't change but the market looks forward and anticipates changes to future EPS. Indeed, projected EPS is the single most important financial factor that affects a share price in both the long term and the short term.

Investors like to see a continually rising EPS, because this a sign of healthy profitability and good business management. If any change occurs that the market anticipates will impact favourably on future EPS, the share price will almost always rise; whereas an unfavourable change will cause a fall. It's also generally the case that the market tends to punish unfavourable news more severely than it rewards favourable news. As a simple example, if an event occurs that is expected to increase EPS by 10%, the share price might rise by 5% in response but if an event is expected to decrease EPS by 10%, the share price might fall by 15%. Perhaps the reason for this is that investors expect the EPS to increase as a natural event and regard a favourable change to EPS as normal. On the other hand, a downgrade to the expected EPS is regarded as abnormal and is punished accordingly. And if investors perceive an event looming that could affect the earnings of most shares, the market as a whole will react in a similar way.

Price-to-earnings ratio

In addition to EPS, a key statistic used by investors is the price-to-earnings ratio (PE), also written as PER. It's the ratio between the share price and EPS as calculated using the following formula:

$$PE = \frac{\text{Share price in cents}}{\text{EPS in cents}}$$

Notes

- Unlike EPS, PE is based on current share price and so will vary with each trade as the share price changes. If the share price goes up, PE will also go up and if the share price falls, PE will also fall.

- In some financial statistics, an average annual PE may be quoted rather than the current PE.

In order to explain the significance of PE, let's divert for a moment to the property market. Suppose you want to buy an investment property and you're shown two properties, A and B, that stack up as follows:

- *A:* Price $160 000, showing a net return of $10 000 per annum

- *B:* Price $240 000, showing a net return of $12 000 per annum.

Assuming you had sufficient funds to buy either property, which one would you consider the better investment?

To answer this question you'd probably calculate the annual return on investment as follows:

- *A:* 10 000 ÷ 160 000 = 0.0625 = 6.25%

- *B:* 12 000 ÷ 240 000 = 0.05 = 5.00%

Clearly, property A gives a higher return on capital invested and, therefore, appears to be the better investment.

Another way of comparing the investments is to calculate the PE for each property. This is:

- $A: 160\,000 \div 10\,000 = 16$

- $B: 240\,000 \div 12\,000 = 20$

What do these PEs mean? They're actually the number of years it would take you to pay for the property from the earnings generated by it. Clearly, the shorter the time, the better the investment. So, again, property A is better than B because it has a lower PE (and so it will take you less time to break even).

So PE gives an indication of the 'value' of the investment, and the lower the PE, the better the value.

Interpreting the PE statistic

In the sharemarket, PE has essentially the same meaning as it has on the property market and provides a measure of investors' perceptions of 'value'. A low PE indicates a share that's underpriced, whereas a high PE indicates an overpriced one. There's always a reason for this—and that reason is almost always future earnings prospects. So low PEs indicate shares where the market is disenchanted with this business and sees little prospect of future increases in earnings, whereas shares with high PEs are seen as having good earnings growth prospects and are liked by the market. Published PEs are based on the current market price and historical earnings. Investors look to the future and build future earnings potential into the current market price and this is reflected in the PE. So high PE shares are essentially based on a certain amount of 'blue sky' potential.

Note

In some cases, high PEs are companies that are relatively 'new kids on the block' that haven't been in business for long enough to establish a profit history over some years but that investors perceive have good future prospects.

To summarise:

- *Low PE:* Value share, high current earnings or low share price and low earnings growth prospects.

- *High PE:* Growth share, low current earnings or high share price but high earnings growth prospects.

Rule of 20

The rule of 20 is a useful rule to rate the 'fairness' of a stock. This rule indicates that 'fair' value is when:

PE = 20 − Inflation rate

So with inflation at, say, 2%, this rule indicates that:

- a fair value share has a PE of about 18

- an underpriced share has a PE less than 18

- an overpriced share has a PE greater than 18.

Generally, you'll find that the average market PE is around fair value as indicated by the Rule of 20. I suggest that for long-term investments, it's usually best to consider shares with PEs not too far away from the market average because they're less risky than shares with PEs a fair way above or below it.

PE growth ratio

As discussed, PEs are based on past earnings and don't take into account possible earnings changes. However, a statistic has been developed that helps you to take into account future growth prospects. It's the PE growth ratio (PEG), which is the ratio of the current PE to the expected annual growth in EPS. It's calculated using the following formula:

$$PEG = \frac{PE}{EGP}$$

Where EGP = earnings growth percentage and is the difference between forecast EPS and current EPS, expressed as a percentage of current EPS.

In formula form, EGP is:

$$EGP = \frac{(\text{Forecast EPS} - \text{Current EPS})}{\text{Current EPS}} \times 100$$

Notes

- If a reduction in future earnings is forecast, earnings growth is negative and a negative PEG isn't meaningful.

- The PEG calculation relies on forecast earnings for the next few years. As everyone knows, it's impossible to predict the future so an element of uncertainty is associated with the PEG, but it does provide a guide.

- In published statistics, the PEG may be given but if it's not, you can calculate it for yourself if a forecast EPS is provided for the year (or years) ahead.

Using PEG, the value of a stock can be rated as follows:

- *Fair value:* PEG about equal to 1.

- *Underpriced:* PEG less than 1.

- *Overpriced:* PEG greater than 1.

Example

A share has a current PE of 17 and an EPS of 38¢. The forecast EPS for next year is 42¢. Rate the 'value' of this share using PE and PEG (assuming an inflation rate of 2%).

Using the rule of 20, a fair PE would be 18 (20 − 2), so this share is somewhat cheaper than fair value.

Now let's see how this share rates using the PEG. First calculate the earnings growth percentage as follows:

$$
\begin{aligned}
\text{EGP} &= \frac{\left(\text{Forecast EPS} - \text{Current EPS}\right)}{\text{Current EPS}} \times 100 \\[6pt]
&= \frac{\left(42 - 38\right)}{38} \times 100 \\[6pt]
&= \frac{4}{38} \times 100 \\[6pt]
&= 10.5\%
\end{aligned}
$$

$$\begin{aligned} PEG \ &= \ \frac{PE}{EGP} \\ &= \ \frac{17}{10.5} \\ &= \ \mathbf{1.62} \end{aligned}$$

So you can see that while this share seems better than fair value based on the PE alone, the PEG statistic indicates that with regard to future earnings this share is actually overpriced.

Share price and discounted earnings

Another way of evaluating a fair share price is based on the idea that the true worth of any business is what can be earned in future profits. So a share's true value is the sum of the future earnings per share. This implies that if a business never makes a profit, the shares are actually worthless. So the only reason shares in a loss-making business are still trading on the market is because investors perceive that the business could possibly make profits in the future.

To obtain a fair share price, it's necessary to discount future earnings because profits received in the future are not as valuable as profits received today. The discounted earnings method involves long-term earnings forecasts and rather complex calculations that are not easily performed by the average investor. Sometimes financial analysts use this method and you may be able to access their reports

Interpreting discounted earnings

If the sum of future discounted earnings is greater than the share price, the shares are good value and well priced. On the other hand, if it's lower, the shares are overpriced and not good value. Because the method involves long-term projections into the future, it cannot be fully relied on; however, it may provide a useful guide to the true value of a business.

Dividend–related ratios

Dividend per share, dividend cover, payout ratio, dividend yield and grossed-up yield were covered in chapter 4 and are important financial statistics that are based on the dividend paid to shareholders. Refer to chapter 4 if you wish to revise these statistics.

Capital invested

The capital invested in a business is the amount of capital the business has available for normal (day-to-day) business activities. This capital is initially derived from shareholder equity and loan capital. It should increase with time because, if the business is profitable, some of the profit should be invested back in the business as reserves.

Note

Do not confuse capital invested with market capitalisation (market cap) because they are entirely different. As mentioned earlier in this chapter, market cap is determined by investors and fluctuates as the share price changes, but capital invested doesn't depend in any way on the share price.

Return on capital

As discussed at the start of this chapter, return on capital is a more meaningful measure of the profitability of a business than profit alone. It measures how efficient a business is in utilising its capital to produce profits.

Return on capital (ROC) is calculated by the following formula:

$$\text{ROC} = \frac{\text{After-tax profit per annum}}{\text{Capital invested}} \times 100$$

Notes

- ROC is also known as *return on investment*.
- ROC may also be calculated using before-tax profit or profit before interest and tax, so you need to clarify which profit figure is being used. However, after-tax profit is the most common one.
- As stated before, earnings is another term for profit.
- A similar statistic is return on assets (ROA), which is based on assets rather than capital invested.

Interpreting the ROC statistic

ROC allows you to compare companies in the same sector grouping regardless of their size, on an 'apples to apples' basis. Ideally, ROC should be around 8% or higher and preferably showing a rising trend.

When comparing the profitability of companies in different sectors, ROC is less meaningful because the assets needed for the business can vary widely. For example, a service-based business such as an employment agency may require only a small asset base and show a high ROC, whereas a manufacturing business may require very high capital investment and accordingly have a low ROC.

Note

ROC is a statistic of little significance for the banking sector because most of a bank's assets are in the form of loans and advances to customers and their ROC is usually very low.

Return on equity

Return on equity (ROE) is very similar to return on capital (ROC) and is calculated using the following formula:

$$\text{ROE} = \frac{\text{After-tax profit per annum}}{\text{Shareholders' equity}} \times 100$$

Shareholders' equity (known also as *proprietorship* or *net assets*) is the amount of capital contributed to the company by the shareholders, plus accumulated reserves. Reserves are essentially retained profits (profits that have been re-invested and not distributed to the shareholders).

The basic accounting equation is:

Assets = Liabilities + Shareholders' equity

This then means:

Shareholders' equity = Assets – Liabilities

Interpreting the ROE statistic

From the preceding equation, it's clear that shareholders' equity must be less than assets and capital employed; therefore, ROE will be higher than ROC. Ideally, ROE would be around 10% or higher and preferably showing a rising trend.

A useful general rule is that a well-run business should be showing a ROE at 3% or more above current fixed-interest rates or bond yields. A continually rising ROE is an indicator of healthy profitability and a well-managed business.

Example

The capital employed by a business is \$484 million, shareholders' equity is \$216 million and after-tax profit is \$17.6 million. The return on capital and return on equity ratios are as follows:

$$ROC = (17.6 \div 484) \times 100 = \textbf{3.64\%}$$
$$ROE = (17.6 \div 216) \times 100 = \textbf{8.15\%}$$

Interpretation: Return on capital is poor and indicates that the business is not utilising its assets very profitably. The business needs to improve profitability (or reduce assets) to improve ROC. Return on equity is better but borderline. Before investing in this business, you should check trends in these statistics. If the trends have been falling or are static, this business doesn't appear attractive.

Understanding loan–related statistics

As discussed previously, most businesses obtain capital from two sources: loans (loan capital) and shareholder investment plus reserves (equity capital). Loans are also known as *debts*, and can be of two types: interest-bearing debt and non-interest-bearing debt. The features of each are as follows:

- Interest-bearing debt is essentially long-term debt obtained by means of a loan from a bank or other lending institution.

- Non-interest-bearing debt is essential short-term debt provided by business creditors who generally don't require immediate payment for goods and services but conventionally allow time before invoices need to be paid. This time is usually about a month but could be as much as three months.

The amount of interest-bearing debt compared to the amount of equity capital is known as *gearing*. A highly geared business has a large amount of interest-bearing debt compared to equity capital. Interest payments are an outgoing expense that reduces profitability, so it would seem logical that it would be better for a business to have little debt and to obtain all the capital it needs as equity capital. Indeed, this approach will increase the dollar value of profits (because interest payments are a small expense) but, as you may not suspect, this approach will reduce the return to shareholders. That's to say, without loan capital, EPS, DPS and return on equity will decrease. You'll see why if you study learning exercise 8.17.

A basic rule about loan capital that applies to any business is:

> ***If the business can get a return on capital greater than the interest rate payable on loans, having loan capital increases profitability.***

So if a business pays 6% interest on loans and can generate a return on capital of, say, 8%, loan capital increases profit by $2 for every $100 of loan capital. On the other hand, if the business can't generate a return on capital greater than the interest payable on its loans, loans are a disadvantage and reduce profits. For example, if loan interest is 8% and the business can generate only 6% return on capital, the loan capital reduces profit by $2 for every $100 of loan capital.

Even if a business can generate a good return on capital, it's not advisable to be too highly geared. A happy medium needs to be found. History shows that highly geared businesses are vulnerable to increases in interest rates or economic downturns and so, from a shareholder's viewpoint, they're more risky.

Debt-to-equity ratio

One common way of measuring the gearing of a business is from the debt-to-equity ratio (DE). It's calculated in the following way:

$$DE = \frac{\text{Long-term debt}}{\text{Shareholders' equity}} \times 100$$

Long-term debt is actually long-term loan capital. DE calculated in this way is a percentage that measures the amount of long-term debt compared to equity capital.

Note

As is common, DE as calculated by this formula is a percentage.

Interpreting the DE statistic

As you can see from the preceding formula, if DE is 100%, loan capital is equal to equity capital. This is usually considered to be about the limit of reasonable gearing.

In summary:

- DE of around 50% is conservative and low risk.

- DE of 100% is the limit of reasonable gearing and risk.

- DE of somewhat over 100% is becoming uncomfortable and risky.

- DE much higher than 100%—say, approaching 200% or even higher—is very risky because the business is vulnerable should a downturn occur in business activity.

Interest cover

Another statistic that provides a very good measure of business indebtedness is the interest cover (IC), which measures how well the business can cover the interest payable on loans from its trading profits—that is, before interest and tax outgoings.

IC is calculated using the following formula:

$$IC = \frac{EBIT}{Interest\ payable\ on\ loans}$$

Where EBIT = earnings before interest and tax. Conventionally, EBIT includes non-operating income but excludes abnormal profits/losses.

Note

Using this formula, the calculation gives a decimal ratio, but sometimes IC is expressed as a percentage by multiplying by 100.

Interpreting the IC statistic

Interest cover and debt-to-equity ratio are inversely proportional—that is, a high IC indicates a low DE (low level of gearing) and a low IC is accompanied by a high DE (high level of gearing). However, unlike DE, IC can be negative if the business isn't making a profit.

So you can evaluate IC in the following way:

- A high IC (anything greater than about 2) is comfortable.

- An IC much below 2 is relatively risky and indicates that a high proportion of earnings are used to pay back interest on loans. This isn't a good situation because insufficient profit is left to put into reserves or to distribute to shareholders.

- An IC of 1 indicates that all earnings must be used to pay interest on loans and nothing is left to go into reserves or to distribute to shareholders. In other words, the business is marking time and all profit is going to the lending institution.

- An IC of less than 1 (or even negative) indicates a loss-making business and, needless to say, one that's very risky.

Note

Because of the unique capital structure of the banking sector, you shouldn't place too much significance on IC for a banking share. Indeed, this statistic isn't usually published and instead a capital adequacy ratio is used. This is the amount of capital held that's available to return to customers who withdraw funds or terminate loans compared to the amount of capital that's been loaned. To protect customers who deposit funds in banks, the Reserve Bank sets a minimum value for this ratio and banks are required to adhere to this minimum.

Current ratio

The debt-to-equity ratio and the interest cover are statistics that give an indication of the level of gearing. Both are based on long-term debt and ignore short-term debt that requires no interest payments. However, short-term debt is still a debt that needs to be repaid and if there's more short-term debt than funds available to repay the debt, the business is in dire straits. Creditors can take legal action to recover the debt and this could result in liquidation. So it's important to measure the short-term financial viability of a business, and a statistic called the current ratio (CR) may be used for this purpose. It's calculated using the following formula:

$$CR = \frac{\text{Current assets}}{\text{Current liabilities}}$$

Current assets are assets that can be readily converted into cash in the short term, as opposed to fixed assets such as land and buildings that can't be as readily sold. Current liabilities are debts that need to be repaid in the short term, such as staff salaries or supplier's invoices. Long-term loan capital is a not a current liability, because the loan doesn't need to be repaid in the short term. However, the interest payable this month is a current liability.

Note

Current ratio as calculated by the preceding formula is a ratio and is seldom given as a percentage.

Interpreting the CR statistic

Generally speaking, from an investor's viewpoint, the higher the CR the better—because the lower the risk of liquidation. A CR greater than 2 can be regarded as healthy and anything less than 1 should be regarded with caution.

Notes

- It's seldom necessary for you to calculate these ratios because they are usually quoted in financial statistics.

- Property developers often have problems with the current ratio—it's not much use owning a property that's worth many millions of dollars, if you can't pay staff or creditors who are becoming impatient! So too, new technology, biotech and resource exploration companies may have a very promising new product under development, but can go bankrupt before the product produces profits, simply because they run out of money and are unable to meet their immediate debt obligations.

- Another ratio sometimes quoted is the quick ratio and it's regarded as even more of an acid test of short-term financial viability than the current ratio. It's essentially the same as the current ratio except that inventories are excluded from current assets. The reasoning behind this is that when the chips are down, inventories may not readily be converted to cash—there may simply be no buyers for them!

Net tangible assets per share

As formerly stated, business assets can vary widely. A service-based or research business may require few assets, whereas a manufacturing or infrastructure business may require a large amount of plant and equipment and, therefore, a large capital investment. A useful financial statistic here is the net tangible asset backing per share (NTA). It's calculated using the following formulas:

$$\text{NTA} = \frac{\text{Net tangible assets}}{\text{Number of ordinary shares}}$$

$$= \frac{\text{Total assets} - \text{Intangible assets} - \text{Liabilities}}{\text{Number of ordinary shares}}$$

Assets are things of value owned by the business, including both tangible and intangible assets. Tangible assets include land, buildings, plant and equipment, fixtures and fittings, stock and accounts receivable. Intangible assets include the value of customer goodwill, the value of patent or trademark rights and the value of any unique technology that's owned by the business.

Liabilities are what the business owes to others, in both the short term and long term, and includes loan repayments and accounts payable.

The dollar difference between assets and liabilities is the net assets, which, as we have already seen, is equal to the shareholders' equity. Usually, when determining the net asset backing per share, only the tangible assets are included. Intangible assets are usually excluded because they may not actually have a saleable value should the business go into liquidation.

Notes

- NTA can be negative, which can be the case if most of the assets of the business are intangible and/or the business has a high level of debt.

- NTA as calculated by the preceding formulae is really the theoretical 'fire sale' value of each share. That's to say, if the business liquidates, it's the theoretical cash that each investor should receive for each share they own.

Interpreting the NTA statistic

To put the NTA in perspective, you can compare the NTA to the share price. That is, from the ratio:

$$\frac{\text{Price}}{\text{NTA}}$$

In some financial listings, this statistic is calculated for you, but if it's not, you can readily calculate it. If this ratio is 1, the share price is equal to the NTA. Theoretically, this indicates no liquidation risk because should the company become insolvent, after the assets are sold, a shareholder should receive cash equal to the share price. While this is ideal from a shareholder's viewpoint, it's a rare situation and usually applies only to investment companies whose assets are primarily in the form of the investments owned by them.

For blue or green chip stocks, the ratio can commonly be in the order of 4 or more because the NTA doesn't take into account the value of goodwill. For speculative or service-based stocks, the ratio could be much higher because the business may own few tangible assets. So when evaluating the Price/NTA ratio you need to consider the sector and when comparing shares in the same sector, you can consider those with the lower Price/NTA ratio to be safer in terms of liquidation risk.

Notes

- For an investment company, if the NTA is above the share price the shares are said to be trading at a premium and if it's below, the shares are trading at a discount.

- If the business is well-established and well-managed, the risk of liquidation is very low so this statistic is not very relevant.

Developing a health test for your shares

I will now outline a set of criteria that I call my 'health test' for shares. You can use this test with fundamental analysis to evaluate longer term shares you own or are considering including in your portfolio. Of course, you're free to modify my criteria and develop your own test according to your preferences and risk tolerance.

My suggested health test is as follows.

History:

- The business has been operating for more than three years.

Product:

- The products have good market acceptance that's likely to continue.

Market valuation:

- The market cap is greater than $100 million.

Profitability:

- The business is making a profit — that is, it has positive earnings.

- ROC is greater than 8% and/or ROE is greater than 10%, and preferably trending up but certainly not trending down.

- EPS growth rate is greater than 5%.

Dividend:

- The dividend yield is greater than 3%.

- The franking level is preferably 100% (fully franked) or a high level of franking.

- The payout ratio is less than 0.8 (dividend cover greater than 1.25).

Debt:

- IC is greater than 2 and preferably above 3.

- DE is less than 100% (preferably less than 80%).

- CR is greater than 1.

Price value:

- PE is not too far away from the sector average; generally in the range of 10 to 25.

- PEG is less than 1 (or close to 1).

- Pr/NTA is ratio no more than 4 and preferably lower.

Shareholder return:

- Annual shareholder return (capital gains + dividends) is greater than 10% for the past year and also over the past three years.

Notes

- If you formulate your own 'health test', dividend yield is an optional criterion and depends on whether you value dividends as a regular source of income or whether you're more interested in capital gain.

- If you use a 'health test', most likely you will find that a share may pass the test on most criteria but fail on some. You then need to consider the deficiencies and if a rational reason exists for them. Finally, you need to decide if the deficiencies are of sufficient importance for you to eliminate the share or whether you'll overlook the deficiencies because of other positives.

- Fundamental analysis is a useful tool but it's worth remembering that published statistics are historical and the sharemarket is forward looking. So you also need to look at the future of the company and get a feeling for how the fundamentals of the business might change with time.

Learning exercises

8.1 For what type of investors is fundamental analysis most relevant and for whom is it irrelevant?

8.2 What are you assuming when you evaluate shares on the basis of sound fundamentals?

8.3 What are the two main types of fundamentals and how can you evaluate each?

8.4

    a. What is the benefit of using ratios in financial statistics rather than raw values?

    b. Sometimes a decimal ratio is shown as a percentage. What is the difference and how can you convert a decimal ratio to a percentage?

8.5 Outline some of the general fundamentals you might consider when evaluating a business.

8.6 How can an average investor simplify the masses of financial data available for any business and what two methods can (or should) be used when evaluating them?

8.7 A business seems financially healthy according to the published statistics yet the share price is trending down at a time when the sector is steady. What conclusion might you draw?

8.8 What are the two periods into which the financial year is broken?

8.9

    a. How is market capitalisation (market cap) calculated?

    b. How do you interpret the market cap statistic?

    c. If the share price increases, how will market cap and capital invested in a company change?

8.10 A listed company has 15.7 million shares on issue.
Earnings for the financial year, before interest and tax, were
$1.36 million and loan interest was $0.28 million. The tax rate
on profits is 30% and the payout ratio is 80%. The dividend is
fully franked and the share price is $0.62.

   a. What are the earnings per share and dividend per share?

   b. What is the yield and the grossed-up yield?

8.11 Three shares, A, B and C, have the following PEs:

- *A:* 6.5

- *B:* 15.2

- *C:* 35.4.

Just using these values, can you come to any conclusions as
to how you think the market views each of these shares?

8.12 What risks do you see in buying/holding shares with a very
high PE (well above market average for the sector) or a very
low PE (well below market average for the sector)?

8.13 Earnings statistics for three shares, A, B and C, are given in
the following table. Use PEG analysis to decide if the current
price of each is justified and which of them appears to be the
best buy at current prices.

Share	Current PE	Current EPS	Forecast EPS next year
A	18.6	12.2¢	14.5¢
B	25.0	24.6¢	28.3¢
C	12.3	58.0¢	56.0¢

8.14 A company floats and issues 20 million shares at 50¢ each.
On the day of listing, the share price closes at 65¢. Two weeks
later, the share price drops back to 55¢ at the close of trade.

Complete the following table.

Time	Equity capital	Market cap
Close of trade on day of listing		
Close of trade two weeks later		

8.15 What effect does an increase in a company's earnings have on the share price, earnings per share, dividend per share and yield? Do you think they will go up, down or stay about the same in each case? Assume that the number of shares on issue and the payout ratio don't change.

8.16 Briefly discuss three ways that the 'fairness' of a share price based on earnings can be evaluated, and state the advantages and disadvantages of each method.

8.17 A business requires $2 million in capital. It is able to generate a return of 20% on capital. Loan interest is 10%, the payout ratio is 70% and the tax rate is 30%. Compare the dividend per share and dividend yield to investors at the end of the year in the following two scenarios by completing the following table and commenting on the result. At the end of the year, the share price has risen to $1.50.

- *Scenario 1:* The business raises all capital needed as equity capital by issuing shares at $1.00.

- *Scenario 2:* The business raises 50% of the capital needed as equity capital by issuing shares at $1.00 and 50% of the capital needed by means of loan capital.

	Scenario 1	Scenario 2
Shares issued		
Loan capital		
Profit before tax and loan interest		
Interest on loan		
Profit before tax		
Tax		
After-tax profit		
Distributed profit		
Earnings per share		
Dividend per share		
Yield		

8.18 What is the gearing of the company given in learning exercise 8.17 for both scenarios?

8.19 The total capital of a company is $273 million, the shareholders' equity is $68.3 million and the after-tax profit is $14.5 million. Determine the return on capital and return on equity and comment on the results.

Note: In learning exercises 8.20 to 8.23, data about seven companies (A–G) was taken from published financial data.

8.20 The Debt/Equity ratios (DEs) for the companies are as follows:

- *A (property developer/holding):* 68.5
- *B (infrastructure/energy stock):* 207.1
- *C (property construction):* 19.4
- *D (newly established small consumer products):* 1.7
- *E (consumer products):* 254.2
- *F (medicinal products):* 76.1
- *G (small bank):* 1693

Comment on each of these DEs.

8.21 The interest cover ratios for companies A to F are as follows:

- *A:* 22.1
- *B:* 3.12
- *C:* 144.3
- *D:* –48.5
- *E:* 11.3
- *F:* 7.02

Comment on each of these ICs, in conjunction with the level of debt as indicated in the previous exercise.

8.22   The NTA and share prices for companies A to G are as shown in the following table. Calculate the Pr/NTA and comment.

Company	Price ($)	NTA ($)	PR/NTA	Comment
A	1.40	1.26		
B	10.82	3.17		
C	1.03	0.86		
D	0.035	0.07		
E	5.35	0.19		
F	5.60	1.29		
G	7.48	3.63		

8.23   The current ratios for companies A to F are as follows:

- *A:* 2.01
- *B:* 0.67
- *C:* 1.62
- *D:* 3.26
- *E:* 2.43
- *F:* 1.11

Comment on each of these in conjunction with the other debt ratios previously considered.

8.24   Based on the fundamentals you consider to be important, formulate your own 'health test' for shares (or modify mine to suit your preferences).

Learning exercises solutions

8.1   Fundamental analysis is most relevant for long-term investors. It's irrelevant for traders interested in short-term capital gains only.

8.2   You are assuming that a business with sound fundamentals will do well in the long run.

8.3   The two main types of fundamentals are general fundamentals and financial fundamentals. You can evaluate general fundamentals by obtaining as much information as you can about the nature of the business, its history and its products. You can evaluate financial fundamentals using published key financial statistics.

8.4

    a.   The advantage of using a ratio is that it eliminates the size factor and allows you to compare businesses of varying sizes on an 'apples to apples' basis.

    b.   The ratio scale is from 0 to 1, whereas the percentage scale is from 0 to 100. You convert a ratio to a percentage by multiplying by 100.

8.5   General fundamentals would include size, length of time in operation, product acceptance/demand and opportunities for earnings growth. (A more detailed list is provided on pages 181–182.)

8.6   Masses of financial data can be simplified using key financial statistics. These can be evaluated using a snapshot approach or a trends-over-time approach.

8.7   You should exercise extreme caution in this situation. The published statistics are based on historical information whereas the share price depends primarily on future expectations. Also, the published figures could have been 'massaged' by clever (but still legal) accounting practices.

8.8   The two periods are the first six months (interim period) and last six months (final period).

8.9

    a.   Market cap is calculated by multiplying the number of ordinary shares on issue by the share price.

    b.   Market cap is really the market value of the business—that is, the value of the business as rated by investors.

    c.   The market cap will increase but the capital invested will not change.

8.10   The solutions for each scenario are as follows:

    a.   Earnings after interest are $1.36 - 0.28 = \$1.08$ million

    Tax $= 0.3 \times 1.08 = \$0.324$ million

    After-tax earnings $= 1.08 - 0.324 = \$0.756$ million

    EPS $= 0.756 \div 15.7 = \$0.0482 = $ **4.82¢**

    DPS $= 0.8 \times 4.82 = $ **3.85¢**

    b.   Yield $= 3.85 \div 62 \times 100 = $ **6.21%**

    From table 4.3, the grossing-up factor for the fully franked dividend is 1.429

    Therefore, the GUY $= 1.429 \times 6.21 = $ **8.88%**

8.11   The solutions for each scenario are as follows:

    A: The market views this as a value share. The share is underpriced in regard to its historical earnings, with little prospect of future earnings growth.

    B: This is an average type of share with reasonable historical earnings and reasonable future earnings growth potential.

    C: This is perceived as a growth share. That is, the share is overpriced in relation to its historical earnings. Historical earnings don't justify the current share price but some 'blue sky' potential exists for future earnings growth.

8.12   A very high PE indicates the share price is based on 'blue sky' potential. The risk is that the potential may not be realised and then the share price could fall considerably. A very low PE indicates that investors are disenchanted with the company. Even though historical earnings justify the share price, investors can't see earnings growth potential and may even consider that earnings could go down. The risk is that this perception may prove to be true and that the share price could fall in the future.

8.13 See the following completed table.

Share	Current PE	Current EPS	Forecast EPS next year	Change next year's EPS	EGP %	PEG ratio
A	18.6	12.2¢	14.5¢	2.3¢	18.85	0.99
B	25.0	24.6¢	28.3¢	3.7¢	15.04	1.66
C	12.3	58.0¢	56.0¢	–2¢	–3.45	–3.57

Conclusions:

» A is fair value (PEG around 1).

» B is overpriced (PEG greater than 1).

» C is in decline and PEG analysis is not meaningful because PEG is negative. Justification of the current share price depends on whether the current downtrend in EPS can be reversed at some time in the future.

8.14 See the following completed table.

Time	Equity capital	Market cap
Close of trade on day of listing	$10 million	$13 million
Close of trade two weeks later	$10 million	$11 million

Note: Equity capital is not affected by changes in share price whereas market cap is.

8.15 An increase in earnings usually has the following effects:

» share price rises

» EPS rises

» DPS rises

» yield stays about the same because the increased dividend is accompanied by an increased share price.

8.16   The three ways are:

1.   *Rule of 20:* Subtract the inflation rate from 20 and so decide the fairness of the PE. For example, if the current inflation rate is 3%, a PE of 17 is fair, if below 17, the share looks undervalued and if above, the share looks overpriced. The advantage of this method is that it's simple. The disadvantage is that PE is based on past earnings and the stock market looks forward rather than backward when setting share prices.

2.   *PEG ratio:* Compare the PE to the percentage forecast earnings growth to obtain the PEG ratio. A PEG ratio of 1 indicates fair value, below 1 indicates good value and above 1 indicates an overpriced share. The advantage of this method is that it's based on future earnings and not historical results. The disadvantage is that earnings forecasts are just that and will not necessarily take place. Also, it's often difficult to obtain earnings forecasts, particularly for small market cap companies.

3.   *Discounted future earnings:* All future earnings are estimated and discounted according to the length of time in the future in which they will occur. All discounted values are added to give the total discounted value of all future earnings per share. If the share price is about equal to the total discounted value, the share price is fair. If above it, the share price is too high (expensive) and if below it, the share is underpriced (a bargain). The advantage of this method is that it's based on long-term future earnings. The disadvantage is that this method is difficult to apply because it requires an estimate of earnings for some time into the future and these are difficult to obtain (and may prove unrealistic in any case).

8.17   See the following completed table.

	Scenario 1	Scenario 2
Shares issued	2 million	1 million
Loan capital	0	$1 million
Profit before tax and loan interest	$0.4 million	$0.4 million
Interest on loan	0	$0.1 million

	Scenario 1	Scenario 2
Profit before tax	$0.4 million	$0.3 million
Tax	$0.12 million	$0.09 million
After-tax profit	$0.28 million	$0.21 million
Distributed profit	$0.196 million	$0.147 million
Earnings per share	14¢	21¢
Dividend per share	9.8¢	14.7¢
Yield	6.53%	9.8%

Comment: You can see that in scenario 2, the business makes less dollar profit because it has to pay interest on the loan capital. However, because only half the number of shares are issued compared to scenario 1, the EPS and yield are much higher. Therefore, from an investor's point of view, scenario 2 is the better one.

8.18 In scenario 1, the gearing is zero (no loan capital) and in scenario 2, the gearing is 100% because of the equal amount of loan capital and equity capital.

8.19 $ROC = 14.5 \div 273 \times 100 = \textbf{5.31\%}$

$ROE = 14.5 \div 68.3 \times 100 = \textbf{21.2\%}$

Comment: ROC is rather low and needs to be improved. ROE is very good.

8.20 Possible comments on the DE ratios are follows:

  » *A:* An acceptable amount of loan capital.

  » *B:* A high amount of loan capital and warrants caution.

  » *C:* A low debt level, indicating the company does not have a great deal of loan capital.

  » *D:* A very low amount of loan capital.

  » *E:* A high amount of loan capital and warrants caution.

  » *F:* An acceptable amount of loan capital.

  » *G:* Banks always have a very high DE and you shouldn't place any significance on it.

8.21   Possible comments on the interest cover ratios are as follows:

» *A:* An excellent interest cover, indicating that this company will have no problems meeting its debt commitments.

» *B:* Acceptable level of interest cover (provided current profit levels are maintained).

» *C:* A very high interest cover (as to be expected) because this company has a low amount of debt.

» *D:* A negative interest cover, indicating that the company is not making a profit and, therefore, could not use profits to repay loan interest. Fortunately, it has a low level of debt.

» *E:* A very good interest cover, even with the large amount of loan capital. This indicates that the company is making sufficient profit to comfortably cover loan interest.

» *F:* A very good level of interest cover for the reasonable amount of debt.

8.22   See the following completed table.

Stock	Price ($)	NTA ($)	PR/ NTA	Comment
A	1.40	1.26	1.11	The price is close to the NTA and indicates that investors are not placing a great premium on these shares above their asset backing.
B	10.82	3.17	3.41	A rather high Pr/NTA, which indicates that investors place a considerable premium on these shares.
C	1.03	0.86	1.20	The price is close to the NTA, indicating that investors are not placing a great premium on these shares above their asset backing.
D	0.035	0.07	0.50	PR/NTA is less than 1, indicating that investors are really not impressed with the prospects for this company.
E	5.35	0.19	28.2	A very high PR/NTA, which I would consider unacceptable—it indicates the shares are too highly priced in relation to the assets.
F	5.60	1.29	4.34	A rather high PR/NTA, which, in my opinion, is bordering on the limits of acceptability.
G	7.48	3.63	2.06	Acceptable PR/NTA.

8.23   Possible comments on the current ratios are as follows:

» *A:* A sufficient level of current assets to cover current liability.

» *B:* Too low a level of current assets in relationship to current liabilities.

» *C:* Acceptable current ratio.

» *D:* A good current ratio that suggests that even though this company is making a loss, at present sufficient liquid assets are available to cover current liabilities.

» *E:* A sufficient level of current assets to cover current liability obligations, indicating that the company is making sufficient profit to comfortably cover current liabilities.

» *F:* Borderline current ratio.

8.24   No solution provided because health test formulated will depend on the individual.

Chapter 9

Using technical analysis to guide your trading decisions

In this chapter I discuss an approach known as *technical analysis* or charting. This approach ignores the fundamentals of a company and considers price trends only. The aim is to detect price trends and identify trading signals (entry and exit points) that can be used as a basis for trading decisions.

Comparing fundamental and technical analysis

The basic principles of fundamental and technical analysis are outlined in table 9.1 (overleaf).

Share traders (as opposed to investors) use technical analysis because they're interested in short-term trading, so longer term fundamentals have little relevance. This is exemplified in the following quote from Christopher Tate in *The Art of Trading* (John Wiley & Sons Australia):

I am by nature and training a chartist or, if you prefer, a technical analyst. It is my belief that price action will tell you everything you need to know about a stock. I have no faith whatsoever in fundamental analysis for a variety of reasons but most of all, it does not take into account the underlying psychology of the market. It may be semantics but people make and move markets, not balance sheets.

Table 9.1: Fundamental and technical analysis

	Fundamental analysis	Technical analysis
Source of profit	Capital gains and dividends	Capital gains only
Usual time period	Medium–long term	Short–medium term
Criteria	Sound fundamentals	Trends and signals
Information needed	General fundamentals and key financial statistics	Charts and technical analysis tools

Understanding trend trading

The basic idea of technical analysis is to identify trends and trend changes, and use these as a basis for trading decisions. As a rather simple analogy, consider travelling in a vehicle. If you want to go forward, you board a forward moving vehicle and the faster it's moving the better. If it starts to slow down, you need to decide if it's now time to get off. If it stops, you're going nowhere and you need to decide if you still want to stay on board in the hope that the vehicle will start moving forward again. If it starts to reverse, it's definitely time to get off—unless you have strong reason to believe this is only a temporary reversal and the vehicle will soon stop and start moving forward again.

You can apply this analogy to the sharemarket:

- *Upward share price trend:* The vehicle is moving forward.

- *Upward trend faltering:* The vehicle is slowing down.

- *Sideways trend:* The vehicle is oscillating forward and backward but going nowhere.

- *Downtrend:* The vehicle is going backward.

The basic principle of trend trading on the sharemarket is that, like a moving vehicle, an established trend is more likely to continue than it is to stop suddenly or reverse. In the vast majority of cases, capital gains are made in an uptrend and losses in a downtrend but it's possible to change this by trading CFDs, options or warrants, or entering into short-sell contracts. With these trading instruments, you can profit from trends other than uptrends. However, this type of trading is suitable for experienced investors only and won't be considered here.

Discovering the value of technical analysis

Two conflicting schools of thought relate to the value of technical analysis, namely:

- Technical analysis is akin to reading tea leaves or tarot cards and should be disregarded entirely.

- Technical analysis provides a meaningful and useful tool that should be used by all share traders and investors.

Generally speaking, most active share traders rely heavily on technical analysis while most share investors would lie somewhere in the middle of these two conflicting viewpoints. There's no guarantee that trends based on past performance will continue into the future, but it's a more likely scenario than one based on sudden trend reversal. Over a period of time, the probabilities indicate that technical analysis will assist you to make better trading decisions. I suggest that if you're a longer term investor, you use both fundamental and technical analysis—you don't need to consider them to be mutually exclusive. If you're going to adopt this approach, check the fundamentals with regard to your benchmark 'health test' (as outlined in chapter 8) and use technical analysis to help identify appropriate trading opportunities.

Gaining benefits from charting

Charts are the backbone of technical analysis as they provide a picture that's not evident with numerical data and they enable you to more readily identify trends and trading signals. The internet has revolutionised the access ordinary investors have to up-to-date charts. In many cases, charts can be customised in several ways but this depends on the charting software.

Note

If you want to expand your knowledge of fundamental and technical analysis and share trading using the internet, please refer to my book *Online Investing on the Australian Sharemarket*, now in its fifth edition.

Price chart

The most widely used chart for technical analysis is the price chart. This chart is drawn with time on the *x*-axis (horizontal axis) and price on the *y*-axis (vertical axis).

Time axis

A linear scale (a scale where the divisions are equally spaced) is used for the time axis. Daily time divisions are most common but sometimes one-day (or intra-day) charts are available and these show the price fluctuations on a trade-by-trade basis during each day. Weekly time divisions are also used, and these time divisions make the chart clearer when it's drawn over a long time period.

Most charting software allows you to choose the period in time back from the present over which the chart will be drawn (unless it's an intra-day chart). Time periods you may want to consider are the most recent:

- month or two
- three or six months
- year or two
- three, five or 10 years.

You can also choose to display all data—that is, as far as data is available.

A perplexing question regarding technical analysis is, 'What time period should I use—which is best?' The usual answer is that the chart time frame should match your investment time frame—if you're a short-term trader, use a short time period and if you're a longer term investor, choose a longer time period.

An approach I often use is a three-step one, namely:

1. Use a weekly chart for the last three years or more to identify long-term trends.

2. Use a daily chart over the last year to get a better focus on the last 12 months.

3. Use a daily chart over the last three to six months to fine-tune the most recent trends or changes in trends.

Price axis

Two scales are used for the y-axis—linear and logarithmic. The linear scale is most common and it's just like the scale on a ruler—that is, the divisions are the same distance apart. For example, the distance between $1 and $2 is the same as the distance between $20 and $21. In a logarithmic scale, the spacings get closer together as the price increases so that the distance between $0.10 and $1.00 is the same as the distance between $1 and $10. The advantage of this is that the relative price movement is the same distance apart. With a linear scale, the absolute price movement is the same distance.

As we have seen, return on capital invested depends on percentage profit, which in turn depends on relative price movement and, therefore, a logarithmic scale is most appropriate for a longer term investor. However, most charting software uses a linear scale and if the time period isn't very long and the price range isn't very great, the difference isn't significant enough to worry about.

Notes

*   Sometimes you may be able to change the range of prices shown on the chart.

*   If a name change or merger takes place, the shares are usually considered to be new ones and so the chart may go back in time only as far as to the time of the change.

*   If a split or consolidation occurs, price charts are usually adjusted automatically for the relative change in value of the shares.

Types of price charts

Four prices are relevant for a price chart:

1. *Opening:* the first sale price.

2. *High:* the highest price.

3. *Low:* the lowest price.

4. *Closing:* the last sale price.

Notes

- If the chart is drawn using a daily time scale, these will be the prices for that day and if a weekly time scale is being used, these will be for the week.

- For a daily chart if the closing price is higher than the opening price, this is known as an 'up day' and if lower, it's a 'down day'.

The four most common price chart formats using these prices are:

- *Line chart:* A line is drawn through the closing prices (or actual prices in an intra-day chart). In some cases, the space below the line on a line chart is shaded. This chart is often called an 'area chart' or a 'mountain chart' because it looks like a mountain.

- *Bar chart:* A vertical bar is drawn and the length of the bar indicates the range of prices (lowest to highest).

- *OHLC chart:* This is the same as a bar chart except that two small tabs are superimposed on the vertical bar. The tab to the left indicates the opening price and the tab to the right, the closing price.

- *Candle chart:* This is essentially the same as the OHLC chart but is drawn in a slightly different way. Instead of using tabs to indicate opening and closing prices, a wide bar is superimposed on the vertical bar. Different colours are used for this bar, with green or white commonly used for an up day, and red or black for a down day.

These chart formats are also shown in figure 9.1.

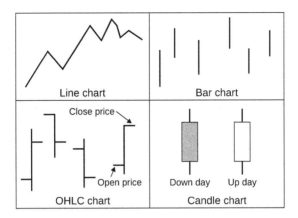

Figure 9.1: Common price chart formats

Each of these charts has different features and you need to experiment to find the one you like best for the time period you are using. A line chart is easiest to interpret but omits important price range data so most technical analysts prefer to use a bar chart or a variant of it such as an OHLC or candle chart. The candle chart provides the most striking visual impact but has the problem that if the chart is drawn over a longish time period, the bars tend to jumble together.

Percent chart

The four price charts I've described in the preceding section are most commonly used but other types of price chart may also be available. A useful one is the percent chart, which doesn't show dollar prices, but rather the percentage price change from an initial price (at the start of the charting period). This enables you to see at a glance the percentage profit (or loss) you would have made had you bought those shares at the start of the time period. The chart is also very useful for comparing two or more shares, or comparing shares with indices regardless of their price or value, because each line starts from the same point. For example, you can easily compare the capital gain profitability of a $1 share with a $100 share, whereas this is not as easy on an ordinary price chart.

Figure 9.2 (overleaf) shows a percent chart comparing two banks, CBA and ANZ, over a 10-year period. CBA is shown as a mountain (shaded) chart and ANZ as a line chart.

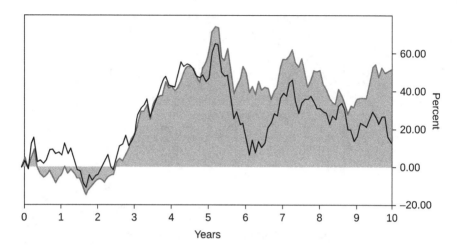

Figure 9.2: Percent chart
Source: ASX

You can see that over the first five years or so they were running almost neck and neck but after that ANZ dropped much more than CBA. You can also see that at the end of the 10-year period, CBA would have given you a capital gain of about 50% but ANZ would have only provided a very modest capital gain of about 10%.

Volume charts

Technical analysts often consider volume trends in conjunction with price trends. Volumes are usually shown in bar chart format below prices on a price chart. Please refer to figure 9.7, later in this chapter, for an example.

A question often asked is, 'Does volume indicate the number of shares bought or the number of shares sold, or is it the sum of the shares bought and sold?' In fact, you can't buy a share unless someone sells you one, so each share traded is a share that's bought and also sold. Therefore, volume is the number of shares bought or the number of shares sold, since they're equal.

The link between volume trends and price trends (for a share or the market as a whole) are usually considered to be as follows:

- Rising volume with increasing prices indicates a strong bull market (uptrend).

- Rising volume with decreasing prices indicates a strong bear market (downtrend).

- Falling volume with increasing prices indicates a bull market that's faltering.

- Falling volume with decreasing prices indicates a bear market that's faltering.

These variations are illustrated in figure 9.3.

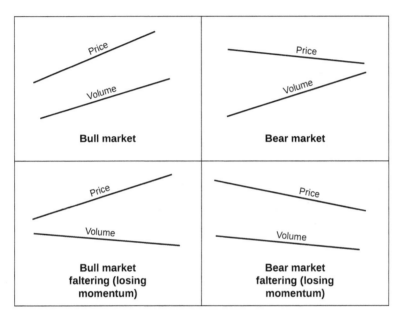

Figure 9.3: Links between price and volume

Volume spikes

Sometimes sudden and dramatic increases in volume occur and these are known as *volume spikes*. They're usually of significance because they indicate a sudden increase in trading interest. For example, if a mining company announces an important new discovery, there's usually a sudden spike in the share price, accompanied by a sudden spike in volume indicating increased trading activity. Confusingly, sometimes volume spikes occur for no reason that's apparent from the price action.

Effect of a dividend

A dividend usually causes a sudden change in share price and this will be evident on the price chart. As discussed earlier in the book, two dates are significant, namely the date at which the dividend is declared and the ex-dividend date. Possible effects of a dividend on the price of a share whose price was rising are shown in figure 9.4.

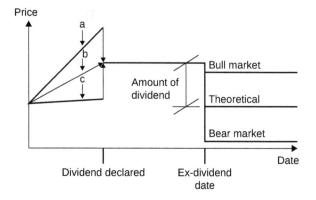

Figure 9.4: Effect of dividend on share price

If there are no surprises, the announcement of the dividend should have no effect on the share price. This is shown by line b. However, if the dividend is less than anticipated, as shown by line a, the share price will usually drop. If the dividend is greater than anticipated, the share price will usually rise as shown by line c.

Theoretically, if the dividend's unfranked, the share price should drop at the start of trading on the ex-dividend date by exactly the amount of the dividend. This is shown by the line marked 'theoretical'. For example, if the shares closed on Tuesday at $2.26 and Wednesday is the ex-dividend day for a dividend of $0.10 per share, the opening price on Wednesday should be $2.16. However, in a bull market, the shares could open higher, and in a bear market they may open lower. These possibilities are also shown in figure 9.4.

Notes

- The normal fall in share price when shares go ex-dividend is not indicative of a change in trend.

- If the dividend is franked, the fall in share price when the shares go ex-dividend can be greater than the dividend itself. For example, with a fully franked dividend of $0.10, the share price could drop by anything up to about $0.14 because of the extra value investors place on the franking credits.

Support and resistance levels

Share prices often bounce around for some time within a horizontal price channel. The lower level in this channel is known as the *support level* and the upper one as the *resistance level*. As these names suggest, the support level is the price where the shares are perceived to be good value so buyers step in and the price rises. The resistance level is the price where the shares are perceived as no longer being good value so sellers step in and the price falls. Often, after some time bouncing between support and resistance levels, a price breakout occurs and this signals a significant change. If the price rises and then starts bouncing around again, it's often the case that the old resistance level becomes a new support level. If the price falls and then starts bouncing around again, the old support level often becomes a new resistance level.

The following analogy may be useful: imagine a multi-storey carpark with holes in the floors. You're located on the middle level and you throw a highly elastic ball at the floor. The ball bounces, hits the roof and bounces back down again. It does this a number of times. This represents horizontal support and resistance levels, with the share price bouncing around between them.

Suppose the ball finds a hole in the roof and shoots upward to the next level. This is analogous to an upward breakout. The old roof now becomes a new support level and the new roof becomes a new resistance level. The ball may now continue to bounce around the new support and resistance levels, or it may find another hole and go through it again—upward, if it found a hole in the roof, and downward if it found a hole in the floor. These effects are illustrated in figure 9.5. You can see the original support and resistance levels (marked 1), but at point *x* an upward price break occurs through the original resistance level. The sidetrend continues with new support and resistance levels (marked 2) where the old resistance level becomes a new support level.

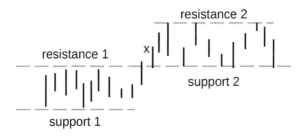

Figure 9.5: Support and resistance levels

Notes

- The price won't always bounce in a sidetrend fashion again after a breakout. An upward breakout often signals the start of a new uptrend and a downward breakout may be the start of a new downtrend.

- To be regarded as a true sidetrend, the support and resistance levels need to be relatively close together.

- Short-term traders often trade between support and resistance levels by buying when the price is around the support level and selling when the price is around the resistance level. This type of trading produces short-term profits and helps to reinforce the support and resistance levels.

Identifying patterns and trends

Over a period of time, price fluctuations often result in identifiable patterns and trends on a price chart. In addition to the sidetrend already discussed and illustrated in figure 9.5, there are three other basic patterns, as shown in figure 9.6.

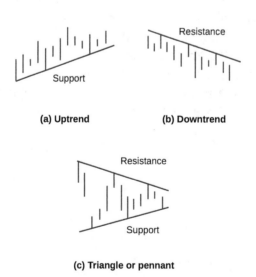

Figure 9.6: Three basic chart patterns and trends

Uptrend

If the support line isn't horizontal but slopes up, the share price is in an uptrend. The resistance level may or may not be recognisable; however, in an uptrend, an upward sloping resistance level is often identifiable as well as the upward sloping support level.

Downtrend

If the resistance line slopes down, the share price is in a downtrend. The support level may or may not be recognisable; however, in a downtrend, a downward sloping support level is often identifiable as well as the downward sloping resistance level.

Note

Uptrends are identified when the *support* line slopes up and downtrends when the *resistance* line slopes down.

Triangles or pennants

Triangles or pennants occur when support and resistance levels are identifiable but they aren't approximately parallel. Converging levels are a sign of decreasing volatility and that investors are reaching consensus about a fair price. This pattern is often known as a 'pennant' because it looks like a pennant-type flag. Diverging levels are a sign of increasing volatility and that investors can't reach consensus about a fair price. The triangle pattern, whether converging or diverging, seldom lasts very long and a breakout will occur from the pattern. This usually signals a significant change in investor sentiment.

Notes

- In figure 9.6 I've illustrated a converging channel (pennant), because this is the most common.

- The basic patterns I've described have many variations and combinations. These are given names based on their shape, such as teacup, or head and shoulders (and many others). If you're interested in delving deeper, I suggest you refer to my book *Charting Made Simple* (John Wiley & Sons Australia), which provides a simplified guide to technical analysis using charts.

Identifying trends

Sometimes a clear trend will be readily identifiable but usually trend identification is more difficult. This is because share prices bounce around with lots of random scatter as trading results in short-term price fluctuations. This scatter tends to mask a more significant underlying trend that may be present. Another problem is that there are no right or wrong chart interpretations; for example, some analysts ignore prices that lie outside the 'normal range', whereas others may include all extreme prices. Interpretation also depends on the time period and whether you are analysing the longer or shorter term. As a consequence, two people can examine a chart and identify different trends and come to different conclusions.

Indeed, you could conclude that if share prices were to move in regular and easily recognisable patterns, trend identification would be easy and the result would be the rather impossible situation of all trades being profitable because everyone would know precisely when to buy and sell to make a profit and avoid a loss!

Many methods are used to identify trends; some are based on statistical trend analysis and others are based on personal chart examination. Two methods in common use are the 'eyeball' method and the moving average method.

Eyeball method

With this method, you examine the chart and try to identify support and resistance levels and trends by personal examination. If you want to draw a trendline, you need a minimum of two points that you can join, but the more points you can line up, the better the confirmation of the trend. For this purpose, it's best to use a bar chart (or variant of it) rather than a line chart, because trend lines should be drawn using points at the extremities of the price bars (not just closing prices). If you can identify a trend line, you should next look for indications of a price break signalling a change in trend. You can then decide whether or not you want to trade the shares and if you want to buy or sell.

Notes

- The more practice you have at identifying trend lines, the more confident you should become about using the eyeball method.

- Some charting software allows you to draw lines on the chart; otherwise, you can copy the chart into another program or print the chart and draw lines using a pencil and rule.

Moving average method

In this method, charting software allows you to superimpose moving average lines on a chart and use these lines to identify trends and changes in trend. Many websites have this facility and this method is so popular and useful that I'll discuss it in some detail.

A moving average line is obtained when closing prices are averaged over successive periods and all the average points charted and joined. It's usually curved (not straight) and its direction indicates the direction of the trend.

Several types of moving average are used, with the two most popular being the simple moving average and the exponential moving average.

Simple moving average

The way a simple moving average (SMA) is obtained is best illustrated by example. To simplify the maths, I'll calculate a three-day SMA (see table 9.2) but in practice, such a short time period is rare and would be used only by day traders.

The figure in row 3 (1.10) is the average of the previous three days (1.00, 1.20 and 1.10), and this process continues for each moving average.

Table 9.2: Simple moving average

Day	Closing price	3-day moving average
1	1.00	
2	1.20	
3	1.10	1.10
4	1.05	1.12
5	1.12	1.09

The figure in row 4 (1.12) is the average of 1.20, 1.10 and 1.05, and the figure in row 5 (1.09) is the average of 1.10, 1.05 and 1.12. Clearly, in my example, days 1 and 2 don't have a moving average figure because three days of data are needed in order to obtain the first average.

Note

In the example shown in table 9.2, I've calculated a daily moving average using daily closing prices. In a weekly chart, the weekly closing price would be used instead.

Exponential moving average

When calculating a SMA, all prices are given equal weight. So with a 31-day average, the price 31 days ago influences the average as much as yesterday's price. Some analysts feel that this creates a moving average that's too insensitive to recent price movements and argue that what happened 31 days ago isn't as significant as yesterday's price move. Also, a single price affects the SMA twice—namely, when it's first included and then again when it's excluded.

The exponential moving average (EMA) is designed to overcome these difficulties because it's calculated using a formula where prices are weighted. Recent prices are given more weight than older prices so as time goes on, prices decay exponentially and their effect on the average fades away gradually.

While the way SMAs and EMAs are calculated is dramatically different, in practice they don't usually result in very different trend interpretations. It's another aspect of technical analysis that you might want to experiment with yourself. You can do so easily, because most charting software gives you the choice of which average you want to use.

Note

It's important to realise that a moving average is the average for a past time period. For example, a 31-day SMA point is really the average price applying to the middle of the averaging period—namely, on day 16 (15 days ago). This highlights why some analysts prefer the EMA because it gives more weight to recent prices.

Moving average time periods

Moving averages smooth out short-term scatter (ripples) and allow underlying trends to be identified more readily. The longer the time period of the moving average, the more smoothing that occurs, and the shorter the time period, the less smoothing. Taken to the limit, a one-day moving average would be the same as a daily price, with no smoothing at all. The difference in smoothing can be seen in figure 9.7.

In this chart, the shorter moving average is a 5-day EMA and the longer moving average is a 30-day EMA. You can see how the short-term moving average closely follows the price action and looks very much like a line of best fit, whereas the longer term moving average smooths out the ripples and doesn't respond immediately to short-term price moves. Instead, it allows you to identify the longer term price trend more readily.

The differences between short- and long-term moving averages are summarised in table 9.3 (overleaf). (See the following section for an explanation of whipsawing.)

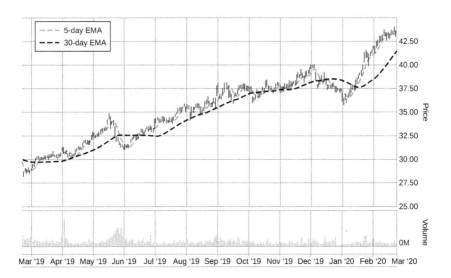

Figure 9.7: Price chart with moving averages
Source: ASX

Table 9.3: Short- and long-term moving averages

	Short-term MA	Long-term MA
Smoothing	Little smoothing	Much smoothing
Sensitivity	Trend changes can be detected more rapidly	Trend changes take longer to detect
Advantage	You can enter or exit trends more quickly and so make more trading profit	You're less likely to be whipsawed
Disadvantage	You're more likely to be whipsawed	Prices may have moved significantly before you detect a trend change so you'll generally make less trading profit

Whipsaw

A 'whipsaw' occurs when you get a buy signal based on price trends and enter into a trade but, soon after, you get a sell signal and need to exit the trade. (See the section, 'Trading signals from moving averages', later in this chapter, for more on buy and sell signals.) Similarly, you could get a sell signal but soon after a buy signal. Needless to say, you'll most likely lose on the combined transactions (especially when you take into account trading costs) so naturally you should try to avoid whipsaws.

One method of reducing the risk of a whipsaw is to use a time delay—that is, not to act on a trading signal immediately but wait for confirmation. You can delay for a short period of time (for example, three to five days) or else wait until the price has moved by a certain amount (for example, 3%) before you trade. However, reducing the risk comes at a cost, because some of your potential profit can be eroded if you delay acting too long.

Suggested time periods

As you've seen from table 9.3, short- and long-term moving averages each have advantages and disadvantages, so you may be wondering what time periods you should use. Like most things associated with share trading, there are no right or wrong answers but I suggest you consider the following time periods:

- *5 to 11 days:* For short-term trends.

- *13 to 31 days:* For medium-term trends.

- *50 to 250 days:* For long-term trends.

Trading signals from moving averages

Moving averages can be used to obtain trading (buy and sell) signals. A common way of doing this is from two moving averages, as shown on the chart in figure 9.7. One moving average should be relatively short term (in the range of 7 to 21 days) and one of longer term (in the range of 31 to 150 days). The time periods you choose depend on the time frame of your proposed trade. For example, if you're interested in short-term trading, you could use an 11-day moving average and a 31-day moving average on a three- to six-month chart. If you're interested in longer term investing you could use a 21-day moving average and a 100-day moving average on a one- to two-year chart. It's really a matter of experimentation and another reason the internet is such a wonderful resource for share investing—you can do this type of experimenting to your heart's content at virtually no cost.

With two moving averages, buy and sell signals are as follows:

- *Buy signal:* The short moving average moves above the long moving average, and the price, short moving average and long moving average are all moving in an upward direction. This is known as a *golden cross.*

- *Sell signal:* The short moving average moves below the long moving average, and the price, short moving average and long moving average are all moving in a downward direction. This is known as a *dead cross.*

Notes

- Some charting software allows you to draw more than two moving averages simultaneously, in which case more complex trading signals are possible. For most purposes, I think you'll find two moving averages are sufficient.

- Frequently, a spike in volume indicating increased trading action will accompany a golden cross or dead cross, but this is by no means always the case.

Filters

Moving averages are an important primary tool to identify trading signals; however, they aren't infallible and whipsaws can and do occur. As mentioned, you can reduce the likelihood of a whipsaw by not acting on a trading signal immediately. Another way of reducing the likelihood of a whipsaw is to use one or two secondary tools in addition to the primary one. These tools are also known as *filters* because they act as a second line of defence in an attempt to improve reliability. At last count, over 50 different filters were obtainable with technical analysis software. Popular ones include MACD (moving average convergence divergence), RSI (relative strength index), OBV (on balance volume) and momentum, just to name a few.

If you use a filter, two results can occur:

1. The filter confirms the signal indicated by the primary tool and gives you more confidence in it.

2. The filter casts doubts on the signal obtained from the primary tool because it gives a different interpretation. This is known as a *divergence* and it decreases your confidence in the primary signal. Often, traders use divergences as a warning not to proceed with the trade based on the primary tool signal. However, if you're more adventurous, you can also regard a divergence as a trading opportunity, allowing you to get a jump ahead of the herd.

I'm only giving you an introduction to charting and technical analysis, so I'll not go into detail about filters here. If you want to know more, please refer to my books *Online Investing on the Australian Sharemarket* and *Charting Made Simple*.

Dead cat bounce

This is a rather descriptive name (and one that won't be appreciated by cat lovers) to identify an occurrence that often happens when a share price has been in a downtrend mode for some time. The name derives from the agility of cats to fall from a height and bounce back up without being hurt when reaching the ground. To complete the gruesome analogy, if a dead cat falls from a height, it will also bounce a little when it hits the ground but it's still a dead cat—and the bounce is known as a *dead cat bounce*. When a share (or the market) has been in a downtrend for some time, and then starts to move upward, this can signal a trend change. However, it could also be just a 'dead cat' bounce if the trend reversal is only a temporary bounce, and soon after the uptrend falters and the downtrend resumes.

It's something to watch for because it frequently occurs with downtrending shares. After a run of bad news, a hint of good news can cause a bounce in price as investors breathe a sigh of relief and quickly jump in to buy the shares at a price that appears to be 'bargain basement'. The price starts to rise as a result of the buying pressure but, soon after, falls again as short-term traders take quick profits and the cold, hard reality returns that there are no real grounds for optimism at this stage—the cat was dead after all.

The best way of avoiding being sucked into a dead cat bounce is to apply a price or time delay before you take action. Wait until you're sure that the bounce is not just a temporary one before you trade. You won't trade at the best possible price but, on average, you'll avoid a lot of pain.

Learning exercises

9.1 Explain how you can use both fundamental and technical analysis when (a) buying or (b) selling shares.

9.2 In order to refresh your understanding regarding relative and absolute price movements, consider the following scenarios:

- The price of share A rises from 5¢ to 7.5¢ in a period of three months'.

- The price of share B rises from $16 to $20 in the same period.

Which of these two scenarios gives greatest capital gain?

Prove your answer by calculating the profit made in each case had you invested $4000 in each.

9.3

a. What are the four prices used for share price charts?

b. Describe briefly the four main types of chart and how these prices are used on each.

9.4 Charts can be drawn in many ways, and many different indicators and filters can be drawn. Charts can be interpreted in different ways with different conclusions being reached by different investors. Finally, trends can suddenly falter or reverse for no apparent reason.

a. Therefore, technical analysis is an inexact science and the conclusions you reach using it can be unreliable, so why use it at all?

b. If you're a longer term investor, what's a better strategy than using technical analysis alone for your trading decisions?

9.5 What are the three common time divisions used for price charts and when would you consider using each?

9.6 What's the difference between a percent chart and a normal price chart and when would you consider using a percent chart?

9.7 How can you draw an uptrend line and a downtrend line on a price chart?

9.8 What is meant by a 'dead cat' bounce and how can you avoid falling into the trading trap accompanying it?

9.9

    a. How is volume normally shown on charts?

    b. When is a volume spike likely to occur and what does it indicate?

    c. Complete the following table showing links between price and volume by inserting the words 'increasing' or 'decreasing' in each blank cell:

	Price	Volume
Bull market		
Bear market		
Bull market faltering		
Bear market faltering		

9.10 The directors of a company declared an interim dividend of 6¢ per share (fully franked) on 21 February, and the ex-dividend date was 7 March. This dividend was anticipated by the market.

What changes would you expect to see on the price chart of the shares on 21 February and 7 March?

9.11

    a. When a share price is drifting sideways, what is meant by support and resistance levels and how would you identify these on a price chart?

    b. If there's an upward breakout through a resistance level but the shares drift sideways again, what's a likely new support level? With a downward breakout, what's a likely new resistance level?

9.12 If you're drawing trendlines by eye:

    a. What's the minimum number of points you can use?

    b. What types of chart are best?

    c. How would you identify an uptrend?

    d. How would you identify a downtrend?

9.13 Examine figure 9A and draw any trends you can identify and mark points where you think a break in the trend has occurred.

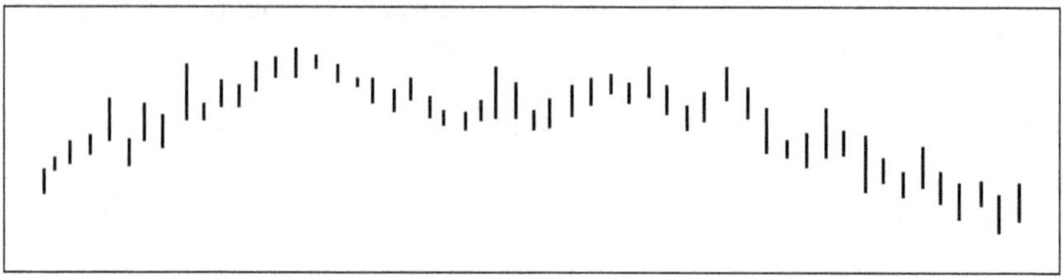

Figure 9A

9.14 Figure 9B is an OHLC bar chart drawn for a one-year time period. Analyse this chart and draw any patterns or trends you can identify. Do these shares look like a good investing proposition now?

9.15 What's the difference between an exponential moving average (EMA) and a simple moving average (SMA) and what advantages are claimed for the EMA?

9.16 What are the advantages and disadvantages of using a long-term moving average compared to a short-term one when identifying trends and changes of trend in a price chart?

9.17 What are appropriate moving average time periods to use to detect trends if you're interested in the following?

    a. Short-term trading

    b. Medium-term trading/investing

    c. Long-term investing

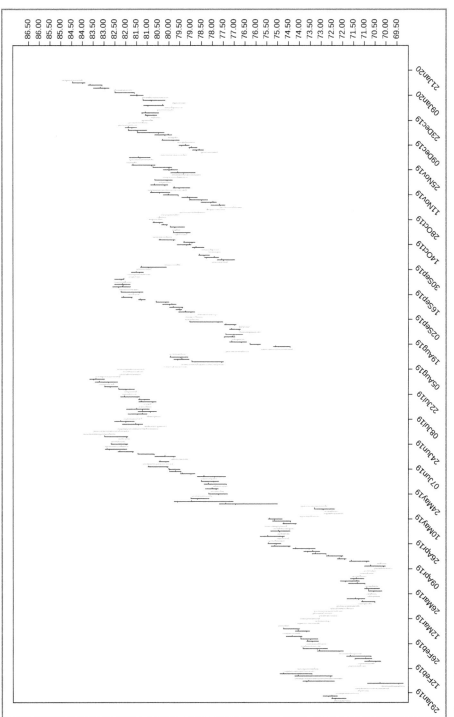

Figure 9B
Source: Incredible charts

9.18 What's meant by a golden cross and a dead cross and what trading signals can you obtain from them?

9.19

    a. What's meant by a whipsaw?

    b. What two main methods can you use to minimise the likelihood of a whipsaw?

9.20 Fill in the last two rows added to table 9.2 to include days six and seven.

Table 9.2: Simple moving average

Day	Price	3-day moving average
1	1.00	
2	1.20	
3	1.10	1.10
4	1.05	1.12
5	1.12	1.09
6	1.15	
7	1.10	

Learning exercises solutions

9.1

    a. *Buying shares:* Use fundamental analysis with your benchmark 'health test' to zero in on shares that are most likely to be good investments for you. Then use technical analysis to time your trading entry point.

    b. *Selling shares:* Use fundamental analysis to keep tabs on your share portfolio and to make sure that your 'health test' still applies for all shares. Use technical analysis to detect if a share price is in a downtrend mode and, if so, to time your exit point if you decide to sell.

9.2   In absolute terms, the price of share A rose by only 2.5¢ whereas the price of share B rose by $4.

    Therefore, you might conclude that much more profit would be made on share B. This is a false conclusion! In relative terms, share A rose by 50%, whereas share B rose by 25%. Therefore, share A would, in fact, show twice as much profit, and the rise from 5¢ to 7.5¢ is twice as significant as the rise of share B from $16 to $20.

    If you had invested $4000 in each:

    » *Share A:* 80 000 shares, now worth $6000, profit $2000.

    » *Share B:* 250 shares, now worth $5000, profit $1000.

9.3

    a. The four prices are opening price, closing price, highest price and lowest price.

    b. The four most common price chart formats using these prices are:

      » *Line chart:* A line is drawn through the closing prices (or actual prices in an intra-day chart).

      » *Bar chart:* A vertical bar is drawn and the length of the bar indicates the range of prices (lowest to highest).

      » *OHLC chart:* This is the same as a bar chart except that two small tabs are superimposed on the vertical bar.

The tab to the left indicates the opening price and the tab to the right, the closing price.

- » *Candle chart:* This is essentially the same as the OHLC chart but a coloured wide bar is superimposed on the vertical bar to indicate opening and closing prices.

9.4

a. Certainly, technical analysis is an inexact science and you can never be certain of the conclusions you come to using it. While there's no guarantee that trends based on past performance will continue into the future, it's a more likely scenario than one based on a sudden trend reversal. Over a period of time, the probabilities work in your favour and technical analysis will assist you to make better trading decisions.

b. For a longer term investor, rather than relying on technical analysis entirely, your best strategy is to use it in conjunction with fundamental analysis.

9.5 The three common time divisions are:

- » *Hourly:* Also known as an intra-day chart, this shows blow-by-blow price action. Use for day trading.

- » *Daily:* Summarises daily price action and is the most common. Use for most charting.

- » *Weekly:* Summarises weekly price action. Use for long-term charting.

9.6 A percent chart shows the price move as a percentage of the price at the start of the charting period. You would consider using a percent chart in order to show the percentage change in price rather than the dollar change and so compare the capital gain (or loss) of different shares (regardless of their price) on an 'apples to apples' basis. You can do this directly if several shares are shown simultaneously (or compare a share with an index).

9.7 You draw an uptrend line by joining the lower extremities of the price bars when this line slopes *upward*. You draw a downtrend line by joining the upper extremities of the price bars when this line slopes *downward*.

9.8   A 'dead cat' bounce occurs when the share price (or market as a whole) falls for some time, and then starts to move upward but the change in trend is temporary and not sustained. The best way of avoiding being sucked into a dead cat bounce is to apply a price or time delay before you trade.

9.9

a.   Volume is normally shown on charts as a bar chart below the prices.

b.   Volume spikes are likely to occur when some significant change occurs. They indicate increased trading interest. However, they also occur frequently for no apparent reason.

c.   See the following completed table

	Price	Volume
Bull market	Increasing	Increasing
Bear market	Decreasing	Increasing
Bull market faltering	Increasing	Decreasing
Bear market faltering	Decreasing	Decreasing

9.10   No change on 21 February because the dividend was in accordance with market expectations. On 7 March, the opening share price will probably drop by 6¢ to 8¢ below the closing price on 6 March.

9.11

a.   A support level is a consensus level where the market perceives the shares are good value at that price. A resistance level is a consensus price level where the market perceives that the shares are overpriced. When the price drifts sideways, you can identify support and resistance levels as horizontal lines at the extremes of price bars on a price chart.

b.   It's likely that in an upward breakout when the price drifts sideways again, the new support level will be the old resistance level. In a downward breakout, the new resistance level will be the old support level.

9.12 When drawing trendlines by eye, the following applies:

a. The minimum number of points you can use is two (but three or more is better).

b. The best types of chart to use are those showing the price range, such as a bar chart, OHLC chart or candle chart.

c. You identify an uptrend by a support line that's sloping upward.

d. You identify a downtrend by a resistance line that's sloping downward.

9.13 The lines and points are shown in the following figure 9A solution. Firstly, an uptrend can be identified but the trend is broken at point *x*. A sideways drift is then broken at point *y*, when a downtrend occurs.

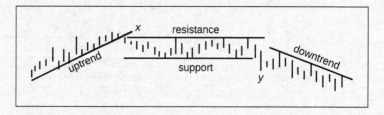

Figure 9A: Solution

9.14 The trendlines I've identified are superimposed on figure 9B's solution.

This chart exhibits a series of three channels with a slight upward slope. The first channel is broken upward and the second downward, but the downtrend is short lived and replaced by a steep uptrend to the third channel. At the end of the time period, the third channel is broken upward again indicating a new high. That is a good sign that a new channel at higher price levels may be established so these shares could be a good investment now.

9.15 In a simple moving average, all prices are treated equally whereas in the exponential moving average, prices are weighted so that the older the price the lesser the effect it has on the average.

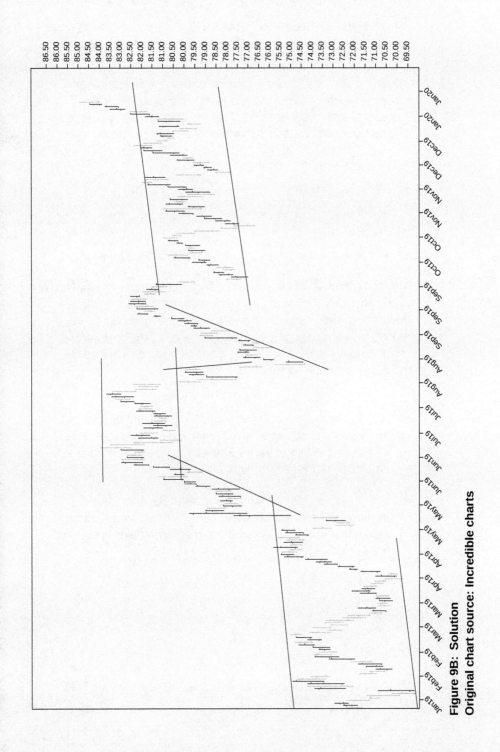

Figure 9B: Solution

Original chart source: Incredible charts

Advantages claimed for the EMA are that it's more sensitive to recent price moves and that a single price doesn't affect the average twice (as it does with the SMA).

9.16 Advantages of a long-term moving average are that you're more confident of the trend and less likely to be whipsawed. Disadvantages are that trend changes take longer to detect and so you won't be able to trade at the most profitable price.

9.17 Appropriate time periods are:

   a. *Short-term trading:* A time period of 5 to 11 days.

   b. *Medium-term trading/investing:* A time period of 13 to 31 days.

   c. *Long-term investing:* A time period of 50 to 250 days.

9.18 A golden cross is when the short-term moving average moves above the long-term moving average (and both are moving upward). A dead cross is when the short-term moving average moves below the long-term moving average (and both are moving downward). The golden cross is a buy signal and the dead cross is a sell signal.

9.19

   a. A whipsaw occurs when you identify a buy signal and enter into a trade but soon after you get a sell signal and you need to exit the trade. Similarly, a whipsaw occurs when you get a sell signal but soon after a buy signal.

   b. The two main methods you can use to minimise the likelihood of a whipsaw are to delay acting when a trading signal first appears on the chart or to use a filter to confirm the primary signal.

9.20 The SMA in row 6 is $(1.05 + 1.12 + 1.15) \div 3 = \mathbf{1.107}$.

The SMA in row 7 is $(1.12 + 1.15 + 1.10) \div 3 = \mathbf{1.123}$.

Chapter 10

Developing trading strategies

In this chapter, I discuss trading strategies that you can consider in order to improve your share investing profitability. These strategies combine the techniques of fundamental analysis and technical analysis.

Understanding the psychology of winning and losing

As I pointed out in chapter 5, human psychology is an important factor in the sharemarket, so understanding the psychology of winning and losing is also important. It's been well established by numerous experiments that people love to win and hate to lose. I think you'll agree that nothing is very profound about this idea. What's interesting is that people are motivated not to lose what they already have to a much greater degree than they are motivated to win what they don't already have. The difference in motivation can be a factor of as much as two to three times.

This motivational preference applies to share investing and results in a well-known behaviour of many investors—the tendency to hang onto losing shares for too long and to sell winning shares too soon. People are often reluctant to sell losers because money's not actually lost until the shares are sold. Losses are just paper losses and not real losses until the sell transaction occurs. So the pain associated with a losing share can be avoided by not selling and may be justified by thinking, *It's possible the price could rise again.* On the other hand, people tend to sell a winning share too soon because, in the same way, profit isn't cash in the bank until the sell transaction occurs. The sell decision may be justified by thinking, *The price could go down and I will lose my profit (or most of it) if I don't sell now.*

A rather negative well-known saying is also:

You can't lose money by taking profits.

In a sense, this saying is true but, on the other hand, if the price continues to rise after you've sold, you are losing the profit you could have made if you had held on.

Another counterproductive attitude investors often have when trying to decide whether to sell is to take the purchase price into consideration. For example, suppose you bought some shares when the price was $1 and it is now $2. You can think *I have doubled my money—time to cash in my profit.* Of course this is true—you have made a good profit and you can't lose it by cashing in—but what if the price keeps rising and later the price is $10? Think of the profit you have lost by selling at $2! This is by no means an exaggerated example—many shares have had large price rises over long time periods. For example, CSL shares rose from about $35 to $280 over a 10-year period. What if you had sold when they were $70?

Note

I'm not suggesting by any means that you should hold onto a winning share indefinitely; I'm just pointing out some common attitudes that are counterproductive and that you should try to avoid.

The psychology of making more profit

Being aware of the common attitudes I have pointed out can make it easier to counter them and make more profit. To do so, you really need to be as dispassionate as you can about your trading decisions.

Try to avoid buying shares just because you 'like' them, unless you have good grounds to believe your liking is justified. If you have bought a share that goes up in price, it's not too difficult to hang onto it until the uptrend falters. Most investors have greater difficulty making good decisions with losers. If you're holding a loser and there doesn't seem to be any light at the end of the tunnel, and if you can take the loss on the chin and sell, you're well on the way to becoming a more successful share investor.

A good way of making more dispassionate selling decisions is to ignore what you paid for the shares relative to the current price. Try to base your decision solely on the future outlook. If you're happy with future prospects, hold on, or even consider buying more shares. If you're not happy with the outlook, then sell—regardless of what you originally paid for the shares.

Making friends with the trend

As previously discussed, trading with the trend usually proves to be the best strategy in the long run. Success is often a question of probabilities and you want the probabilities to be in your favour. Once a trend starts, it's more likely to continue than to suddenly reverse because share prices tend to have a certain amount of momentum. I'm not saying sudden trend reversals can't happen, but they are less likely than an established trend continuing until some major change occurs. If you're alert and follow chart trends using technical analysis, you can often detect a warning signal that a trend change may be imminent and you may be able to act on it in a timely fashion.

A well-known saying in the stock market summarising this idea is:

The trend is your friend.

Following this idea leads to probably the most important trading strategy you can adopt and that is to buy shares only when the price is rising and to sell only when the price is falling. This is such an important strategy that I'll state it again:

Buy in a rising trend, sell in a falling trend.

The corollary to this rule is:

Don't buy in a falling trend and don't sell in a rising trend.

Of course, there's no guarantee that if you follow this strategy, all your trades will be profitable, but you'll generally do better by following it than you will by ignoring it.

Notes

- When you use this strategy, you don't buy at the best price or sell at the best price. This is because you're not buying at the bottom of a trend or selling at the top of a trend. Instead, you'll be buying above the bottom and selling below the top. In fact, it's difficult (perhaps impossible?) to pick the bottom and top of a trend change in real time.

- The practice of trying to buy at the bottom of a trend change is known as 'bottom fishing'. It's generally a dangerous practice and you shouldn't assume that because a price is well below some previous support level, it couldn't fall even further. It can and frequently does!

- A trader who trades against the trend is known as a *contrarian* and a strategy based on this idea is known as a *contrarian strategy*. This gives you the possibility of beating the market but at a higher risk than trend trading.

Day trading

Day trading is the practice of both buying and selling the same parcel of shares in one day with the aim of profiting from short-term price fluctuations. If you are good at it, you can make a significant profit on small price changes. For example, if you can make a profit of only 2% in a day, this is equivalent to an annual profit of nearly 500%! Another advantage of day trading is that you can trade large parcel values of shares without outlaying much (or indeed any) of your own money.

This is because the T+2 rule for settlement of transactions is based on the day of the transaction and isn't calculated on an hourly basis. For example, if you buy $50 000 worth of shares shortly after the market opens and sell them before the market closes for $52 000 net, you'll make a profit of $2000. This profit will be paid to you two days later as a cash settlement without you having to outlay any of your own money! On the other hand, if the shares go down in price and you sell them for $48 000 net, when settlement occurs two days later you'll not be required to pay $50 000 because the $48 000 credit will be treated as a contra transaction and you'll be required to pay the difference of $2000 only.

Note

Apart from the cash outlay aspect of day trading, many day traders don't like to keep open positions overnight because of the uncertainty of how the market will open the next day.

Trading systems

If you don't have the confidence to make your own trading decisions, you can buy a trading system or software package that does it all for you. All you have to do is to purchase the package, load it onto your computer (or smartphone or tablet) and then follow the instructions on how to use it. These systems vary in price from several hundreds to several thousands of dollars. In addition, ongoing fees are usually charged to cover upgrades and data management.

Many trading systems are available for purchase in Australia. Most of them use technical analysis and/or fundamental analysis as a basis for recommendations.

While it's tempting to think that 'experts' must know more than you or are cleverer than you, it's helpful to reflect that trading systems depend on algorithms (computer programs) that have been written by some person (or persons) using their own ideas. In essence, a trading system is trying to predict future price moves and, as we all know, the future cannot be predicted with any level of certainty. No system is infallible and no evidence suggests that any particular system produces consistently better results than another—despite the often grandiose advertising claims. There is also no evidence that the more expensive the system, the better the results from it. Another thing to watch is that many of the facilities provided in a purchased system are available for free on a trading or public access website.

Notes

- Anyone can make good profits with the wisdom of hindsight simply by focusing on the winners and the most favourable time periods and not mentioning the losers! Remember that if you are thinking of draining the pond, don't ask the frogs for an opinion.

- A mushrooming practice that has sprung up in recent times is the free so-called live webinar. At first sight, this may appear to present an unbiased view of the market or some particular shares but, as discussion goes on, you discover that it's actually plugging some particular (and expensive) system that you need to subscribe to in order to get the results. Also I discovered that some so-called live webinars aren't live at all but pre-recorded.

Subscription services

Some subscription services operate in Australia where subscribers are given tips or recommendations about shares to buy or sell. These tips can be provided on a regular basis or when some special trading opportunity presents itself. They are usually based on technical and/or fundamental analysis, sometimes using some 'special' indicators or systems. A problem for a prospective subscriber is that getting an unbiased evaluation of these services is very difficult and often it's a case of 'suck it and see'. If at all possible, try contacting a subscriber (current or past) for an evaluation. In some cases, you may be able to trial the service free of charge for a short period of time and, if this is possible, by all means do so before you commit yourself to any sizeable subscription cost.

Director trades

In Australia, directors of publicly listed companies can own and legally trade shares in the companies in which they are directors, provided that they don't use inside information to their advantage when doing so. It seems logical that a director buying shares in a company they direct must think that the shares are a good buy at the time. On the other hand, if a director sells them, this could be a warning that it's time to exercise caution. The director may simply be selling to obtain cash but it could also be that they feel that the shares have reached a high point and it's time to take profits.

A trading strategy based on director trades is to buy when the director buys and sell when they sell. When directors trade shares in their own companies, the ASX must be informed and the ASX will in turn make the information available on its website. From there, the information can be picked up by and appear on other trading or information websites.

A few words of caution are appropriate:

- You need to consider the amount of money involved in a director's trade. A few thousand dollars isn't significant but hundreds of thousands or millions certainly are.

- Directors often receive company options as part of their salary package and some director trades may involve trading these options or converting them to fully paid shares, so you need to check the details as these trades aren't really significant.

Averaging

Averaging is a trading strategy where you buy or sell parcels of shares in a company at different times (and prices). For example, suppose you decide you'd like to invest $6000 in shares in a company. If you cost average, you don't buy a single parcel of $6000—instead you buy a parcel with a value of, say, $2000 or $3000. You then see what happens to the share price. If the price rises, you buy another parcel of the same value until you have invested the capital you intended. The time between purchases could be a matter of weeks or months or even years. When averaging is applied to purchases in this fashion, with the parcel value of each purchase being approximately the same, it's known as *dollar cost averaging*.

Averaging can also be used as a selling strategy, where it's known as *price averaging*. For example, if you hold $6000 worth of shares in a company and you decide to sell using a price averaging strategy, instead of selling all the shares at once, you sell some shares now and then and wait and monitor the market before deciding when (or indeed if) you'll sell some more.

The advantage of averaging is that it allows you to have 'several bites of the cherry'; that is, it reduces the volatility associated with daily price movements. The disadvantage is that it increases your trading costs and the strategy may increase or reduce your capital gains profit depending on how the price moves after your initial trade. This is shown in table 10.1, which illustrates the effect of cost averaging when you buy or sell (compared to buying and selling the full parcel at the first transaction point).

Table 10.1: Effect of cost averaging on price and profit

Transaction type	Price movement after initial trade	Effect on average price	Effect on profit
Buy	Up	Increases average buy price	Reduces profit
Buy	Down	Decreases average buy price	Increases profit
Sell	Up	Increases average sell price	Increases profit
Sell	Down	Decreases average sell price	Reduces profit

If you study this table, you may wonder about the value of averaging if the probability of the price moving either up or down after the initial transaction is equal. Half the time, averaging will produce more profit and half the time less, but due to the additional trading costs, the net result should be that in the long run, you will make less profit by using an averaging strategy. Despite this, I believe averaging is a worthwhile strategy to consider, because you're not committing full trading funds to the initial trade. Averaging provides additional flexibility because you're able to see how the market moves before you plunge in deeper.

Notes

- It's generally not a good idea to cost average buy transactions when the price is falling, despite the fact that it appears to increase your profit. The reason is because if you do this, you are buying in a falling market and, as I've said before, that's not a strategy I recommend. It's better to wait until the trend reverses before buying more. Similarly, you shouldn't sell when the price is rising but wait for it to reverse.

- If you participate in a DRP and receive shares in lieu of dividends, you're effectively cost averaging — particularly if you hold shares in the company for a long time — because you receive different parcels at different prices.

Taking advantage of deferred execution

Deferred execution or conditional execution is a common strategy you may want to consider. The basic idea is similar to averaging in that you don't trade immediately but your trade is conditional and depends on how the market moves. In a sense, it's like having an insurance policy on your shares because if the market moves against you, your losses are restricted.

The two most common deferred execution or conditional strategies are applied to the sell transaction and are known as *stop loss orders* and *profit stop orders*.

Stop loss orders

As the name suggests, a stop loss order is one designed to limit losses with shares should the price fall. It's a deferred selling order at a price below the current share price. If the price falls to your stop loss level, you sell all (or some) of your shares. For example, suppose you're holding 1000 shares that you bought for $7.50. The shares have risen in price and the current market price is $8.50, so you're making a paper profit of $1.00 per share. You don't want to sell right now because you want to make more profit if the price rises further. However, you want to protect your profit and not lose too much of it should the share price fall. In this case, you could set a stop loss price of, say, $8.00. Depending on how the market moves you act as follows:

- *Share price rises:* You don't sell but continue holding your shares.

- *Share price falls but doesn't reach $8.00 or less:* You don't sell but continue holding your shares.

- *Share price falls to $8.00 or less:* You sell.

Note

The name 'stop loss' is a bit of a misnomer really because you can use this type of order with shares where you have made good capital gains (not just to stop further losses).

Stop loss price

The biggest problem with a stop loss order is deciding on a suitable stop loss price. If you set a price too close to the current trading price, you can be stopped out on day-to-day price fluctuations that aren't really significant. On the other hand, if you set a stop loss that's a fair bit below the current trading price, you're unlikely to be stopped out on a day-to-day price fluctuation but you'll lose more of your profit if the stop loss triggers. This problem really has no solution but you can ameliorate it by not committing all your shares to one transaction—that is, average the sell through having multiple stop loss points (see the section 'Multiple stops', beginning on the opposite page).

Types of stop loss

Several different types of stop loss are used, and I'll now outline the most common ones.

Fixed stop

A fixed stop (as the term suggests) is a fixed price you set as your stop loss (as in the example I gave in the earlier section). A common way of setting a fixed stop is to calculate it based upon a percentage of the current price, and often 10% is used. So with the earlier example, if you were using a 10% stop loss, then 10% of $8.50 is $0.85 so you'd set a stop loss of $7.65 ($8.50 – $0.85).

Another way of setting your stop price is to try to identify a support level and to set your stop loss price just below this level. This means if the price breaks below the support level, your sell order will be triggered. This is a logical way to set your stop loss price but it depends on identifying a support level and one isn't always apparent.

Trailing stop

With a trailing stop, you set the stop loss at a certain amount below the current price. You keep resetting your stop loss if the price rises but the golden rule is that you don't reset it lower if the price falls. Continuing the earlier example, you could set your trailing stop at, say, 50¢ below the last sale price. So if the share price rises to $8.75, you raise your stop loss to $8.25 and if the price rises to $9.00, you raise your stop loss to $8.50. You continue to do this if the price keeps rising and sell only should the price fall back to your most recent stop loss level and your stop loss triggers.

Note

You can also use the percentage method with a trailing stop. For example, you can use 10%, meaning if the share price rises to $8.75 in the example, you raise your stop loss from $7.65 to $7.88 and if the price rises to $9.00, you raise your stop loss to $8.10.

Multiple stops

With multiple stops you divide your total shareholding up into parcels of smaller size and set a different stop loss level for each parcel. For example, if you're using a multiple trailing stop strategy, you could decide to sell half your holding if the price drops by 50¢ and the other half of your holding if the price drops by a further 50¢. Using multiple stops in this way is essentially the averaging principle applied to selling.

Advantages and disadvantages of stop losses

Like every share trading strategy, stop losses aren't infallible (or even a good idea) in all circumstances. Setting stop losses has both advantages and disadvantages and I'll now outline these.

The advantages of stop losses include the following:

- If you place a stop loss order with your broker, you don't have to monitor the market constantly — your order will activate automatically. This is very convenient if you're going away on a holiday or if you're just too busy with other things to monitor the market continually.

- Losses can be limited in case of a price downturn.

- The emotion tends to be taken out of the selling decision, because you don't need to agonise about it once you place your stop loss order.

Stop loss disadvantages include:

- Not all brokers accept stop loss orders.

- The additional brokerage cost associated with them will likely be substantial.

- In times of a rapid market sell-off, a stop loss may be ineffectual because the price can shoot below your stop loss trigger point before the trade can be executed at the price you've specified. This typically occurs during a sudden market sell-off with price gaps. In this situation, you mightn't be able to obtain a price anywhere near your stop loss price and you may not be able to avoid a substantial loss.

- A stop loss can result in you selling at the very lowest price (or close to the very lowest price) the shares reach. Frequently, a share price may spike suddenly downward before recovering a short time later. If your stop loss activates at a low point, you may find that you've sold at the bottom of the market. This can be very frustrating when you sell and soon after, you see the price heading back up again into territory where you could have made a lot more profit if you hadn't sold.

- If you set stop losses for all your shares, in times of a general market downturn, all your shares can reach the stop loss point and be sold. Then you may find yourself up for a huge capital gains tax bill that financial year (as well as large trading costs).

On balance, I think the advantages of stop losses outweigh the disadvantages with speculative shares. So I suggest you consider setting stop losses as an important part of your trading strategy with these types of shares. For core portfolio shares, I prefer to regard stop losses as alert points rather than trading points. Ask yourself: if you bought these shares as a long-term investment because of sound fundamentals, should you sell just because the price has fallen to some arbitrary level? It's a decision I like to contemplate rather than act on with a knee-jerk response. If the price tracks down to the alert point, I check any announcements or fundamental reasons for the price drop and decide whether these justify re-evaluation. I also examine the chart and try to identify how the moving averages are trending and if a significant break of trend can be identified before I make a decision on whether or not it's time to sell.

Using a stop loss strategy

Many brokers provide a stop loss trading facility but you can also apply the strategy without actually setting stop loss orders with a broker. To do this, you decide on a trigger price and minimum price. Then you need to monitor the share price closely and activate a sell order as soon as a share price reaches the trigger level. Another method is to set up an email or mobile phone alert system where you specify an alert price as your trigger price for shares you nominate. You should then receive an email or SMS alert should the price fall to this level. For this to be effective, you need to check your emails or messages frequently so you can act on the alert in a timely fashion.

Resetting stop losses

As I have said, resetting stop losses down is not a good idea, because this is tantamount to giving up on the original stop loss. It's tempting to think that perhaps you should wait a little longer to see if the price recovers before your stop loss activates, bearing in mind that you'll most likely be reluctant to sell if you are making a loss. To avoid this trap, I suggest adopting a golden rule as part of your trading strategy:

Adjust stop losses in an upward direction but never downward.

Profit stop orders

A profit stop is a deferred selling order designed to lock in profit. For example, you buy some shares for $7.50 at a time when the price is trending up. You plan to make at least $1.00 profit per share, so want to sell at $8.50 or above. The price continues to rise so, using a profit stop strategy, you place a profit stop order at a price of $8.50. The idea is that if the price reaches your target, you take profits and sell.

Setting your profit stop price

Like a stop loss, you can use several methods to set the profit stop price. Some you can use are:

- *Fixed price:* This is some price above the current price where you are making your targeted profit. You can also use an identified resistance level or a price just below it as your profit stop price.

- *Percentage price:* This is a price that is a certain percentage above the current price. You can keep adjusting this price upward if the price rises but doesn't reach your trigger price.

- *Multiple stops:* You break your total holding up into a number of parcels, and set a different profit stop price for each parcel.

Profit stop advantages and disadvantages

The advantages of using profit stops are as follows:

- If you've placed a profit stop order with your broker, you don't have to monitor the market constantly — your order will activate without any further input from you. This can be convenient if you're going away on a holiday or if you're just too busy to monitor the market regularly.

- You lock in profit and convert a 'paper profit' to an actual profit; that is, you crystallise your profit and insure yourself should the price fall.

- The emotion tends to be taken out of the selling decision, because you don't need to agonise about it once you place your order.

Profit stop disadvantages include:

- You'll make less profit should the price continue to rise after you've sold.

- Profit stops can violate the principle of not selling in a rising market and selling only when the price is trending down.

- The price may not rise to your profit stop level. Indeed, if the price falls, you'll make less profit than if you'd have sold once you detected the change in trend.

An alternative to a profit stop order

If you don't want to place a conditional order, you can still use the profit stop strategy by simply placing a sell order that's good until execution. If you set a selling price that's above the current market price, there'll be no buyers and your order won't transact but will sit somewhere down in the queue of sellers. However, if the price rises in the future, your order should transact as soon as buyers come into the market prepared to buy at your specified price.

However, this arrangement can hit a couple of snags. For example, some brokers won't accept orders if the price is too far away from the current market price. Another problem is that if it takes too long for the price to rise to your specified level, the order could automatically be purged (cancelled). Should this happen, you need to reactivate the order—that is, place it again as a new order.

Note

Profit stop orders or sell orders of the type described in the preceding sections can be purged if the dividend status of the shares changes from cum-dividend to ex-dividend before your profit stop activates. Another thing to watch is that your broker may have specified time limits for orders so you need to ensure you know what they are. In my experience, you won't necessarily be notified when an order is purged, so you may be under the impression that your order is still active when, in fact, it's no longer at market.

Profit stops as a trading strategy

Profit stops are a trading strategy that's often advocated but personally I'm not in favour of them unless you're trading volatile speculative shares.

For the less speculative or volatile shares in your portfolio, I believe a better strategy is expressed by the saying:

Stop your losses but let your profits run.

It's impossible to pick the top (or bottom) of the market in real time. It's usually not a good idea to sell when a share price is rising (or reaches a new high) because you think that the price won't rise any further. It can and often will and there's no logical reason to assume that it won't.

Trading strategy with speculative shares

If you are interested in buying some speculative shares for a fast profit because you think the price will most likely rise, a trading strategy worth considering is placing a stop loss order and a profit stop order immediately after buying the shares. For example, suppose you buy some speculative shares for $7.50. You could now place a stop loss order for, say, $7.30 and a profit stop sell order for, say, $7.70. If you are right and the price rises to your target level, you make 20¢ profit per share. If the price rise takes place in one day, you could make a tidy profit without outlaying any of your own money!

If you are wrong and the price falls to your loss level, you have limited your losses to 20¢ per share. If you can be right more often than you are wrong, the long-run result will be an overall profit.

> ## Note
> You can also make a profit in the long run if you are wrong as often as you are right (or even more often), provided you practise good money management (as discussed in chapter 13).

Other types of conditional orders

I've already discussed two commonly used types of conditional (or deferred execution) orders—stop loss orders and profit stops. These are both conditional sell orders. As well as these, two other common types of conditional buy orders are 'buy on rise' (a buy gain order) and 'buy on fall' (a supporting buy order). These four basic types of conditional orders are shown in table 10.2.

Table 10.2: Common types of conditional order

Order type	Order name	Interpretation	Purpose
Buy on rise	Buy gain	Buy if the price rises to the limit you've set above the current market price	Ensure you're buying into a rising market
Buy on fall	Supporting buy	Buy if the price falls to the limit you've set below the current market price	Buy shares you want at a low price
Sell on rise	Profit stop; Profit target; Resistance sell	Sell only if the price rises to the limit you've set above the current market price	Crystallise paper profits
Sell on fall	Stop loss	Sell if the price falls to the limit you've set below the current market price	Avoid greater losses if the price continues to fall

In addition to these four basic types of conditional order, other more complex types can be used by advanced traders. These more complex types may take into account volumes as well as prices or have built-in time delays, which aim to prevent order triggering on brief price spikes on low volumes. Another option is straddle orders, which allow you to simultaneously place both conditional buy and sell orders. Many other types of deferred execution orders can be used, with many different methods of setting them so the whole subject is rather complex. However, despite the sophistication involved in some of the more complex orders, I've found that they won't necessarily produce better outcomes than the simpler ones.

Planning your trades

I discussed planning your share investment in some detail in chapter 6, where I indicated that an important part of share investing should be to plan goals or targets and the mix of shares in a portfolio. Now I will consider in greater detail a trading strategy for each trade you make. That is, before you trade a parcel of shares, you need to have a plan and stick to it. A very good saying I suggest you follow at all times is:

Plan your trade and trade your plan.

You may wish to consider having several different trading plans (as indeed I do). For example, you could have one trading plan for longer term core portfolio shares, and another for short-term speculative shares.

I strongly recommend that you write down your trading plans and keep them prominently visible so you can refer to them before you place any orders. This will help you to focus on your plans and stick to them. Writing down a trading plan is the easy part; sticking to it is the difficult part. Human emotion tends to come into play and unless you're disciplined in your approach, personal feelings can override adherence to your plan and may tempt you to divert from it.

Notes

- One of the great advantages of having a written trading plan is that it tends to take some of the emotion out of your trading decisions because, in effect, you are just 'following orders'.

- It's a very good idea to duplicate your trading plan so that you have an individual copy for each order.

- It's a very good idea to 'paper trade' for a while. This is where you track and test the outcomes of your plan and trading system before actually placing orders with a broker.

I suggest a written trading plan for each share type (for example, long term or speculative) could have the following headings and information:

- *Trading cash:* The amount of money you'll allocate for trading each different type of share.

- *Time period:* The length of time you plan to hold shares you buy. The time period could be short term (up to a month or less), medium term (up to six months or so), or long term (12 months or more or indefinitely).

- *Parcel value:* The amount of money you'll allocate for any particular trade.

- *Buy criteria:* The strategies you'll use to decide what shares to buy and when.

- *Profit target:* The minimum profit you want to make on each trade. This should relate to the trading time period and may be expressed as a percentage of the parcel value or in dollars.

- *Sell criteria:* The strategies you'll use to decide when to sell, including whether or not you'll place stop loss or profit stop orders.

Sample trading plan

Here's an example of a hypothetical trading plan for short-term speculative shares:

- *Trading cash:* $10 000.

- *Time period:* Maximum of four months for any parcel purchased if the shares don't achieve the profit target.

- *Trade value:* Maximum of $2000 for any single parcel.

- *Buy criteria:* Concentrate on volatile, low market cap stocks. Study the price chart and draw trendlines. Consider only buying shares that are in uptrend mode. Use 11-day and 31-day EMAs and buy when a golden cross appears with them.

- *Profit target:* Minimum 20% per trade.

- *Sell criteria:* Set 10% trailing stop losses or sell if a dead cross appears on the chart. Also sell if the price has not risen 10% within two months or the profit target of 20% has not been achieved within four months.

Note

The benefit of having an individual plan for each of your trades is that you can specify actual dollar values and calendar dates rather than unspecified periods or dollar values (such as a price rise of 10%) or time periods (such as 'one month' or 'four months'). For example, a suitable strategy for shares you have just bought might be, 'I will sell if the price hasn't risen to $1.08 by 16 June or to $1.18 by 16 August'.

Learning exercises

10.1 What are two essential differences between trading speculative shares and punting (such as betting on a horse race)?

10.2 What's the attitude of most people with regard to winning and losing money and how does this attitude tend to affect share-trading decisions?

10.3 What's meant by 'paper trading' of shares and what is the advantage and disadvantage of doing this?

10.4 What's meant by 'bottom fishing' with shares and what's the danger involved with it?

10.5 What's the golden rule with regard to buying or selling shares in an uptrend or downtrend?

10.6 You have a share investment portfolio of five shares, A to E. Your original purchase price and quantities are shown in the following table, as well as current prices and values.

You have to raise $12000 urgently and you decide to raise this money by selling some shares. Consider your portfolio and decide which shares you will sell in order to raise the cash you need.

	A	B	C	D	E
Quantity	1000	10000	20000	5000	10000
Original price ($)	10.00	1.00	0.50	2.00	1.00
Original cost ($)	10000	10000	10000	10000	10000
Current price ($)	20.00	2.20	0.60	1.50	0.60
Current value ($)	20000	22000	12000	7500	6000
Profit/loss ($)	+10000	+12000	+2000	−2500	−4000

10.7 Why is it impossible for any trader, analyst or market system (no matter how sophisticated) to identify a top or bottom share price in real time?

10.8   Describe briefly the following strategies:

    a.   Cost averaging

    b.   Dollar cost averaging

    c.   Price averaging

10.9

    a.   What's the main benefit of averaging and what's the main disadvantage?

    b.   Why is it generally not a good idea to cost average buy orders after a price fall? When might you consider doing so?

10.10 You have 5000 shares that you originally bought for $1.00 each and the current price is $1.20. Your trading cost is $30 per parcel. Compare the profit you will make if you sell all your shares now with the profit you would have made if you had decided on a price averaging strategy in each of the following two scenarios:

    •   *Scenario 1:* You sell half your shares now and the remaining half when the price rises to $1.30.

    •   *Scenario 2:* You sell half your shares now and the remaining half when the price falls to $1.10.

10.11 What's meant by a deferred execution (or conditional) order and what are the two main types?

10.12

    a.   What are the three main types of stop loss order?

    b.   What's the golden rule with regard to resetting stop loss prices?

10.13 What's the main benefit of a profit stop order and what's the main disadvantage?

10.14 You've bought some shares for $1.00. You decide to use a trailing stop of 10% with conventional sell orders. Outline what you would do in each of the following scenarios:

    •   *Scenario 1:* The price falls to $0.92.

    •   *Scenario 2:* The price falls to $0.88.

- *Scenario 3:* The price rises to $1.06.

- *Scenario 4:* The price rises to $1.20 and then falls to $1.10 a few days later.

- *Scenario 5:* The price rises to $1.30 and then falls to $1.15 a few days later.

10.15 Draw up written trading plans for both long-term core shares and short-term volatile shares you intend to trade.

You may wish to refer to the end of this chapter where I suggest the headings you could include in your plans and provide a hypothetical trading plan for speculative shares.

Learning exercises solutions

10.1 The two essential differences between trading and punting are:

1. When you bet on a horse, you don't get equity in the horse whereas when you buy shares you do get equity in a business enterprise.

2. After you've placed a bet, you can't change it or modify your strategy but with shares that option is open to you so long as the shares keep trading on the market.

10.2 Most people hate to lose much more than they love to win. This results in a tendency to hold losers for too long and sell winners too soon.

10.3 Paper trading is making hypothetical trades without actually placing any orders. The advantage of this is that you can test your system without committing any actual dollars. The disadvantage is that the results won't necessarily be matched by your actual trades, where emotion may affect your actions.

10.4 'Bottom fishing' is the term used to describe the strategy of buying shares when they seem to have bottomed at a low point so as to get them at a 'bargain basement' price. The danger lies in assuming that because the price appears to have bottomed that it can't fall further—it can and frequently does!

10.5 The golden rule is that you should buy in an uptrend and sell in a downtrend. You should not buy in a downtrend or sell in an uptrend.

10.6 At first sight shares D and E look like the most likely candidates to sell because they have been the worst performers. But you shouldn't make a final decision based on the data given in the table. Current profit or losses on your shares are irrelevant when you're trying to decide which ones to sell. You should look at the future prospects for each and sell the ones that have the lowest future profit potential.

10.7　It's logically impossible to identify a top in real time because you can't know that the top has been reached unless the share price subsequently moves down and this will be some time later. Similarly, you can't know that a bottom has been reached until some time later when the share price moves up. No system and no person can overcome this logical limitation and identify the top or bottom price in real time.

10.8

   a.　Cost averaging is the strategy of buying different quantities of shares in the same company at different times (and prices) so you effectively average the buying price.

   b.　Dollar cost averaging is cost averaging where the parcel value is approximately the same in each case.

   c.　Price averaging is the strategy of selling different parcels of shares in the same company at different times (and prices) so you effectively average the selling price.

10.9

   a.　The main benefit of averaging is that you get to 'suck it and see'; that is, you obtain some flexibility and don't commit to an 'all or nothing' approach. The main disadvantage is that you can lose some profit or make a greater loss if the market moves in a direction you didn't foresee.

   b.　It's generally not a good idea to cost average a buy order when the price has fallen because this violates the principle of not buying in a downtrend. You should consider buying only when you're confident that the downtrend has reversed.

10.10　If you sold all your shares at $1.20 your profit would be

$$P = 5000 \times (\$1.20 - \$1.00) - 2 \times \$30 = \$940$$

  » *Scenario 1:* Sell half your shares at $1.20 each and the remainder at $1.30:

$$P = 2500 \times (\$1.20 - \$1.00) + 2500 \times (\$1.30 - \$1.00) - 3 \times \$30$$
$$= \$1160$$

    Therefore, additional profit is equal to $1160 − $940 = **$220**

  » *Scenario 2:* Sell half your shares at $1.20 each and the remainder at $1.10:

$$P = 2500 \times (\$1.20 - \$1.00) + 2500 \times (\$1.10 - \$1.00) - 3 \times \$30$$
$$= \$660$$

Therefore, additional profit is equal to $\$660 - \$940 = -\$280$ (that is, you would lose this much profit using the price averaging strategy).

10.11 A deferred execution or conditional order is an order that does not activate immediately but is conditional on some criteria you specify, usually based on price. The two main types of conditional orders are stop loss orders and profit stop orders.

10.12

    a.   The three main types of stop loss order are fixed stop, trailing stop and multiple stop.

    b.   The golden rule is that stop loss prices may be reset in an upward direction but they should not be reset in a downward direction.

10.13 The main benefit of a profit stop order is that you crystallise your profit and protect yourself from a market downturn. The main disadvantage is that you could be reducing your profit by selling too soon.

10.14 The results of each scenario are as follows:

    » *Scenario 1:* The price falls to $0.92. You do nothing, but continue to monitor.

    » *Scenario 2:* The price falls to $0.88. You should have already sold when the price fell to $0.90.

    » *Scenario 3:* The price rises to $1.06. You reset the stop loss to $0.95.

    » *Scenario 4:* The price rises to $1.20 and then falls to $1.10 a few days later. You reset the stop loss to $1.08. You hold and continue to monitor.

    » *Scenario 5:* The price rises to $1.30 and then falls to $1.15 a few days later. You reset the stop loss to $1.17. You sell at this price.

10.15 No solution provided because trading plan formulated will depend on the individual.

Chapter 11

Buying and selling shares

You've completed your planning, decided on your investment strategies and written down your trading plan. Perhaps you've paper traded for some time and fine-tuned your strategies. You've decided whether to trade offline or online and registered with your broker (or brokers) of choice and have the necessary capital available in a trading account. Now it's time to put your plan into action and actually buy and sell shares. In this chapter, I outline the nuts and bolts of doing so.

Understanding the basics of trading shares

Trading shares involves two basic types of trade:

1. *Purchase or buy trade:* You make this trade when you want to own some shares you do not currently have or when you want to add to the number of shares in a stock you already own.

2. *Sell trade:* You make this trade when you want to rid yourself of some shares you own or when you want to reduce the number of shares you have in a stock.

In the following sections, I outline some of the mechanics involved with these basic trades, such as placing orders, settlement, trading hours and order processing.

Parcel size: Selling shares

For a sell order, the minimum parcel size is governed by the number of shares you own. In normal circumstances, you cannot sell more than you own but you can sell fewer. The exception to this is called *short selling*, where you sell shares you don't own but buy them back a short time later. This is not a normal procedure and it's often banned during periods of high market volatility. It's also a high-risk strategy and I suggest you refrain from considering it unless you are an experienced day trader. For normal types of sell orders, you have to be meticulous about the number of shares you actually own. The problem is that if you try to sell just one more share than you own, you may 'stir up a bees nest' and get into some difficulties. On the other hand, if you sell just one share fewer than you own, your order will transact without any problems but you will be left holding one share. Unless the shares are very costly, this share will be just a real nuisance to everyone (including yourself).

Therefore, I strongly suggest you check with your stockbroker or your online portfolio and confirm the number of saleable shares you actually own just before you place your sell order.

Note

A trap for the unwary to watch out for is when you have joined the dividend reinvestment plan. If you haven't kept tabs on the number of shares due to you under the plan, you may find that after the sell order transacts you will be awarded these shares. So you will be left holding a small parcel of shares that could be of nuisance value only.

Buy order

Two limitations are placed on the parcel size of a buy order:

- If you are trading ASX-listed shares, the minimum parcel value for shares you don't already own is $500. If you already own shares in the company, you can top up any number you like.

- On settlement, you must have the funds available to pay for the shares plus the brokerage (unless you have loan arrangements in place with your broker to extend you credit).

Note

You have to be very careful to ensure you haven't made an error when placing your order. For example, an extra zero could mean you have placed an order with parcel value of $100000 rather than the $10000 you really intended! Therefore, it is excellent practice to check the order value before you confirm the order.

Settlement

Under ASX trading rules at the time of writing, settlement is T+2, which means that when shares are traded, cash transfers between brokers take place on the second business day after the transaction. So, if you sell shares, cash proceeds will be transferred to your broker two days after the sale. If you buy shares, you need to provide the funds with your broker to pay for them within those two days. Therefore, it is prudent to ensure that you have the funds available to pay for any shares you buy when you place your order.

Notes

- Originally settlement was T+5 but this was eventually reduced to T+3. Then in 2016 it was reduced to T+2 and this is the settlement period at the time of writing. There has been talk of introducing real-time settlement in the future, which would have a lot of advantages, but still depends on whether the financial institutions can arrange it.

- In some cases, a delay may occur with your broker when transferring cash from shares sales into your account. So you should not rely on receiving cash in your account exactly on the second day after a sales transaction.

Trading costs

Two costs are payable when you buy or sell shares. These are:

- brokerage

- GST (10% of the brokerage).

Notes

- Most online brokers include the GST in their transaction cost and it's not an extra charge.

- Stamp duty is not applied to ASX trades.

- You don't pay transaction costs when you're allocated shares directly from a prospectus, when you take up an option or rights issue, or when shares you own change their name or are taken over.

Trading small parcels

Brokers (both online and offline) have a certain minimum charge for each transaction so when you trade relatively small parcel values, the average cost per share can be affected. I've illustrated this in tables 11.1 and 11.2, where I've shown the costs of trading different small parcels of shares at a nominal market price of $1.00 each. In table 11.1, I've assumed a minimum charge of $55 ($50 brokerage and $5 GST) with an offline broker, whereas in table 11.2, I've assumed a minimum charge of $20 with an online broker.

Table 11.1: Average cost per share for $55 minimum trading cost

Parcel value ($)	Brokerage and GST ($)	Total cost ($)	Average cost per share ($)
500	55	555	1.11
1000	55	1055	1.06
1500	55	1555	1.04
2000	55	2055	1.03
2500	55	2555	1.02
3000	55	3055	1.02

Table 11.2 Average cost per share for $20 minimum trading cost

Parcel value ($)	Brokerage and GST ($)	Total cost ($)	Average cost per share ($)
500	20	520	1.04
1000	20	1020	1.02
1500	20	1520	1.01
2000	20	2020	1.01
2500	20	2520	1.01
3000	20	3020	1.01

You can see that the average cost per share reduces as the parcel value increases. However, the law of diminishing returns kicks in and, at a certain point, the difference is so small it becomes negligible. With a $55 trading cost, that point is reached with a parcel value of about $2500 and with a trading cost of $20, that point is reached with a parcel value of about $1500. So if you're trading online for around $20 per trade, you can economically trade small parcels with a value as low as $1000, or preferably about $1500. However, if you're trading offline for about $55 per trade, your parcel value needs to be a minimum of about $2000, or preferably about $2500 in order to get a reasonable average cost per share.

Bids and offers

A *bid* is the price a buyer is prepared to pay for the shares required (similar to a bid at an auction).

An *offer* is the price a seller is prepared to sell the number of shares they want to offload. That is, the seller is offering for sale a certain number of shares at a certain price.

Market price

When agreement is reached between a buyer and a seller on the price of the parcel, the transaction will occur and the price at which this occurs is the market price. As different transactions take place, the market price can rise or fall.

Trading hours

Normal share trading takes place only during the times at which the market is open (ASX trading hours are nominally 10 am to 4 pm on business days).

However, online brokers provide access to their websites at any time, which means you can place buy and sell orders with them using the internet on a 24/7 basis at any time that's convenient to you. Offline brokers should also have provisions for contact outside trading hours such as phone, email or text message.

Note

Orders placed outside trading hours (either online or offline) won't transact at the time you place them but will go to market as soon as the broker processes them and the market opens.

When to trade

Despite the fact that your broker may accept orders at any time, I recommend that you avoid placing orders outside of the exchange trading hours. Instead, getting an idea of market direction before you trade is wise, and that means not placing an order until the market's been open for some time. Before the market opens, you may see apparent nonsense—such as bids that are higher than offers. This means that buyers are prepared to pay more than the price at which sellers are willing to sell! This type of anomaly probably occurs as a result of carry-over orders in the system. So you can't really get an idea of market sentiment at times when the market is closed and that's why it's not a good idea to place orders outside of market trading hours. For example, the orders at market on, say, 7 pm Sunday evening may be very different from those at market when trading commences at 10 am on the following Monday morning, even though no trading has taken place in the intervening period. If you act on the information available on Sunday evening, you could enter into a trade at an unfavourable price or even trade shares you would not have traded had you had the up-to-date information available at market opening.

So for various reasons, bids and offers at market opening may be very different from those that appear even 10 minutes later.

I also suggest you avoid placing orders in the 10-minute (or so) period before the market closes. This is often a period of frenetic activity as day traders close their positions to avoid carrying open positions into the next day's trading. It can be a turbulent period and, like turbulence in water, is best stayed out of.

Note

I suggest that, if possible, you do not place orders until the market has been open for at least an hour, because this will allow you to get a reasonable idea of market direction. Of course, this direction can change later but at least you are aware of market direction at the time you place your order.

Order processing

The size of an order doesn't affect the priority of execution; instead, automatic computer-based trading systems attempt to match bids, offers and quantities. Orders with a match are transacted first. If a number of matches occur simultaneously, orders transact in time sequence priority—that is, according to the time when they were received. This is also known as *FIFO priority*—first in, first out.

Note

Nowadays, throughout the world almost all orders are processed automatically by a computer using an algorithm, without any human intervention.

Tick size

Tick size (or price step) is the minimum price increment of any order that will be accepted. At the time of writing, ASX tick sizes were:

- 0.1¢ for share prices up to 10¢

- 0.5¢ for share prices from 10¢ to $2.00

- 1¢ for shares prices over $2.00

For example, you could place an order for 9.6¢ or for 51.5¢, but you couldn't place an order for 51.6¢ because for prices over 10¢ the minimum tick increment is 0.5¢.

Understanding the types of order you can place

Despite all the complexity and sophistication of trading shares, you can really place only three different types of order:

- limit order

- market order

- conditional (or deferred execution) order.

Limit order

With a limit order you specify a price limit, which is a maximum buy price or a minimum sell price. If the share price doesn't reach your specified price limit, your order won't transact. In addition to your price limit, many brokers allow you to specify a time limit. For example, if you specify 'good for the day' and the order isn't transacted on the day you place it, it'll be purged. If you don't specify a time period, usually a maximum time limit is specified by the broker. For example, if this time limit is four weeks and your order doesn't transact during this time, it'll be purged. As I pointed out in chapter 10, automatic purging can also occur if the status of the shares changes before order transaction occurs (for example, cum-dividend to ex-dividend).

Market orders

With a market order (or 'at-market order'), you are prepared to accept the best price available at the time you place your order. This means if you're buying, you accept the lowest offer and if you're selling, you accept the highest bid. Time limits don't usually apply to market orders because in almost all cases, they transact very quickly. The only exception to this is when a match isn't possible—when simply not enough shares are on the market to fulfil the order. Though very unusual, this can happen when the order is for a large quantity of shares in an illiquid stock (one with low turnover or volume).

Notes

- A limit order you place won't necessarily transact if your bid or offer can't be matched. So you usually place a market order when you really want to buy or sell and you aren't particularly concerned about a small difference in price.

- Many brokers won't accept market orders if you try to place them outside of ASX trading hours.

Comparing limit and market orders

Limit and market orders each have advantages and disadvantages, so to help you decide which you'd prefer, I've compared them in table 11.3.

Table 11.3 Advantages and disadvantages of limit and market orders

Order type	Advantages	Disadvantages
Limit order	You know the maximum price you'll pay if you buy or the minimum price you'll receive if you sell. If your order doesn't transact quickly, you get some breathing space to re-evaluate prices as the market moves.	You can miss out on the trade if the market is moving against you. Also, your order may be purged if it doesn't transact within a reasonable time period.
Market order	You're sure of the trade taking place (unless you're trying to trade a large number of shares in an illiquid stock) and you get the best price if the market is moving against you.	The trade price is uncertain and if prices are moving quickly against you, you may have to pay more than you planned when you buy or receive less than you planned when you sell. You don't get any breathing space to re-evaluate prices as the market moves.

Order strategy

A strategy you can consider is to place limit orders most of the time even if you specify a price close to the last sale price (or even the same as it).

The advantage of doing this is that you know the transaction price, and if the order doesn't transact, you can re-evaluate the situation and re-think your strategy.

If the market is moving quickly in an unfavourable direction and you want to get in or get out at the best price you can, a market order will be most appropriate. For example, if you want to buy shares that are in an uptrend mode, it makes sense to place a market buy order and get in without delay. Similarly, if you hold shares you want to offload and the price is falling, a market order is probably the best strategy.

Specifying your order duration

A decision you need to make before placing an order is the order duration—that is, how long you'll leave the order in the market. If you're placing a market order, this is not usually a consideration because the order generally transacts very quickly (literally within seconds). If you're placing a limit order or conditional order, you need to decide if you want the order to remain for as long as it may take to transact, or to be purged after a certain lapse of time.

I don't think it's a good idea to leave orders in the market indefinitely, and I suggest most of your orders should be 'good for the day' or have a maximum time limit of about a week. The market can move a great deal in a short time and the move may be unfavourable to you. For example, consider the following scenario: you place a buy order when the price is rising and you state your price limit. Your order doesn't transact because the market gaps above your limit but you leave your order in the system. A few days later, the price reaches a peak and starts to fall. When the price tracks down to your bid price, your order transacts. The result is that you've bought shares in a falling market—generally not a good strategy! If the price continues to track down, you note with dismay that you've bought the shares at a higher price than you could have had you cancelled your initial order and placed a new buy order at a later date after the share price had bottomed out and started rising again.

Having said this, in some circumstances it can be a good strategy to leave a limit order in the system for some time. An example of this is when you confidently identify clear support and resistance levels for a sideways trending share. Suppose you place a buy order at a price around the support level but your order doesn't transact because the price gaps above your bid price. You decide to leave your order in the system. Subsequently the price rises to the resistance level and then drops back down toward the support level. When the price reaches your bid price, the order transacts. If you are correct about the sideways trend and the support and resistance levels, the price should recover later and track back up toward the resistance level. Because you left your original order in the system, you bought the shares at a good price and will now be making a profit.

Notes

- As I previously pointed out, automatic order purging can take place if the status of the shares changes before transaction. This is most likely if your order stays in the market for some time.

- If your broker doesn't have a time limit with orders, you need to keep track of them yourself and cancel any that remain in the system for longer than you want.

- Another situation where you might choose to leave your order in the system for some time is with illiquid shares with few trades taking place and most likely a large spread. In this case, no trades may take place for a day or more, so 'day only' orders may be ineffectual.

Conditional orders

As discussed in chapter 10, conditional (or deferred execution) orders have advantages and disadvantages, and you may not wish to place them for all (or even most) of your trades considering the likely substantial extra brokerage cost. This cost may be charged as an upfront cost when you place the order or as a higher execution cost should the order transact.

I feel conditional orders are most useful if you don't have the time (or motivation) to monitor the market regularly. Of the various types of conditional orders, stop losses are undoubtedly the most widely used and the most useful. If you're new to share trading, placing only limit or market orders for a while is probably best until you become more confident. Then, as you gain more experience, you might like to try placing stop losses on some of your more speculative shares and decide if you want to use this type of order.

If you decide you want to place conditional orders, you need to ensure that your broker will accept the type of order you want to place, and you may need to make special arrangements. In some cases, you may have to answer a short quiz designed to test your understanding of these types of orders. Many brokers (both online and offline) provide a conditional ordering facility; however, many also don't or may provide only for one or two types.

When you place a conditional order, you need to specify two prices:

- *A trigger price.* This is the price at which the order will trigger and go to market.

- *A limit price.* This is the price limit for the trade once it triggers.

For example, say you own some shares that are showing a good paper capital gain and are currently trading for $9.40. You're worried about a price drop so you decide to place a stop loss order with your broker. You might set a trigger price of, say, $9.00 and a limit of $8.80. This means that if the price drops to $9.00, a sell order will go to market and if buyers can be found, your shares will be sold for $9.00. If there are insufficient buyers, your shares will be sold at the best price obtainable above $8.80. If the price drops below $8.80, any shares that weren't sold will be held over and sold only if the price rises to $8.80 (or above) before the order cancels.

Note

A conditional order doesn't actually go to market until it triggers and, therefore, will have a lower transaction priority than limit orders for the same price that were already in the market.

Market depth and spread

Market depth refers to the number of buyers and sellers and the quantity of shares each wishes to buy or sell at a given price.

Spread is the gap between the highest bid and the lowest offer—that is, the trading price differential between buyers and sellers most closely in agreement and, therefore, most likely to trade. With liquid shares, the spread is often only a cent or even half a cent but with illiquid shares it can often be substantial.

Note

Share prices are always quoted in dollars, even for shares that are trading for a few cents or even less than one cent.

Understanding why you want to trade

You may have a number of reasons for wanting to trade shares, such as:

- You have a 'gut feeling'.

- You have had a tip from a friend or analyst.

- Your fundamental or technical analysis shows a buy or sell signal.

- You have some spare cash you want to invest and get a better return than you will get from a bank.

- You need some cash and the easiest way to get it is by selling shares.

- You want to re-jig your portfolio and sell some shares and buy some others to replace them.

Whatever the reasons I strongly suggest you use both fundamental and technical analysis before you actually place any orders.

Timing your trade

It's important to time your trade. As previously pointed out, I recommend you don't buy when shares are in a downtrend and that you don't sell when shares are in an uptrend. I think it's also a good idea not to place a buy order if the shares have fallen in price today or sell if they have risen unless for some particularly good reason.

Considering market action

By looking at an index such as the All Ordinaries index, you can get a feel for the way the overall market is moving. Then you need to look at the particular share or shares you are interested in. If the share is a large cap one and included in the All Ords, it will most likely move in the direction of the overall market but this isn't necessarily the case. The best way to get a feeling for market action for a share you are interested in is by looking at the market depth screen. This is a snapshot summary of the market action for a share at any point in time and provides the following information:

- A list of the bids, offers and quantities of shares bid and offered at each price. This is seldom a complete list and usually only the 10 or so bids and offers closest to the last sale price will be shown. This list may also show the total number of bids and total number of offers in the market and their value in dollars.

- Last sale price and whether this is higher or lower than the closing price yesterday — that is, whether the price has risen or fallen.

- The price rise or fall in dollars and also as a percentage.

- The number of shares traded so far today and the total value of all trades.

- The highest and lowest trade prices for the day so far.

- The opening price — that is, the first trade price.

Intra-day chart

If you are trading online and trading has been going on for some time you should be able to access an intra-day chart from your broker's site. This chart shows trade prices as the day progresses. Obviously this chart isn't a great deal of value at the start of trading because there won't be enough data to get a really good idea of market action. But as the day progresses the chart is very useful as it allows you to get a visual impression of how prices have been moving far better than looking at rows of figures.

Predicting price action

Shares are a practical application of supply–demand theory for an elastic commodity. Supply of any commodity is determined by the number of shares sellers offer for sale (at a given price) and demand is determined by the number of shares buyers want to purchase (at a given price). Shares are an elastic commodity because supply and demand are closely related to price. This is different from relatively inelastic commodities such as essential food items or fuel, because for them supply and demand often don't change much with price.

For an elastic commodity like shares, the basic relationship between supply, demand and price is as follows:

- With increasing prices, demand falls and supply rises.

- With decreasing prices, demand rises and supply falls.

- The balance (or equilibrium) between supply and demand governs the price and quantity traded.

The basic economic supply–demand relationship applied to share trading means that:

- If the number bid exceeds the number offered (at prices around the last sale price), the price can be expected to rise. If the excess of buyers over sellers is persistent, this creates a bull market for the shares.

- If the number offered exceeds the number bid (at prices around the last sale price), the price can be expected to fall. If the excess of sellers over buyers is persistent, this creates a bear market for the shares.

If when you're thinking of placing your trade you know the number of shares bid and offered around the last sale price, you can get an idea of whether there's an excess of buy or sell pressure and, therefore, the most likely price movement. However, there's always a degree of uncertainty in the longer term because buyers and sellers can enter or exit the market at any time, and within a short time period the balance can change markedly.

The direction of price movement is a lot more difficult to predict with illiquid shares because there's usually a large spread and few trades. In this case, it's probably better to look at the longer term price movements and try to get an idea of overall price direction. It also makes sense to place a limit price order at a price that may be a fairly large price differential away from the last sale price and hold out for a week or two and see if your order transacts. If it does, you will probably have made the trade at a good price.

Deciding on your buy or sell price

The motivation of share traders is really no different from that of traders of any other commodity. If you're a buyer, you want to buy at the lowest price and if you're a seller, you want to sell at the highest price. The price you're prepared to bid or offer in either case depends upon how keen you are to buy or sell and how you judge the market is moving. For example, if you want to buy and the market is moving down I suggest you wait, but if you really want to buy, bid a price well below the last sale price. On the other hand, if the market appears to be moving up, jumping in right away is best—most likely with a market buy order. You also use the same type of strategy if you are a seller—if the market is moving down, jump in immediately; if moving up, either delay action or place an offer well above last sale price.

Specifying your order quantity

Naturally, before you place an order, you need to decide on the number of shares you wish to trade. As shown in tables 11.1 and 11.2, it's uneconomical to trade small parcels, and you generally wouldn't place orders with parcel values less than $1000 unless you're getting rid of a small parcel of shares or are buying a small number of shares to top up an existing shareholding. Although you can't place a new buy order of value less than $500, you can place a sell order of any value.

As already mentioned, when you want to sell all your shares it's really important to check that the number of shares you specify in your order exactly matches the quantity you own. You can't sell more shares than you own and your order won't transact if you try to do so (unless you're allowed to place a short-sell order). However, selling fewer shares than you own is never a problem. For example, suppose you own 4320 shares but your records show only 4300. You place a sell order for 4300 shares and this order transacts. Some time later you realise that you still hold 20 shares, and these shares will most likely be of nuisance value only because the cost of trying to sell them may be greater than what you'd get for them. Therefore, I always check my portfolio holding record with my broker before I place a sell order because my online portfolio is always up to date and accurate.

Note

CHESS statements, usually take several weeks to be updated, so you can't rely on them to be exactly up to date. For example, if you're in a DRP and have recently been allocated shares in lieu of dividends, or if you've recently traded shares, the CHESS statement you access may not show the exact quantity you actually own.

Placing your order

Once you've made up your mind on all the details I've discussed, placing an order is a comparatively simple matter. If you trade online, all you need to do is to move from the market depth screen to the order screen, enter your order details and hit the order button. You'll then be asked to confirm the details of your order to help minimise the risk that you've unintentionally made an error. Once you've confirmed the order details, that's it—your order will go to market.

If you trade offline, all you need to do is contact your broker by whatever means you've arranged and provide details of your order. If you've done so by telephone, you'll most likely get immediate verbal confirmation to ensure no communication misunderstanding has occurred. In addition, most offline brokers tape all phone orders as backup security.

Confirming your order

You can usually set up your online account so you receive email confirmation of your order.

If you place an offline order by phone or email, requesting confirmation of some sort is a good idea to ensure that your order has actually been received and will be acted on.

Trade confirmation

If you trade online, you'll be able to receive a trade confirmation by email after the order transacts. You'll also be able to check the order status at any time by logging on to your online trading site and using the 'order status' facility.

If you trade offline and place a market order by phone, the trade will most likely take place almost immediately and the broker will confirm the trade before you hang up. If you've placed a limit order, you'll need to make arrangements with the broker to confirm the trade by phone or email after it transacts.

Regardless of whether you trade online or offline, after a trade takes place you'll receive a contract note confirming all the details of the transaction. Traditionally, your broker mailed out this document to you but nowadays email is most often used.

Sometimes your order can transact in more than one parcel, and in this case each parcel will be treated as a different transaction and each trade will be listed separately on the contract note. If trading takes place on different days, each transaction will have a different contract note. This means that a single order could have different dates of acquisition (buy order) or disposal (sell order). However, the share registry (and CHESS) will amalgamate parcels in the same shares and your CHESS statement will show your total holding.

Note

You won't pay additional brokerage for orders that transact in several parcels on the same day, but if the order transacts on different days and there are separate contract notes, some brokers charge additional brokerage.

Amending or cancelling your order

If your order doesn't transact within a few days, it's most likely your price is outside the current trading range. That is, your bid is too low or your offer is too high. In this case you have four possible strategies:

- You sit tight and wait to see if your order transacts at some time in the future if prices move toward your price.

- You amend or cancel your order—for example, raise your bid or lower your offer.

- Your order exceeds the specified time limit and is cancelled by your broker.

- Your order is automatically purged because the status of the shares changes.

If you decide to amend or cancel your order no cost is involved because brokerage is charged on transacted orders only. However, if you amend your order after partial transaction, your amended order will be treated as a new order and you will have to pay another lot of brokerage.

For example, let's say you place an order to buy 10 000 shares at $1.00 limit. This price finds a seller for 5000 shares and so you obtain these shares but then there are no more sellers at this price. After a while, the market price rises to $1.10 and shows no indication of dropping back. You now feel you have little chance of obtaining the additional 5000 shares at $1.00 so you decide to amend your order and raise your bid to $1.10. No problem—except that you'll pay brokerage on the initial parcel of 5000 shares purchased for $1.00 and also on the second parcel of 5000 shares purchased for $1.10.

Learning exercises

11.1

    a.   What's meant by T+2 settlement?

    b.   You buy some shares of total cost $8770 on Monday morning and sell some others of net value $9640 on Tuesday afternoon. How much cash will be debited or credited with your broker and on what days? What would have happened if both transactions had taken place on Monday morning?

11.2   Your brokerage charge (including GST) for a parcel value up to $10 000 is $35.

    How many shares can you buy at a price of $1.56 per share so that your cost per share does not increase by more than 1¢ when you include trading costs? What will be your total cost for the transaction?

11.3   State which of the following bids or offers is valid or invalid. Correct the invalid ones to the nearest valid one.

    a. $0.052

    b. $0.113

    c. $0.345

    d. $0.667

    e. $0.765

    f. $2.085

    g. $5.96

11.4

    a.   How does the size of an order affect the execution priority?

    b.   If a number of limit orders are in the system all specifying the same price, which will be executed first?

11.5   Outline the circumstances when it's generally not a good strategy to place a limit buy order or a limit sell order and give reasons why in each case.

11.6 Explain how the price will change if a significant number of (a) buyers or (b) sellers place market orders for the same shares.

11.7 You own some shares currently trading for $3.35 and you place a stop loss order with a trigger price of $3.20 and a limit price of $3.10. Several days later you check prices and you find that the shares are trading for $3.00 yet none of your shares were sold. What's the likely explanation?

11.8 What are the minimum and maximum parcel sizes you can place for a sell order and for a buy order with ASX-listed shares and what determines these parcel sizes?

11.9 When is a good time of the day to trade and why isn't it a good idea to place orders outside of market trading times?

11.10 You own some shares and after a while the price begins to fall. You decide to sell and place a limit sell order. After a few days the order hasn't transacted and the price continues to fall and you are now making a loss on the shares. What is your best strategy?

11.11 For the scenario given in learning exercise 11.10, you decided to sell your shares. Soon after the price stops falling and starts to rise again. What actions might you consider now?

11.12 Under what circumstances do you think it might be a good idea to leave a limit order in the system for some time?

Learning exercises solutions

11.1

    a. T+2 settlement means that money changes hands between brokers two working days after the trade transacts.

    b. Your account would be debited $8770 on Wednesday that week and credited $9640 on Thursday. If both transactions had taken place on Monday, your account would be credited $870 on Wednesday that week.

11.2 1¢ = $0.01. To spread $35.00 in such a way that the cost of each share does not increase by more than $0.01, you will need to buy $35 \div 0.01$ shares, which is **3500 shares**.

Your total cost is: $3500 \times \$1.56 + \$35 = $ **$5495**

Note: Cost per share = $\$5495 \div 3500 = \$1.57$

11.3

    a. $0.052: valid (5.2¢)

    b. $0.113: invalid, closest valid $0.115 (11.5¢)

    c. $0.345: valid (34.5¢)

    d. $0.667: invalid, closest valid $0.665 (66.5¢)

    e. $0.765: valid (76.5¢)

    f. $2.085: invalid, closest valid $2.09

    g. $5.96: valid

11.4

    a. The size of an order doesn't affect the execution priority.

    b. If a number of limit orders in the system all specify the same price, they will be executed in FIFO sequence—that is, first in, first out.

11.5 It's generally not a good strategy to place a limit buy order when the price is in an uptrend mode. The reason is you could miss out on the trade because the price won't reach your limit. If you really want the shares, you'll end up paying more if you bid later on.

It's generally not a good strategy to place a limit sell order when the price is in downtrend mode. The reason is you could miss out on the trade because the price won't reach your limit. If you really want to sell, you'll end up receiving less if you offer later on.

11.6
    a. Market buy orders tend to put upward pressure on prices so a significant number of market bids will result in a substantial price rise as buyers soak up the available offers.

    b. Market sell orders tend to put downward pressure on prices and a significant number of them will result in a significant price drop as sellers absorb the available bids.

11.7   The most likely explanation is that the price gapped down below $3.10 before your order could be fulfilled. For example, the shares may have closed at $3.22 one day and then opened at $3.08 the next day.

11.8   The minimum and maximum orders are as follows:

» *Sell order:* There is no minimum sell order. The maximum is determined by the total number of shares you own—that is, you can't sell more shares than you own.

» *Buy order:* The minimum value is $500 (for shares you don't already own) and this is an ASX rule. The maximum is governed by the funds you have available for the trade. If your order value exceeds your available funds, you will be in a spot of bother.

11.9   A good time to trade is at least an hour after the market opens so that you can get a good idea of current market action and sentiment. It's also best to avoid the often turbulent period of trading just before market close.

It's not a good idea to place orders outside of market trading times because the orders at market when it is closed may be very different from those at market when trading commences on the next trading day, even though no trading has taken place on the ASX in the intervening period. If you act on the information available when the market is closed, you can enter into a trade at an unfavourable price or even enter a trade you would not have entered otherwise.

11.10 Your best strategy is to cancel the original order and place a market sell order so the shares will be sold quickly. You simply have to accept the loss.

11.11 You now have to decide whether the rise is just a temporary change in the downtrend (dead cat bounce) or based on a genuine change of sentiment and the start of a new uptrend. If you feel the latter is the case, you need to decide whether to jump on board and maybe place a market buy order, stay away entirely, or wait a while but still keep tabs on the shares.

11.12 Leaving a limit order in the system for some time can be a good strategy when you've identified clear support and resistance levels for a sideways trending share. In this case, leaving your order in the system can result in you obtaining the shares at a good price at around the low point if you're buying or selling them around the high point if you're selling.

Chapter 12

Using market and sector indices

The Australian sharemarket is made up of a diverse range of listed companies, and these can be divided into various groups of similar type according to the nature of their business. These various groups are known as *sectors*. The performance of the market as a whole or of each sector can be measured by a statistic known as an *index*. In this chapter, I outline the nature of these indices and, most importantly, how you can use them to your advantage as a share investor.

Looking from the top down

A 'top-down' approach is one where you look at market performance, then sector performance and finally performance of shares within a sector. It's a different approach from a bottom-up or fundamental analysis approach (as discussed in chapter 8), which is based on analysing shares from the grass roots upward rather than first considering the broader, overall picture.

Although the two approaches seem basically different, you can use them both and include technical analysis as well when making investment decisions. You can use a top-down approach with market performance to decide when to invest most heavily in shares and when to lighten your share investment. If this analysis indicates that it's time to invest more capital into shares, you can evaluate sector performance to decide which sectors offer the most potential. You can then look at shares within the best performing sectors using technical analysis as a tool to guide your decisions. Once you've identified shares with the most potential, you can sort them into order of preference using fundamental analysis and your 'health test' to decide which ones to include in your portfolio. You can then use technical analysis to time your entry point. If your analysis indicates that you should be reducing your capital investment in shares, you can adopt this approach to decide which sectors are under performing and decide on the best shares to sell.

Understanding indices

An index is a calculated statistic based on the value of a number of shares. The index value of itself is not really important, but a change in value is significant because it indicates the change in value of the shares in the companies comprising the index.

Indices are split into two main types: market indices and sector indices.

Market index

As the name suggests, a market index comprises a diverse group of the larger market cap shares. A change in the index indicates a change in market value of the group and is indicative of the change in value of the broader market.

Sector index

As the name suggests, a sector index comprises shares in similar types of industry. A change in the index indicates a change in market value of this type of industry and doesn't necessarily reflect the change in value of the broader market.

Notes

- Australian market and sector indices are identified by a code in the same way that a code is used as a shorthand way of identifying a share.

- Australian indices aren't calculated by the ASX but by Standard and Poor's—a company that specialises in compiling indices and in rating stocks and markets. This is indicated by the letters 'S&P' in the name of the index, although this prefix is frequently omitted.

- Australian market and sector indices may change from time to time as new indices are added or existing ones removed or changed. The Australian indices I quote in this chapter are up to date at the time of writing.

Calculating indices

To understand how an index is calculated, consider the following example: At some point in time, your share portfolio is worth $125 300. A year later, it is worth $134 200.

You can calculate the change in value of your portfolio in dollars or as a percentage (relative to the initial value):

- Change in value = $134 200 − $125 300 = $8900

- Percentage change in value = $8900 ÷ $125 300 × 100 = 7.1\%

Another way of measuring the change in value would be to give your portfolio some initial points value—say, 1000 points. This could be called your *benchmark portfolio index value*. Then one point of your portfolio index has a value of $125.30. A year later, your portfolio value in points is $134 200 ÷ $125.30 = 1071 points

So the change in value of your portfolio in points over the year was +71 points. Since the initial value of your portfolio was 1000 points, the change in value was 7.1% (as before).

Notes

- You could also divide your portfolio up into sectors and use the same method to measure changes in value of each sector.

- The benchmark dollar value of one point in your portfolio index doesn't change with time; only the value of the index changes as the share prices of the shares in the index changes.

The method I've outlined is essentially how a market or sector index is calculated and how changes in an index are determined. While calculating indices for your portfolio or sectors in it would be pointless, the benefit of having Australian market or sector indices is that dollar values and changes in value can be quoted in points rather than billions of dollars.

Because benchmark point values are different for the various indices, it's not really meaningful to compare changes in the points value of one index with another. Rather, you obtain a true 'apples to apples' comparison by the relative change in value (percentage change in the points value) of each index. For example, if I tell you index A went up by 127 points and index B went down by 67 points, that gives you no real idea of the relative change. But if I tell you index A went up 1.2% and index B went down 1.6%, you now have a meaningful comparison of the change that occurred.

Weighted indices

Australian indices are usually 'weighted', which means that shares with higher market cap within the index influence the index more than shares of lower market cap. To see why, consider the following example. A portfolio of value $60 000 consists of just two shares with the following values:

- A: $50 000

- B: $10 000

If some time later, the price of share A goes up 10%, while B goes down 10% the portfolio will now have a value of $64 000.

However, if share A goes down 10% and B goes up 10% the portfolio now has a value $56 000.

So you can see that similar price movements can have a dramatic difference in portfolio value because A influences the portfolio value much more than B. In fact, B needs to rise or fall five times as much as A to have the same effect on portfolio value.

The same principle applies to the Australian sharemarket, so indices are weighted according to the market capitalisation of the shares comprising the index.

Note

Not all indices outside Australia are weighted; for example, the Dow Jones is an unweighted index based on the value of only 30 shares. Despite this, the index is widely regarded as a very good measure of the performance of the US market as a whole.

Accumulation indices

As discussed in previous chapters, the total return from share investing is the sum of capital gains (price movements) and dividends. An accumulation index takes this into account by including dividends in the index. Naturally, an accumulation index will show a higher growth rate over time than an index that doesn't include dividends.

Note

Even though accumulation indices give a truer picture of shares profitability, they aren't widely quoted and the most widely used and quoted Australian market and sector indices are based only on prices.

Australian market indices

Usually about 10 or more Australian market indices are available. Many of these are of interest mainly to fund managers because the performance of a fund is often compared to that of an appropriate index. For example, if a fund owns about 50 stocks, it would be logical to compare the performance of the fund to the index that also has 50 stocks in it.

The indices most useful for Australian investors are listed in table 12.1 (overleaf). In this table, I've also provided the make-up and approximate percentage market cap of the stocks in the index compared to the total Australian sharemarket. For example, the S&P/ASX 500 (also known as the 'All Ords') is comprised of 500 stocks (about 25% of all ASX listed stocks) yet because these stocks are the largest market cap stocks, this index represents about 98% of the total Australian stock market capitalisation.

Table 12.1: Australian market indices

Index	Code	Make-up	Market cap (%)
S&P/ASX 500	XAO	500 largest market cap stocks	98
S&P/ASX 300	XKO	300 largest market cap stocks	80
S&P/ASX 200	XJO	200 largest market cap stocks	80
S&P/ASX 100	XTO	100 largest market cap stocks	75
S&P/ASX 50	XFL	50 largest market cap stocks	65
S&P/ASX 20	XTL	20 largest market cap stocks	45

Notes

- The name 'All Ords' is a misnomer since this index isn't made up of all ordinary listed shares.

- A comprehensive list and description of these indices is available on the ASX website.

- Stocks included in market indices are generally chosen according to market cap and liquidity of the shares. That's to say, illiquid shares are usually excluded from the index. The exception to this is the All Ords, where liquidity is not a factor in stock selection for the index.

- The benchmark All Ords index used nowadays was set in 1980 at 500 points.

- As share prices change, market cap changes and the stocks included in the index may also change. Stocks at the lower fringes of the index may be taken out of the index if their share price falls and be replaced by others just out of the index when their share price rises.

- For the preceding reason, the percentage market cap of the stocks in the index also changes with time and the figures I've quoted in the table are approximate and should be used only as a guide.

Using market indices

Australian market indices can be used for several purposes, including the following:

- To measure the performance of the Australian market — for this purpose, the All Ords is most frequently quoted because it represents around 98% of the value of all listed Australian shares.

- To measure the performance of the largest market cap stocks in the Australian market, such as the 20 or 50 largest market cap stocks.

- To provide a benchmark against which the performance of a large fund (such as a superannuation fund or managed fund) can be evaluated. For example, many fund managers rate the performance of their fund against the S&P/ASX 100 or the S&P/ASX 200.

- To provide a benchmark against which the performance of a share portfolio can be evaluated. This is a subjective judgement and you can choose whichever index you think is most appropriate. I use the All Ords because it is widely quoted and therefore convenient. Also, because my portfolio is strongly weighted with large market cap stocks (blue chip and green chip shares), I believe the All Ords provides a good benchmark.

- To provide a benchmark against which the performance of a particular share can be measured.

Note

A very convenient way of gauging company or market performance is from an appropriate chart. If you refer to chapter 3, figure 3.1 shows a chart of the All Ords that provides an instant picture of the Australian market's long-term performance. Some charting sites allow you to chart an index and a share simultaneously. So the chart provides a picture of not only the performance of the index and the share but also their relative performance.

Strategic use of market indices

Because market indices are identified by a letter code (like shares are), you can chart market indices and use technical analysis to identify trends and changes in trends in the index. When you've identified uptrends or downtrends, you're best to follow the general principle of trading with the trend rather than against it. So a logical investment strategy based on market indices is as follows:

Increase your investment in shares when market indices are in uptrend and reduce your investment in shares when market indices are in downtrend.

While this strategy is logical and follows the principle of trend trading, it has a few prickles. If you sell a significant number of profitable shares, you may incur considerable trading costs and also be hit with a large capital gains tax bill in one year. However, the thorniest problem with trying to get into and out of the market is that it's virtually impossible to get the timing right. Statistics over the years show that Pareto's principle (80/20 rule) applies to the sharemarket because significant changes to the market occur on a small number of trading days. So if you're out of the market on significant up days, you'll miss most of the action. Bearing this in mind, perhaps a good strategy is as follows:

Maximise your exposure to defensive shares when market indices are in a downtrend and minimise your exposure to these shares when market indices are in an uptrend.

Notes

- This strategy is reinforced by the CAPM model (discussed in the next chapter), which indicates that the more volatile shares produce better returns in a bull market, whereas the less volatile, defensive ones produce better returns in bear markets.

- Defensive shares are discussed in chapter 1, and they are shares that tend to remain relatively steady even when the general market is trending down.

Using sector indices

Sector indices are comprised of shares in companies that have a common nature to their business. If the company has several diversified sources of revenue, the main revenue earner of the business is taken into account when allocating the sector.

The simplest sector grouping is just two sectors:

- industrials

- resources (mining and oil stocks).

The ASX uses a more sophisticated grouping system that identifies over 10 sectors of the Australian market. The sector groupings aren't static and new sectors are sometimes introduced and sector make-up changed to keep up to date with changes in the market and to keep sectors relevant for investors and fund managers. In the past, ASX sector indices were tailored to the Australian market but nowadays the ASX uses the Global Industry Classification Standard (GICS), which provides a common global standard for categorising sectors. The advantage of this is that Australian sectors align with global industry classifications, giving investors worldwide a more uniform basis for comparison.

Some of the sector classifications used by the ASX and of importance to Australian investors are shown in table 12.2. In this table, I've included the codes and a short description of the make-up of each index.

Table 12.2: Sector indices

Sector	Code	Index make-up
Energy	XEJ	Energy equipment and services. Oil, coal and gas exploration, production, refining and marketing.
Materials	XMJ	Manufacture of chemicals, construction materials, containers and packaging, metals and mining, paper and forest products.

(continued)

Table 12.2 Sector indices (*cont'd*)

Sector	Code	Index make-up
Industrials	XNJ	Manufacture and distribution of goods for aerospace and defence, construction, engineering and building products, electrical equipment and industrial machinery, and provision of services for printing, employment, environment, airlines, couriers, marine, road and rail.
Consumer discretionary	XDJ	Cars and car components, consumer discretionary durables, leisure equipment and apparel, hotels, restaurants, casinos, gambling, and leisure facilities, media, multi-line and speciality retailing.
Consumer staples	XSJ	Manufacturers and distribution of food, beverages, tobacco, non-durable household goods and personal products as well as food and drug retailing.
Health care	XHJ	Manufacture of health care equipment and supplies or providers of health care related services; also research, development, production and marketing of pharmaceuticals and biotechnology products.
Financials	XFJ	Banks and financial services, insurance, property trusts and real estate lending and investment.
Real estate investment trusts	XPJ	Real estate and investment trusts that own property and derive income from rental returns.
Financials excluding property trusts	XXJ	Same as XFJ but excluding companies in the XPJ sector.
Information	XIJ	Computer and internet software and technology services, and providers of equipment for communications and electronic applications.
Communication services	XTJ	Providers of services for telecommunication and allied communication industries.
Utilities	XUJ	Electricity, gas, water and multi-utility producers and providers.
Metals and mining	XMM	Companies in the materials sector involved in the production of aluminium, steel, gold and other precious metals, and the extraction of metals and minerals not elsewhere classified.
Gold	XGD	Companies in the gold industry.

Notes

- This list provided in table 12.2 is not complete — some of the more obscure sectors have been omitted.

- A comprehensive list and description is available on the ASX website.

- Interestingly, household durables, textiles and apparel are included in the consumer discretionary sector, whereas alcohol, tobacco and personal products are included as consumer staples!

- Even though companies included in an index are in the same type of business, there can be considerable differences between them. For example, in the metals and mining sector or in the energy sector, there's a great deal of difference between established producers and speculative explorers.

Sector performance

How can you evaluate sector performance and identify the best performing sectors? A good way of doing this is to chart sectors using their three-letter code and technical analysis to identify sector trends and changes in trend. You can compare sectors by charting two or more of them simultaneously using a percentage chart. This provides an 'apples to apples' comparison that's easy to interpret. Once you've set up the parameters for the charts, you can quickly run through all sectors and identify the best performing ones. Another approach is to chart sector performance relative to an appropriate market index. When comparing sectors, you need to decide on an appropriate time frame, because the various sectors will have different relative performances depending on the time frame you choose. As a guide, I suggest a suitable time frame for long-term investing would be one to three years and for shorter term investing three to six months. For longer term sector performance comparison, a weekly rather than a daily chart is easier to interpret.

Strategic use of sector indices

You can use sector indices to strategically assist both your trading decisions and your investment decisions. If you are trading shares for capital gains, you can identify sectors that are outperforming others and, therefore, have the greatest profit potential. This is sometimes known as identifying *hot* sectors as opposed to *cold* sectors. Clearly, trading shares in the hot sectors makes sense because these shares have the greatest potential for capital gains profits. When doing this, you need to compare sector performance over a relatively short time frame—say, from about three to six months or perhaps the last year or so.

If you're more interested in investing rather than trading, you can use sector indices to assist you when setting up and managing your portfolio. You can essentially use two approaches when doing this: a balanced approach or a concentrated approach. Using the balanced approach, you set up your portfolio with shares in companies in each of the major sectors and keep the value of each company's shares approximately the same. This would suggest a portfolio with shares in about 10 different companies. However, you don't necessarily need to diversify to this extent and you can still get good diversification with a smaller number of different sectors in your portfolio.

When your shares are a mix from various sectors, at times shares in some sectors will outperform others. But in the long run, a well-diversified portfolio should track market performance fairly closely and a balanced portfolio is usually best for long-term investing. As sector performance changes, you may need to re-jig the sectors in your portfolio or change the relative value of shares in each sector.

If you're more adventurous and want to beat the market, you need to have a more concentrated portfolio. As the name suggests, a concentrated portfolio is one where you concentrate your capital in a number of sectors, and/or the value of the shares in some sectors is substantially different from the value of those in others. Most likely, you would have most capital invested in the hottest sectors and less in the colder ones.

While a concentrated portfolio is about the only way you can beat the market over the longer term, this strategy does have several downsides, namely:

- An increased level of risk—that is, a greater risk that your portfolio will underperform the market.

- You may need to switch from one sector to another as the relative performance of the different sectors changes with time and this could have capital gains tax implications.

- It's dangerous to assume that past performance will continue into the future. Quite often the best performing sectors in one year aren't the best performing ones in a following year. Indeed, quite often a reversal occurs from one year to the next and a hot sector goes cold, while a cold sector becomes hot.

Therefore, if you're a long-term investor without the time or inclination to constantly monitor sectors and switch and change, your best strategy could well be to maintain a fairly balanced portfolio.

Learning exercises

12.1 Using the example given at the start of this chapter (refer to the section 'Calculating indices'), after another year, your portfolio has increased in value from $134 200 to $141 500. Calculate the new value of your portfolio and the increase in value of your portfolio in points and as a percentage (relative to the initial value).

12.2 Explain the difference between a market index and a sector index. Also explain how liquidity is taken into consideration when compiling market indices.

12.3 Explain why the All Ords index comprises only about 25% of all listed stocks, yet represents about 98% of the total Australian market cap.

12.4
   a. What's meant by a weighted index? Are Australian market indices weighted?

   b. What's meant by an accumulation index? Are the indices quoted in tables 12.1 and 12.2 accumulation indices?

12.5
   a. What's a convenient way of gauging the performance of a market index over a period of time?

   b. What's a convenient way of gauging the performance of one sector relative to another or of one sector relative to the market in general?

12.6 How can you use market indices in a strategic way to improve your investment returns?

12.7 How can you use sector indices in a strategic way to improve your profitability for short-term trading and also for long-term investing?

12.8
   a. What's meant by a top-down investing approach and how does it differ from a bottom-up approach?

   b. How can you use indices in a top-down approach to guide your investment decisions?

12.9

a. The value of the market index you are using to gauge the performance of your shares at the end of a financial year was 5048 points and your share portfolio value was $240 500. A year later the index was 4835 and your portfolio value was $235 460. How did your portfolio perform relative to the index for this 12-month period?

b. If you received dividends of value $9370 during the year, what was the overall performance of your portfolio?

12.10 The comparative values of various sector indices on 1 July and 31 December are given in the following table.

Calculate the percent index change for this six-month period, and so identify the three hottest and the three coldest sectors in this period.

Notes:

- Comparative values only are shown and most have been divided by 100 for ease of comparison.

- For the purpose of this exercise, just two points in time six months apart have been used and while this will give you an idea of sector performance, it is much better for evaluation purposes to look at and compare index charts.

Sector	Code	Value 1 July	Value 31 Dec	Percent change
Energy	XEJ	111	115	
Materials	XMJ	141	138	
Industrials	XNJ	67.7	69.5	
Consumer discretionary	XDJ	24.4	26.8	
Consumer staples	XSJ	114	122	
Health care	XHJ	339	406	
Financials	XFJ	63.5	59.8	
Financials ex prop trusts	XXJ	71	66.7	
Information technology	XIJ	13.6	14.5	
Real estate investment trusts	XPJ	16.2	15.8	
Communication services	XTJ	13.3	12.6	
Utilities	XUJ	82.7	81.6	
Metals and mining	XMM	46.6	45	
Gold	XGD	63.3	68.5	

Learning exercises solutions

12.1 One point in your portfolio index has a value of $125.30. Therefore, the new value of your portfolio in points is $141500 \div 125.30 = \textbf{1129 points}$.

Increase in portfolio value in points is $1129 - 1071 = \textbf{58 points}$.

Percentage increase in value is $58 \div 1071 \times 100 = \textbf{5.42\%}$.

12.2 A market index is based on a number of stocks in different types of industries whereas a sector index is based on all stocks in the same type of industry. Liquidity is included as a factor in stock selection in most market indices other than the All Ords.

12.3 Clearly a large number of listed companies have very small market caps. This is another example of Pareto's principle (80/20 rule) in that most investor dollars are invested in a relatively small number of large companies. For example, some share prices are $30 or more whereas many of the smaller miners and speculative stocks may have share prices of 10¢ or less. It takes 300 shares trading for 10¢ to have the same market cap as one share trading at $30.

12.4
   a. A weighted index is one that is weighted according to the market cap of the companies in the index. Australian market indices are weighted.

   b. An accumulation index is one where dividends are included in the value of the index, thus giving total investor return. None of the indices in tables 12.1 or 12.2 are accumulation indices.

12.5
   a. A convenient way of gauging the performance of a market index over a period of time is to chart the index over that time period.

   b. A convenient way of gauging the performance of one sector to another or of one sector to the market in general is to chart two or more indices simultaneously using a percentage chart.

12.6 You can use market indices in a strategic way to improve your investment returns by using technical analysis with market indices in the same way as you would for shares. Then you increase your share investment in a market uptrend and reduce it in a downtrend. Also, you invest more in defensive shares in bear markets and less in bull markets.

12.7 For short-term trading you can make strategic use of sector performance by identifying sectors that are outperforming others and, therefore, have the greatest profit potential. If you're more interested in investing rather than trading, you can use sector performance to assist you when setting up and managing your portfolio. You can essentially use two approaches when doing this: a balanced approach or a concentrated approach. In the balanced approach, you include in your portfolio a number of different shares from each of the major sectors and keep the value of each parcel of shares approximately the same. In the concentrated approach, you concentrate your investment capital on a number of sectors only, or, if you do have a portfolio with shares spread among various sectors, you don't have an approximately equal parcel value of each.

12.8

a. A top-down investing approach is one where you firstly evaluate the total market picture, then identify the best performing sectors and then the best performing shares within the best sectors. It differs from a bottom-up approach, which evaluates shares from the grass roots upward without considering the sector or market picture.

b. You can use indices in a top-down approach by first charting market indices to identify market trends. You can then evaluate sector performance using technical analysis with sector charts and compare the various sectors using percentage charts to identify the best performing ones. Finally you can hone in on the best performing shares within the best sectors.

12.9

a. The index went down by $5048 - 4835 = 213$ points.

The percentage drop is $213 \div 5048 \times 100 = 4.22\%$.

Your share portfolio went down by
$240500 – $235460 = $5040

The percentage drop is $5040 \div 240500 \times 100 = 2.1\%$.

Therefore, your share portfolio outperformed the index by
$4.22 - 2.1 = \textbf{2.12\%}$.

b. Your overall profit (capital gain and dividend) is
$9370 – $5040 = $4330

The percentage profit is $4330 \div 240500 \times 100 = \textbf{1.8\%}$ **profit**.

12.10 The percentage change in value of the index is calculated in
the following table.

Sector	Code	Value 1 July	Value 31 Dec	Percent change
Energy	XEJ	111	115	+3.6
Materials	XMJ	141	138	–2.1
Industrials	XNJ	67.7	69.5	+2.7
Consumer discretionary	XDJ	24.4	26.8	+9.8
Consumer staples	XSJ	114	122	+7
Health care	XHJ	339	406	+19.8
Financials	XFJ	63.5	59.8	–5.8
Financials ex prop trusts	XXJ	71	66.7	–6.1
Information technology	XIJ	13.6	14.5	+6.6
Real estate investment trusts	XPJ	16.2	15.8	–2.5
Communication services	XTJ	13.3	12.6	–5.3
Utilities	XUJ	82.7	81.6	–1.3
Metals and mining	XMM	46.6	45	–3.4
Gold	XGD	63.3	68.5	+8.2

Conclusion: During this period the hottest sector by far was XHJ,
followed by XDJ and XGD. The coldest sector was XXJ, followed by
XFJ and XTJ.

Chapter 13
Managing risks

Investing in shares is undoubtedly a more risky form of investment than a fixed-interest bank account or term deposit. However, risk and potential return are almost always also without question related, so if you want higher returns, you need to be prepared to take more risk. If you're prepared to accept the higher level of risk associated with share investing, it is a good idea to understand and manage the risks involved. In this chapter, I outline some strategies for doing so.

How risky is share investing?

Many people won't invest in shares because of the perceived risk. Understanding this attitude isn't hard when corporate collapses and poor performance from some blue chip stocks are highly publicised. Investors who own shares may have their confidence sapped when they see their savings eroding rather than gaining in value for some period of time. Often it's a case of 'once bitten, twice shy' and research indicates that many investors who lose money on the stock market are reluctant to reinvest in shares later on.

Managed funds, with fortunes controlled by a team of financial 'experts', often show extended periods of negative returns, and investors may wonder, 'If the experts can't get it right, what chance do I have?'

Without doubt, during a sudden market collapse or periods of prolonged bear markets, most share investors get their fingers burnt to some extent. However, history shows that after every downturn, the Australian market eventually recovers and tracks upward again, making higher highs. Indeed, downturns can be a source of long-term gains for investors who haven't lost their nerve and who have the confidence to take advantage of the good buying opportunities they usually present.

One of the main reasons shares are perceived as risky is because the stock market receives a huge amount of publicity. Market fluctuations and share prices are reported on a daily basis in the media so people tend to focus on the short-term volatility of shares rather than the long-term picture.

Investing risk

Investing risk is not simply the likelihood of losing money. For example, suppose you buy some shares that aren't paying a dividend, hold them for a year and then sell them for the same price as you bought them. You might say to yourself, 'Well, apart from transaction costs I didn't lose any money'. But you did lose money for the following two reasons:

1. Inflation has eroded the purchasing power of the capital you've invested—with an inflation rate of, say, 3% you've actually lost 3% in terms of purchasing power.

2. Accumulated capital has an intrinsic investment value because it can be loaned or deposited in an account that pays interest. So while your money was 'taking a holiday' in a non-productive investment, you lost the interest you could have received. This is often known as 'opportunity cost'.

You can see that an apparently 'break even' investment is really a loss investment when you consider the effect of inflation and opportunity cost.

So you should think of investing risk not simply as the likelihood of losing money, but as the likelihood of your investment return falling below your investment goal.

Understanding volatility

The riskiness of an investment depends on its volatility. Simply put, volatility is the magnitude of the up and down swings over the short term. To use an analogy, imagine you're in a car travelling up a hill from point A to point B over rocky terrain. The car's going to bounce up and down a lot. But now suppose a smooth road is built over the same route. Next time you travel from A to B, you'll start at the same point and finish at the same point but with much less bounce. With share investing, if point A represents your initial capital invested and point B the higher value of your capital after some time, it's clear that in both cases you've started and finished at the same points and achieved the same return but with a lot more volatility in the first case.

For an investor, the more volatile an investment, the riskier it is—certainly in the short term. We'd all love to see steady growth in the value of our shares and so in our investment capital, but unfortunately in real life, it just doesn't happen. The sharemarket is always volatile to some extent and can go through periods of extended high volatility. In addition, individual shares are usually volatile and some shares are more volatile than others. Generally speaking, the smaller market cap and more speculative shares tend to be more volatile than the larger market cap blue or green chip shares.

After any big shakeup, the market tends to be more volatile and take some time to settle down again. The same effect applies to individual shares and when investors get nervous about any shares or the market as a whole, volatility and hence short-term risk increases.

Measuring volatility

You can get an impression of volatility from a chart—the greater the up and down swings, the greater the volatility. A measure of volatility can also be obtained mathematically by the spread of a distribution. The most precise way of calculating this is by a statistic known as the *standard deviation*. A less rigorous but simpler way of calculating spread is by the range, which is the difference between the highest and lowest values.

As an example, consider the returns on two investments A and B as given in table 13.1 (overleaf).

Table 13.1: Returns from two investments

Year	% Return A	% Return B
1	10	10
2	8	5
3	12	15
4	9	8
5	11	12
Average return	10	10
Standard deviation	1.58	3.81
Range	4	10

In this case, over a five-year period, both investments achieved the same average return (neglecting any differences caused by compounding). However, from the point of view of return on investment, investment B is more volatile than A. The standard deviation of B's return is more than twice that of A's; also, B's range of 10 (15 – 5) is more than twice A's range of 4 (12 – 8).

Notes

- To obtain standard deviations as provided in table 13.1, I used a calculator with statistical functions.

- You can pictorially compare the volatility of A and B by charting the returns, as I've done in figure 13.1. You can see at a glance that B's return is more volatile than A's.

Price and earnings volatility

The volatility of the sharemarket and individual shares has several components, of which the two most important are price volatility and earnings volatility. Clearly they're closely related because share prices are closely related to earnings.

Price volatility

Price volatility is the volatility of share prices for the market as a whole or for individual shares. You can gain a visual impression of this from a chart

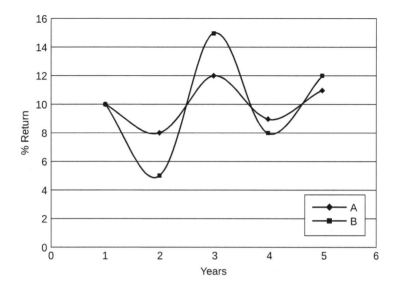

Figure 13.1: Investment returns charted

of a market index or the price chart of a share. Share price volatility relative to the market as a whole can be calculated mathematically in several ways. One way is by a statistic known as the *beta*, which is calculated by dividing the volatility of the share price by the volatility of the market as a whole. A beta greater than 1 indicates a share with a higher price volatility than the market as a whole and so a more risky share, whereas a beta less than 1 indicates a safer share in terms of price fluctuations.

The beta value is usually listed in the financial statistics summary for a share. Theoretically, the beta of the All Ords should be exactly equal to 1, but due to statistical variations it may be shown a little higher or lower than this. So, for example, a share with a beta of 0.8 or so would be one with lower volatility than the general market but a beta of 1.2 would be a share with higher volatility.

A less sophisticated, but still useful way of calculating price volatility is from the range of prices over a period. A formula for doing so is as follows:

$$V = \frac{(H-L)}{L} \times 100$$

Where:

- V = volatility percentage.

- H = highest price over the last 52 weeks.

- L = lowest price over the last 52 weeks.

- (H − L) is the price range.

The lower the value of V, the less volatile the share; the higher the value of V, the more volatile. Using this formula, you'll generally find that blue chip shares have a volatility percentage of around 50% or less, whereas more speculative shares can be well over 100%.

For example, consider a share with a yearly (52-week) high of $35.05 and a yearly low of $22.85.

Using the formula:

$$V = \frac{35.05 - 22.85}{22.85} \times 100 = 53.4\%$$

This is a relatively low value and indicates low price volatility.

Capital asset pricing model

The capital asset pricing model (CAPM) is a theory that links the potential capital gain from shares to volatility. According to this theory, the potential capital gain of a share depends upon three factors:

1. bond yield

2. average sharemarket gain

3. beta of the share.

The conclusions from the CAPM theory are:

- In a bull market where the average sharemarket gain is greater than the bond yield, high volatility shares have the potential to produce better gains than the general market and low volatility shares to produce lower gains.

- In a bear market where the average sharemarket gain is lower than the bond yield, low volatility shares have the potential to produce better gains than the general market and high volatility shares to produce lower gains.

Notes

- The CAPM theory doesn't take into account dividends—only capital gains.

- The average sharemarket gain can be measured by the rise in the All Ords. If the market is going down rather than rising, the gain will actually be a loss (reduction in value).

Earnings volatility

For long-term share investing, a company with stable earnings (profits) that rose somewhat from year to year would be ideal. In this case, earnings stability would be high and earnings volatility would be low. One method of judging earnings stability is to examine a chart of earnings over some years to get a visual impression of the extent of the fluctuations in earnings from year to year. As well as past earnings, future earnings estimates could be included if available.

A more mathematical method of calculating earnings stability is to fit a trend line to past and predicted earnings and then calculate the magnitude of the deviations from this line. This calculation results in earnings stability expressed as a percentage per annum. If the earnings each year followed the trend line exactly, the stability of earnings would be 100% and the volatility would be zero. Earnings stability at greater than that of the market as a whole indicates a company with more stable earnings than the general market and, therefore, relatively low risk.

Note

If the company doesn't make profits or has been trading for less than four years, earnings stability can't be calculated.

Managing risks

A good method of managing share-investing risks is to adopt a three-pronged approach:

1. Know the various risks involved.

2. Manage the risks with sound risk management strategies.

3. Stick to the strategies and don't allow emotions to cause you to deviate from them—that is, adopt a disciplined approach.

The risks associated with share investing can be broken down into three main types:

1. market risk

2. sector risk

3. specific risk.

Market risk

Market risk is the risk associated with the general sharemarket—that is, the risk of a market fall that's significantly greater than normal day-to-day fluctuations. When a fall in the market is significant, all shares tend to be affected (to a greater or lesser extent) and very few shares are immune. When the market falls, your portfolio is most likely to fall in step with it. This is indicated by the market saying:

When the tide goes out, all boats drop.

Significant market falls may result from significant local factors such as an increase in interest rates, change in government or other major change likely to affect the profitability of leading shares. Because the Australian market is so small and we rely a great deal on exports, significant overseas events that affect overseas markets (particularly in the United States or China) often flow on to our market.

You can detect market trends using technical analysis techniques (as outlined in chapter 9) with a suitable market index chart. If you're trying to gauge overall market sentiment, the most suitable index is the All Ords because this index best represents almost the entire Australian market.

Unfortunately, sometimes sudden and unexpected market falls appear to come 'out of the blue'. On the other hand, a warning may be apparent preceding the fall and you may be able to detect this on a chart. Severe downturns often occur after periods of irrational optimism when the market diverts significantly from the long-term trend. Then a correction is bound to come sooner or later. I've illustrated this in figures 13.2 and 13.3.

Another warning of an impending market downturn occurs when the market diverges upward significantly from the long-term price-to-earnings ratio (PE). Over some years, the long-term average Australian market PE has been around 16. The average market PE rising significantly above this

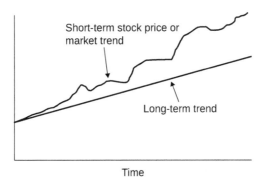

Figure 13.2: Irrational optimism

Figure 13.3: Irrational optimism correction

is a sign of market overheating, because share prices are rising to levels that can't be justified by profits. Similarly, a correction upward often occurs after periods of irrational pessimism.

Market risk strategies

The various strategies for managing market risk are:

- maintain some liquidity

- adopt a long-term approach

- bias your portfolio with defensive shares

- invest in shares that pay good dividends

- use geared instruments.

Maintain some liquidity

As suggested in earlier chapters, it's generally a good idea to keep a proportion of your investment capital in cash or in liquid accounts that won't be affected by the stock market. If you suspect an impending bear market, consider increasing your level of cash by selling some of your shares and moving from an investment phase to an accumulation phase. If you decide to adopt this strategy, it's important to act quickly. If you wait too long and panic selling starts, in all probability you won't be able to sell at a reasonable price and you'll just have to sit tight or sell at a greatly reduced price. Later on when the bear market ends and you're sure the market is in a bull phase, you can jump back in again. Now you can see the advantage of accumulating cash, because when the market recovers you can purchase good quality shares at low prices. This strategy may enable you to offset losses or even use the downturn as an opportunity to make longer term profits.

Adopt a long-term approach

Volatility is essentially a short-term phenomenon and bear markets don't last forever, so another strategy for dealing with market volatility is to adopt a long-term approach and avoid a panic reaction. If you adopt this strategy, you don't need to worry about gauging market sentiment and you won't get unduly concerned if the market takes a sudden dive. Instead of trying to get out of the market and then back in at some later date, you simply sit tight and ride the waves, secure in the knowledge that the market will eventually recover. A fall in your portfolio value is not a real money loss unless you sell. So if you don't sell and simply hold on, there's no actual loss and when the market recovers you are back to square one.

Another argument for the long-term strategy is Pareto's principle (80/20 rule) discussed in previous chapters, which indicates that the majority of market price growth occurs on a relatively small number of days. If you're out of the market on these days, you miss the action. Sudden market upswings are usually as difficult to predict as sudden downswings and by the time it's evident that an upswing is in place, if you're not in the market it will most likely be too late for you to get back in and profit from the upswing.

Bias your portfolio with defensive shares

Defensive shares tend not to be affected as much as speculative ones during a market downturn. So in times of high uncertainty, if you bias your portfolio with defensive shares, your portfolio will tend not to be as greatly affected as the general market.

Invest in shares that pay good dividends

Another strategy for dealing with market risk is to bias your portfolio with shares that pay a good consistent dividend because this tends to counteract the effect of falls in share prices. A fall in a share price based on investor perceptions shouldn't really affect company profitability. If you're getting a yield of 4% or more (giving a grossed-up yield of 7% or so), this yield (and the associated tax rebate) will continue to produce a consistent income and help mitigate the market fall. For example, if the market falls 10% and your shares also fall in value by 10%, this is a significant drop in value. But if you are getting a grossed-up yield of 7% at the same time, the net fall is a far less significant 3%.

Note

This strategy may not be very effective if the price downturn is due to some major event that affects profitability, because if a significant fall in earnings occurs, the company may not be able to sustain the same level of dividend payments.

Use geared instruments

A more advanced strategy of managing the risk of a market downturn is to hedge your portfolio using geared instruments such as index warrants or options. This is rather similar to taking out an insurance policy on your share portfolio. An index put option or warrant enables you to profit from a fall in the index. So if the market falls, you make a profit on the index option or warrant that can counteract a loss in value of your shares. On the other hand, if the market rises, you lose on the index option or warrant but this loss is offset by the gain in value of your shares. If you trade short-sell CFDs on indices or shares, it's also possible to profit from downswings.

The disadvantages to these strategies are as follows:

- In order to trade these types of instruments effectively, you need a level of expertise higher than that of the average investor.

- These types of trading instruments have a much higher risk and if you get it wrong your losses are magnified so they're generally recommended only for experienced traders.

- You'll make less profit when the market recovers.

- Not all brokers (online or offline) provide an options or CFD trading facility.

- The cost of trading these instruments is usually fairly high and higher than the cost of trading shares.

Sector risk

Sector risk is the risk associated with a sector of the market. Each sector is affected by different factors and has a different risk profile. For example, volatility in the price of gold affects gold stocks but should not affect oil stocks. Also, within the gold sector, we can expect that gold producers (selling gold) will be more directly affected by gold price volatility than gold explorers (looking for gold).

You can detect sector trends using technical analysis techniques (as outlined in chapter 9) with a sector index chart. You should be able to recognise longer term trends using moving averages and secondary technical analysis tools (filters) and detect warning signals (such as dead crosses).

Sector risk strategies

The most obvious strategy for dealing with sector risk is to match sector risk with your risk tolerance. Clearly, some sectors are more volatile (and risky) than others so if you want to minimise sector risk, investing only a small amount of your capital in the more risky sectors (or avoiding them entirely) makes sense.

Safer and more defensive sectors are those that are less affected by economic volatility—usually because demand for the product is relatively inelastic. That is, the product is regarded as essential and not discretionary.

Generally speaking, the less volatile sectors include:

- banks (if the majority of the income is from secured loans)

- property trusts

- alcohol and tobacco

- gambling/gaming

- infrastructure/utilities

- manufacturing and retailing of consumer staples.

The more volatile sectors include:

- mining exploration

- tourism and leisure

- biotechnology

- telecommunications

- internet and new technology.

Like market risk, a more advanced strategy for dealing with sector risk is to hedge by trading put warrants, options or CFDs over sector indices, but this strategy is recommend only for the experienced and more risk-tolerant traders.

Specific risk

Specific risk is the risk associated with a particular share that affects only that share and no others (even in the same sector). For example, if XYZ oil exploration company makes a significant new oil find, the share price will usually rise dramatically. However, ABC oil company's shares should not be affected in any way (unless investors switch allegiance, in which case ABC's share price might even go down).

You can assess specific risk in a number of ways, including fundamental analysis. You can check the beta value and calculate the price volatility using the volatility formula (refer to 'Price volatility', earlier in this chapter). Look for fluctuations in profitability, dividends and investor returns over past years and consider future projections and analysts forecasts. You can also use charting and technical analysis to assess trends and the likelihood of a trend continuing or reversing.

Specific risk strategies

Like sector risk, the most obvious strategy for dealing with specific risk is to match specific risk to your risk profile. Clearly, some shares are more volatile (and risky) than others. If you want to minimise specific risk, investing only a small amount of your available capital in the more risky shares (or avoiding them entirely) makes sense. If your risk tolerance is higher, you can consider a portfolio with a mix of relatively safe and relatively risky shares. If you refer to table 6.2 (in chapter 6), you'll see a hypothetical investment mix for various risk profiles.

In my opinion, the more volatile (and hence risky) shares include:

- Shares issued by companies that don't have good fundamentals—in particular those that fail your 'health test' (as outlined in chapter 8).

- Companies running at a loss (not making a profit). Unless the business can stage a turnaround, inevitably it will run out of funds and go bankrupt. Meanwhile, it's trading on 'blue sky' and that's always a risky proposition.

- Low market cap shares in general.

- Shares in a downtrend with no indication of an upside trend change.

- IPOs—unless they're a float of a very sound and well-established business.

- New technology and resource exploration companies where sustainable earnings will occur at some time in the future only when (and if) the new technology or exploration results in a profitable product and a positive cash flow. The risk is that, in the meantime, the company may simply run out of money and be forced into liquidation before any positive cash flow occurs.

- Companies with business activities primarily in an overseas country where the political climate is unstable.

- Companies with earnings highly dependent on weather or other factors beyond managements's control.

- Companies with earnings closely tied to a few customers. The danger here is that if a major customer doesn't renew a contract and takes their business elsewhere, the company will suffer greatly.

- Illiquid shares—because you may not be able to sell at a reasonable price if you want to, due to there simply being no buyers.

Also beware of irrational optimism, which often occurs with individual shares as well as the market as a whole. I suggest you be cautious when you see a share price divert upward for some time away from the longer term trendline or when the PE rises skyward to a level that can't be sustained by profits.

Like market and sector risk, a more advanced strategy for dealing with specific risk is to hedge by trading put warrants or options over your shares, but this strategy is recommended only for the experienced and more risk tolerant traders. Also, options and warrants are not available over all shares, only a selection of the higher cap and liquid ones.

Using risk management strategies to your advantage

In the following sections, I outline some general strategies you may find useful for managing share investing risks and hopefully reduce the stress associated with risk and uncertainty.

Diversification

Diversification is based on the well-known idea of 'not putting all your eggs in one basket' and sharing risk rather than concentrating it. Most diversification occurs when you spread your capital over different asset classes such as cash, fixed interest, property, Australian shares and international shares. This strategy is used by most managed funds, investment funds and investment companies, but the average investor doesn't usually have the funds or expertise to diversify directly to this extent. However, diversifying this way indirectly is possible by investing in managed funds, index funds or investment companies that use this type of strategy.

Diversification applied to a share portfolio means spreading your investment capital between different shares in different sectors. In this way, possible losses in some shares can be offset by gains in others. In fact (as demonstrated in learning exercise 13.19), with good cash management, you can make a profit even when you have as many losers as winners in a sideways trending market.

The relationship between risk and diversification with shares can be expressed mathematically by what's known as *tracking error*. This is actually the probable deviation between the change in value of a portfolio and the change in value of the market as a whole. As you'd expect, tracking error reduces as the number of stocks in a portfolio increases, but as the number increases, the law of diminishing returns kicks in and increasingly less benefit occurs. This effect is shown in figure 13.4.

From figure 13.4, you can see that for a low tracking error (less than 5%), you need to hold at least 10 different shares. Ideal diversification occurs when the market value of each parcel of shares is the same. For example, if your portfolio has a total market value of $100 000 and you own 10

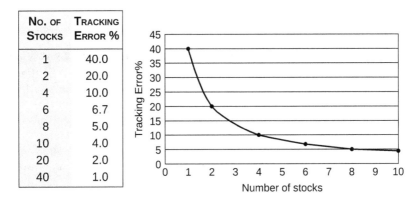

No. of Stocks	Tracking Error %
1	40.0
2	20.0
4	10.0
6	6.7
8	5.0
10	4.0
20	2.0
40	1.0

Figure 13.4: Tracking error

different shares, the market value of each would be $10 000. In practice, ideal balance isn't attainable because share prices fluctuate all the time and it's impractical to constantly re-jig your portfolio to keep the value of each parcel the same.

As well as diversifying the shares in your portfolio, you can also diversify by holding shares in companies that are themselves diversified—that is, they have a range of different products and markets. This provides some internal diversification because a downturn in one product or market shouldn't have a major effect on profits. Historically, internal diversification has been generally successful when a business doesn't diversify too far away from its core competencies. Otherwise, it can be disastrous, particularly when companies take over others with very different products or when they foray into overseas markets with very different conditions from those in Australia.

Advantages and disadvantages of diversification

Diversification undoubtedly reduces the risk that a portfolio will underperform the general market, but there's also a downside: diversification reduces the likelihood that a portfolio will outperform the general market. If you concentrate your portfolio in a small number of high-performing shares, you may be able to beat the market. On the other hand, if these shares underperform, you'll do worse than the market. So it's up to you which way you want to go, but I suggest a portfolio of at least 10 different shares in diverse sectors is a good option if you're a long-term investor (and you want to sleep well at night).

Share partnerships

Another way of reducing the risk of share investing is to belong to a share investing club or partnership. This means you don't shoulder all the risk but share it with others.

The advantages of share partnerships include:

- More capital is available—for example, a club with 10 investors contributing $5000 each has a cash pool of $50 000 to invest.

- Risk is shared—clearly with 10 investors, each investor is bearing only 10% of the overall risk.

- You can bounce ideas around with others and obtain fresh insights and viewpoints. This can be an enjoyable experience as well as an opportunity to broaden your horizons, and tends to prevent you from getting 'into a rut'.

- You get into a disciplined routine of reviewing the performance of the portfolio regularly.

The disadvantages are:

- It takes time (and some cost) to set up a partnership agreement, open a partnership bank account, and obtain a tax file number.

- The partnership must file a separate tax return.

- You need to commit to attending meetings that may not always be held at a convenient time or venue for you (unless internet group conferencing is a feasible option).

Establish a worst-case scenario

A well-known method of minimising the stress associated with risk and uncertainty is to establish a worst-case scenario and come to terms with it. This method can be applied to share investing where, theoretically, the worst-case scenario with any share is that the company will go bankrupt and you'll lose all the money you've invested. This can be a realistic scenario with a penny-dreadful speculative stock but I think you'll agree that it's not a realistic one with blue or green chip shares such as Woolworths, BHP or Commonwealth Bank.

However, it's actually a good idea to use this method before you buy shares in any company. The idea is to try to establish a lowest feasible price should things go pear-shaped and compare this price to the current price. Then you can estimate the maximum loss that could feasibly occur and use this to tailor the amount you'll invest in the shares. This will automatically prevent you from investing large amounts in speculative shares.

You can also apply this idea to an existing portfolio and, if you do so, reducing your holding in some shares and/or increasing it in others may be prudent.

Downside/upside potential

Another risk management strategy with shares is to establish a realistic downside and upside potential for any share. This is best considered when you contemplate purchase, but it can be completed at any time you're reviewing your portfolio. One way you can establish realistic down and upside potentials is to examine the price chart and see if you can identify support levels and resistance levels. The difference between the current price and the support level is the downside potential and the difference between the current price and the resistance level is the upside potential. Then you can calculate the ratio between the upside and downside potential. Ideally, the ratio should be in the order of 2:1 or more and the higher it is, the greater the likelihood of capital gain and the lower the risk of capital loss.

If you cannot establish clear support and resistance levels, another way of estimating upside and downside potentials is from the 52-week high and low values. For example, consider a share currently trading for $26.70, where the 52-week high was $35.05 and the 52-week low was $22.85. Using these values as probable future price limits, the upside potential is $8.35 and the downside potential is $3.85. The ratio between them is 2.2, which is greater than 2, and so indicates a relatively low risk investment with greater potential for gain than loss.

Notes

- While greater potential for capital gains exists when a share is trading close to its 52-week low, you need to ensure it's not doing so because the price is in a downtrend mode.

- If you buy a share after you've identified support and resistance levels, you should consider selling should the support level be breached some time in the future, because it's usually indicative of a change in investor sentiment and the start of a downturn.

Sequential trading

If you maintain a constant parcel value when you trade, and your winning trades and losing trades balance, at the end of the day you will break even (apart from trading costs). However, if you trade sequentially, this logical result changes and you will actually lose overall even when your winning and losing trades balance one another. You're trading sequentially if you buy shares that go up in price, then sell them and re-invest all your capital from that sale in your next share purchase. For example, say you buy $2000 worth of shares. Some time later, the price increases by 50% and you sell the shares for $3000. You're trading sequentially if you now re-invest the full $3000 in your next trade. If your next trade is a profitable one, sequential trading will increase your profit. But if your next trade is a losing one and the price goes down by the same percentage amount as your previous trade went up, you will make a greater loss by trading sequentially.

The additional risk with sequential trading is an inbuilt mathematical risk that's not dependent on the shares traded. To understand the added risk, assume that the next parcel of shares goes down in price by the same amount as the first ones went up—namely, 50%. Do you break even? No—you make a loss of $500 because you'll get only $1500 from the last sale! So while your second investment went down by the same relative amount as the first one went up, you end up making a loss on the combined transaction!

You can avoid the inbuilt mathematical risk associated with sequential trading by not trading sequentially. Going back to my scenario, if on the second trade you invest only the original amount of $2000 and put the profit of $1000 from your first trade aside in your investment cash pool, you'll break even if the next trade is a 50% loss one.

Interestingly, the order of the wins and losses doesn't matter—if you lose 50% on your first trade and gain 50% on the next trade, you still end up with the same $500 loss! So if your first trade is a losing one and your capital is down to $1000, you will have to draw $1000 from your investment cash pool so that your next trade maintains the same parcel value as the first trade, namely $2000. This is another reason you need to maintain some liquid cash in your investment cash pool at all times.

Note

The risk associated with sequential trading applies to any form of investment or gambling/gaming. For example, if you place a gambling bet and win but then put all your winnings on the next bet and that loses, you will lose all your initial cash. But if you had pocketed the profits from the first bet, and bet only the same amount on the next one, you would end up with some cash—namely, the profit you pocketed from your first bet. The same applies to poker machines—if you are lucky enough to strike a jackpot or get a substantial payout early in the play and you pocket the profit (or most of it), you can walk away with cash in your pocket. But if you keep ploughing your winnings back into the machine (sequential trading), you will inevitably walk away with nothing.

Averaging

As discussed in chapter 10, averaging is a trading strategy where you don't buy or sell all shares in a single parcel, but break your trades up into smaller parcels that are bought or sold at different times.

Averaging is essentially a risk management strategy because it reduces the volatility (and risk) associated with daily price movements. It's another way you can reduce risk by 'not putting all your eggs in one basket'—in this case, it's a time basket. Depending on how the market moves, averaging could increase or decrease profitability but certainly your trading costs will be higher because the total brokerage on several smaller parcels will be higher than the brokerage on a single larger parcel.

Conditional orders

Another risk management strategy is to use conditional or deferred execution orders. These are orders where your order doesn't immediately go to market but is placed some time later and then only if some prior conditions that you've set are attained (trigger points). The most common conditional orders are stop loss orders, designed to limit losses should prices downturn. Profit stops can also be considered a risk management tool because once you've sold shares for a profit, you've eliminated the risk of losing that profit should the price subsequently downturn.

As I outlined in chapter 10, conditional orders of all types have both advantages and disadvantages. In particular, stop losses can be an effective risk management tool especially in times of high market volatility and particularly for your more speculative shares.

Cash management

Most investors expend a great deal of effort in choosing the right shares for their portfolios but, contrary to popular opinion, the mix of shares in a portfolio is not necessarily the most critical factor in determining profitability. Sound cash management is far more critical than share selection and if you apply a sound cash management strategy with a diversified portfolio of shares, it's possible to show a good profit even in a trendless market. This is illustrated in learning exercise 13.19.

Cash management is an important aspect of risk management because investing risk has two components:

1. the likelihood (or probability) of a loss

2. the amount of the loss, should it occur.

Highest risk occurs with a high likelihood of a high loss, and lowest risk occurs with a low likelihood of a low loss. In between are many possible combinations that have various levels of risk, between high and low. To see how the amount of the loss affects the risk, consider the following example.

Example

Imagine you're considering two investments, A and B. Investment A has a 20% likelihood of losing all capital invested whereas B has a 5% likelihood.

Considering only the likelihood of loss, A is clearly more risky than B. But suppose you invested $1000 in A and $10000 in B—which is the more risky investment now?

To work this out, you need to calculate the probable loss:

- For A, the probable loss is $0.2 \times 1000 = \$200$.

- For B, the probable loss is $0.05 \times 10000 = \$500$.

Now you can see that even though B has a lower likelihood of loss, because more capital is invested, it's a more risky investment than A. From this follows an important risk management strategy that you can adopt with shares:

Invest less in the more risky shares and more in the less risky ones.

This strategy underpins table 6.2 (in chapter 6), where the hypothetical investment mix is shown based on the risk profile of the investor and riskiness of the shares. You may wish to review this table now.

The percentage capital rule

Another strategy based on cash management is to limit the downside potential on any single parcel of shares you trade (or hold) to only a small amount of your total investment capital. This is often expressed as a percentage capital rule—otherwise known as a *1% rule* or a *2% rule*. While many traders use the 2% rule, the 1% rule provides a higher margin of safety but is not always feasible.

The 1% rule is:

Limit the downside potential on any trade or parcel of shares you hold to no more than 1% of your total investment capital.

The percentage capital rule is most applicable when you consider purchasing shares, but you may be able to use it with some (or all) of the shares in your portfolio. A practically foolproof way of using it is to place stop loss orders where you set the trigger points so that if the stop loss activates, the maximum amount of loss on the trade will be no more than

1% of your investment capital. You can also use this strategy by monitoring your shares regularly and placing sell orders when the price falls and your loss approaches the 1% limit.

Example

Say your total investment capital is $50 000 and you've just bought a parcel of 2500 shares at a price of $2 each, so the trade value is $5000.

Using the 1% rule to set a stop loss limit price, you need to limit your loss on any trade to $500 because this is 1% of your capital.

The parcel value of the shares just purchased is $5000, and you own 2500 shares, so you need to ensure that you don't lose more than 20¢ per share. At the current price of $2.00, your stop loss price is $1.80. This is also a realistic stop loss price because it represents a 10% fall in the current price.

Effect on parcel value

In the preceding example, applying the 1% rule with a realistic 10% stop loss was no problem because the parcel value of the shares you purchased was only 10% of your investment capital. This principle can be stated as a risk management strategy as follows:

> **Limit the parcel value of any shares you buy or hold to no more than 10% of your investment capital.**

In order to apply this strategy you need good diversification with at least 10 different shares in your portfolio of approximately equal value. In this case, no parcel of shares has a value greater than around 10% of your investment capital.

If the parcel value of any shares is less than 10% of your investment capital, you have an extra margin of safety because a 10% stop loss will reduce the potential loss to less than 1% of your investment capital. However, if the parcel value of any shares is greater than 10%, you can't apply this strategy directly. In this case, you have two possible options:

1. Use a higher percentage rule—perhaps a 2% rule or even higher. If you do this, you've reduced your margin of safety and increased your possible loss.

2. Set a stop loss limit of less than 10% of the share price—for example, a fall in price of 5%. If you do this, you don't reduce your safety margin but you increase the risk of being stopped out on a relatively small price fall.

Clearly, neither of these options provides a really satisfactory solution to the dilemma. If you use a higher percentage rule, you can lose more than 1% of your capital on a price fall, and if you use a lower stop loss margin, you increase the risk of being stopped out on a small price fall that may not really be significant.

To summarise these points, in table 13.2 I've shown how the 1% rule and 10% stop loss limit apply for various parcel values. I've assumed an investment capital of $100 000. Therefore, using the 1% rule, the maximum loss on any parcel is $1000.

You can see that you can use the 1% rule with a 10% stop loss if the parcel value of any shares is 10% or less of your investment capital. With a 5% parcel value, you've doubled your margin of safety, because if the 10% stop loss triggers, your loss will be only half the maximum loss allowed by the 1% rule. However, with a 20% parcel value, you can't apply the 1% rule with a 10% stop loss because a 10% price fall will produce a loss that's double that indicated by the 1% rule.

Table 13.2: Parcel values and stop loss limits

Parcel value of the shares	Percentage of investment capital in these shares	Maximum loss on this parcel using a 10% stop loss
$5 000	5%	$500
$10 000	10%	$1000
$20 000	20%	$2000

Note

I strongly suggest you work out these critical values for your own portfolio, according to the total value of the portfolio and the individual parcel value of each of the shares in it.

Learning exercises

13.1　As a share investor trading ordinary shares only, outline a strategy that may enable you to take advantage of a major market downturn to eventually show a profit.

13.2　What are suitable strategies for a long-term investor in the following situations?

　　a.　Prior to a market downturn

　　b.　During a downturn

　　c.　After a downturn ends and the market rises

13.3

　　a.　What are two ways you may be able to anticipate a market downturn before it occurs?

　　b.　If a market downturn occurs, should you buy some more shares and, if so, when is the best time to do so?

13.4　Draw a freehand graph showing a typical market index (or stock price) trending upward. On this graph, illustrate what's meant by irrational optimism. If irrational optimism does occur, also show on your graph what's likely to follow.

13.5

　　a.　What's one of the main reasons shares are popularly regarded as being risky?

　　b.　What are the three main groups of risk with shares?

13.6　You buy some shares, hold them for a year and then sell for the same price as you bought them. Give two reasons (apart from transaction costs) why you didn't really break even but lost money.

13.7

　　a.　What's meant by the volatility of an investment?

　　b.　What's the relationship between volatility and investment risk?

    c. How can you obtain a visual impression of volatility?

    d. What are two ways volatility can be measured mathematically?

    e. What are two important types of volatility that apply to shares?

13.8 What's a three-pronged approach you can use in order to manage share-investing risks?

13.9 Indicate how Pareto's principle (80/20 rule) applies to share prices and how it indicates that a hold strategy can be a good one.

13.10 What are some of the less volatile and more volatile sectors of the Australian market?

13.11 What are some of the more volatile (and hence risky) shares?

13.12

    a. What's meant by diversification as applied to risk management with shares?

    b. How many different stocks should you have in your portfolio in order to obtain good diversification?

    c. How can you obtain diversification with a single share?

    d. What's meant by company diversification?

    e. What's a possible downside to diversification of a share portfolio?

13.13 What's meant by sequential trading and how can you avoid the risk associated with it?

13.14 The statistics shown in the following table are applicable to two industrial shares:

	52-week high	52-week low	Volatility (%)
Share A	8.2¢	1.8¢	
Share B	$13.25	$9.12	

Complete the table, showing the price volatility of these two shares using the volatility formula. Draw conclusions.

13.15 Explain how you can use CAPM theory to your advantage to reduce risks and increase returns if the market is in either a bear phase or a bull phase.

13.16 Consider two shares, A and B, with prices and support and resistance levels as shown in the following table.

Share	Price	Support	Resistance	Downside potential	Upside potential	Ratio up/down
A	$1.86	$1.75	$2.11			
B	$5.34	$5.00	$5.60			

Complete this table and identify the downside and upside potential risk, and whether either of these shares appears to offer a good opportunity for investment.

13.17 You buy $5000 worth of XYZ shares for $1.25. Some time later, the share price rises to $1.65 and you sell. You then buy ABC shares for $0.64 but, unfortunately, the price drops and you sell at $0.54.

Calculate your total profit/loss and compare them in each of the two scenarios:

a. Same parcel size

b. Sequential trading

Note: For this exercise, ignore trading costs and round off your calculations to whole numbers of dollars or shares.

13.18 The current value of your share portfolio is $54342 and you now buy 2500 shares at a price of $3.26.

a. Decide the stop loss price for these shares using the 1% rule.

b. What percentage loss would occur on these shares if the stop loss activates?

c. Is this a realistic stop loss price? If not, suggest an alternative.

Note: For the purpose of this exercise ignore trading costs.

13.19 You have $20 000 to invest in shares. You decide to buy 10 parcels of shares for your portfolio, investing $2000 in each. You decide to adopt a simple trading strategy where if a share price drops by 10%, you'll sell; otherwise, you'll hold. Using the letters A to J to denote these shares, after one year the situation is as follows:

- A up 50%

- B up 20%

- C up 10 %

- D up 5%

- E no move

- F no move

- G down 5%

- H down 10%

- I down 20%

- J down 50%

Note: This is an example of a sideways-trending market where the up and down movements are equally balanced.

Calculate the capital gain or loss using the trading strategy you've adopted and compare it to what it would have been had you adopted a buy and hold (bottom drawer) strategy. For the purpose of this exercise, neglect trading costs.

13.20 Using any method you like, use random selection to choose 20 or so different shares for a portfolio. Write down these shares and their prices on a sheet of paper (or spreadsheet) and put the paper away. Wait six months or more and then write down the prices at this later time. Calculate the capital gains or losses assuming you adopted a buy and hold strategy and also the simple cash management strategy outlined in learning exercise 13.19 with equal purchase parcel values. How did this random portfolio fare? Did it do better or worse than your own portfolio? Which strategy proved best? What have you learnt from this exercise?

Note: Another way you can obtain a random diverse portfolio is to obtain a sector listing of shares and pick one or two at random from each sector.

13.21 If you have a way of obtaining share purchase recommendations or tips, repeat learning exercise 13.20, but this time select a portfolio of shares based on the recommendations. Was the result better or worse than the random selection method?

Learning exercises solutions

13.1   You may be able to profit from a major market downturn if you sell some shares as soon as you sense the downturn is imminent and so accumulate cash. You can then wait until the market starts to recover (as inevitably it will), and buy good-quality shares at low prices. In this way, you should be able to show a good profit as the market rises.

13.2   Suitable strategies are:

a.   *Prior to a downturn:* Sell some shares and accumulate cash.

b.   *During a downturn:* Sit tight and accumulate cash.

c.   *After a downturn as the market rises:* Buy good quality shares at low prices with the cash you've accumulated.

13.3

a.   Two ways of anticipating a market downturn are:

» *From a market index chart:* Look for trend change indications and signs of irrational optimism.

» *From the average market PE:* Irrational optimism is also detectable when the average market PE rises significantly above the long-term average (traditionally about 16).

b.   If a market downturn occurs you shouldn't buy shares straight away. You should wait until you are sure the bounce isn't just a 'dead cat' bounce and that the market has definitely broken out of the downturn phase and is starting to rise again.

13.4   Please refer to figures 13.1 and 13.2 for examples of how your graph could look.

13.5

a.   One of the main reasons shares may be considered as risky is because the stock market receives a huge amount of publicity. Market fluctuations and share prices are reported on a daily basis so people tend to focus on the short-term volatility of shares rather than considering the long-term picture.

    b. The three main groups of risks with shares are:

       1. market risk

       2. sector risk

       3. specific risk.

13.6   You actually lost money for the following reasons:

    » Inflation has eroded the purchasing power of the capital you've had tied up in the investment.

    » While your money was tied up in a non-productive investment, you incurred an 'opportunity cost', which is the interest you could have received had you deposited the money in an interest-bearing account.

13.7

    a. The volatility of an investment is the extent of the up and down swings in value.

    b. The relationship between volatility and investment risk is that the higher the volatility, the greater the risk.

    c. You can obtain a visual impression of volatility from a chart by looking at the extent of the up and down swings.

    d. Two ways volatility can be measured mathematically are by the standard deviation and by the range (highest to lowest values).

    e. Two important types of volatility that apply to shares are price volatility and earnings volatility.

13.8   A three-pronged approach you can use is:

    1. be aware of the risks and their significance

    2. have good risk management strategies in place to control the risks

    3. apply a disciplined approach and stick to your strategies without allowing emotion to cause you to deviate from them.

13.9   Pareto's principle indicates that the majority of market price growth occurs on a small number of trading days. So a hold strategy can be a good one because if you're out of the market on these days you miss the action and won't be able to profit from the major price increases.

13.10 Generally speaking, the less volatile sectors include:

» banks (if the majority of the income is from secured loans)

» property trusts

» alcohol and tobacco

» gambling/gaming (if not internet based)

» infrastructure/utilities

» manufacturing and retailing of consumer staples.

The more volatile sectors include:

» mining exploration

» tourism and leisure

» biotechnology

» telecommunications

» internet and new technology.

13.11 In my opinion, the more volatile (and hence risky) shares include:

» shares issued by companies that don't have good fundamentals

» shares in companies that aren't making a profit

» low market cap stocks

» shares in a downtrend or sideways trending mode relative to the market as a whole with no indication of an upside trend change

» IPOs—unless they're a float of a very sound and well-established business

» new technology and resource exploration

» companies with earnings that are highly dependent upon weather or other factors beyond management's control

» companies that rely heavily on a few customers

» illiquid shares.

13.12

a. Diversification applied to risk management with shares means that you should spread the risk by holding a diverse portfolio of shares.

b. You should have at least 10 different shares in your portfolio in order to obtain good diversification.

c. You can obtain diversification with a single share if you buy a listed investment company or listed managed fund.

d. Company diversification occurs when the company diversifies its products and markets.

e. A possible downside to diversification is that the portfolio won't beat the market. The only way of beating the market is to concentrate.

13.13 Sequential trading occurs when you reinvest all the cash obtained from the proceeds of a sale on your next trade. You avoid the risk by maintaining the same parcel value of each trade.

13.14 See the following completed table.

	52-week high	52-week low	Volatility (%)
Share A	8.2¢	1.8¢	356
Share B	$13.25	$9.12	45

Conclusion: Clearly, share A is far more volatile than share B.

13.15 CAPM theory indicates that if the market is in a bear phase, you can reduce losses by concentrating your portfolio on low volatility shares and when the market is in a bull phase, you can increase your returns by concentrating your portfolio on high volatility shares.

13.16 See the following completed table.

Share	Price	Support	Resistance	Downside potential	Upside potential	Ratio up/down
A	$1.86	$1.75	$2.11	$0.11	$0.25	2.27
B	$5.34	$5.00	$5.60	$0.34	$0.26	0.76

By this method of evaluating the risk, share A clearly presents better profit potential than B because of the higher upside/

downside ratio. Indeed, you'd be wise not to invest in shares B unless you're very confident that a strong uptrend is in place.

13.17 The solutions for each scenario are as follows:

    a. Same parcel size:

You buy 4000 XYZ shares at a cost of $5000.

You sell for $1.65 and get $6600.

Profit on this transaction is $1600.

You buy $5000 ÷ $0.64 = 7813 ABC shares.

Selling them obtains 7813 × $0.54 = $4219.

Loss on this transaction is $5000 − $4219 = $781.

Overall profit is $1600 − $781 = **$819**.

    b. Sequential trading:

Your investment capital is now $6600.

You buy $6600 ÷ $0.64 = 10312 ABC shares.

Selling them obtains 10312 × $0.54 = $5569.

Overall profit is $5569 − $5000 = $569.

The difference in profit is $819 − $569 = **$250**.

That is, you make $250 more profit by not sequentially trading.

13.18

    a. Your outlay for the new shares is 2500 × $3.26 = $8150.

Your portfolio will now be valued at $54342 + $8150 = $62492

Using the 1% rule, the maximum you should lose on these shares is $625.

The minimum you should obtain should the stop loss activate is $8150 − $625 = $7525.

Therefore, your stop loss price is $7525 ÷ 2500 = **$3.01**.

    b. Loss per share for a sale at this price is $3.26 − $3.01 = $0.25

Percentage down stop loss point is
$0.25 \div 3.26 \times 100 = \mathbf{7.67\%}$.

   c. This is not a very realistic stop loss price because
you could easily be stopped out on price falls that
aren't really significant. In this case, it would be
better to use a stop loss price of 10% down, which
would be $0.1 \times \$3.26 = \$0.33$ down, or a price of
$\$3.26 - \$0.33 = \$2.93$. Note that this provides less
protection than provided by the 1% rule.

13.19 If you had adopted a buy and hold strategy, you would have
finished the year with a brea-even result because the rises
and falls would have been balanced.

The result of using your cash management strategy is
summarised in the following table. You have now made a
profit of $1000. This illustrates the importance of good cash
management because even in a sideways trending market
with as many losers as winners, you've still shown a profit on
your portfolio.

Share	Invested ($)	Price move during year	Sell (S) or hold (H)	P/L ($)
A	2000	+50%	H	1000
B	2000	+20%	H	400
C	2000	+10%	H	200
D	2000	+5%	H	100
E	2000	0	H	0
F	2000	0	H	0
G	2000	−5%	H	−100
H	2000	−10%	S	−200
I	2000	−20%	S at −10%	−200
J	2000	−50%	S at −10%	−200
Total	20 000		Total	1000

13.20 and 13.21 You may be surprised at what these exercises reveal.
In any case, before you decide to subscribe to any advisory service, it
is worthwhile testing the recommendations over a period of time with a
paper portfolio based on them.

Chapter 14

Monitoring and improving performance

Setting up a good portfolio of shares is important, but just as important is properly managing your portfolio. In this chapter, I discuss how you can do this efficiently and effectively.

Comparing systematic and ad-hoc approaches

You can manage your shares in one of two ways. One way is a disciplined approach in which you follow a system that you planned. Another way is a non-systematic one, otherwise known as an 'ad hoc' approach. It's not planned and proactive, but is instead based on gut feelings and knee-jerk responses to stimuli. A stimulus is a change of some type that provokes you into considering a response to it; for example, a 'hot tip' or media report, receiving cash (such as from a tax refund), needing cash, a change in market sentiment or simply a change in your mood.

I've illustrated the ad-hoc approach as a flow chart in figure 14.1 (overleaf).

Figure 14.1: Ad-hoc approach to share investing

I suspect that many investors use this approach (for at least some of the time) but, probably needless to say, it's not one I'd recommend—especially for a long-term investor. Instead, I suggest a systematic approach, as illustrated in the flow chart in figure 14.2.

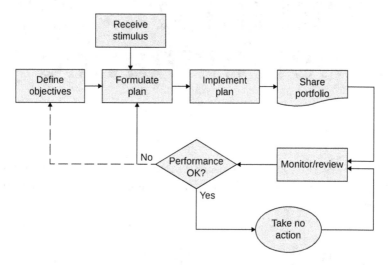

Figure 14.2: Systematic approach to share investing

The systematic approach is as follows:

- define your objectives

- formulate a plan that allows you to achieve your objectives

- implement your plan and set up your share portfolio

- monitor and review your portfolio on a regular basis.

If you're happy with the performance of your portfolio when you review it, well and good; if not, consider what you should do. You may need to sell some shares, buy some more shares in stocks currently in your portfolio or buy some shares you don't currently own. You may need to go back to your plan and see what might be changed in order to improve performance. You might even need to go right back and review your objectives and perhaps make some changes—this eventuality is shown by the dashed line in figure 14.2. However, the golden rule is that you shouldn't change any objectives unless you've given your plan a good trial; otherwise, you're quitting too soon. As I pointed out in chapter 6, you shouldn't change your plan unless you have given it a fair trial.

No doubt you'll receive stimulus from time to time but in the systematic approach, you don't react to it in a knee-jerk fashion. Instead, you refer to your plan and see whether or not the stimulus fits into your plan. Then you can decide whether or not you will act on it.

Note

If you already have a portfolio of shares, you can't really apply the systematic approach to it from the beginning. However, you can apply a systematic approach to your future trades and review your current portfolio in a systematic fashion.

Emotional and rational responses

You can see that the essential difference between the ad-hoc and systematic approaches is that the ad-hoc approach is an emotional one whereas the systematic approach is a rational one. As I have often pointed out, the less emotional you can be in your share trading and investing, the greater your likelihood of success. Because the systematic approach is rational rather than emotional, in the long run it will give the best results so I strongly suggest you adopt it.

Keeping good records

An important aspect of a systematic approach is to have a proper record-keeping system. The three main reasons for this are:

1. You need relevant information about shares you own or have traded so you can refer to this when you're evaluating your performance. If you don't have a good record-keeping system, you mightn't have

the information you need, or if you do have it somewhere, you might waste a lot of time searching.

2. You need records of capital gains and dividends for income tax purposes.

3. If shares are part of your estate, your executors need records of all transactions for shares owned at the time of your death (no matter how long ago the shares were acquired).

Electronic or paper documents?

At this point, you need to decide whether you will keep records in electronic form or as paper documents. This is a matter of personal preference. When you buy shares you don't already own, the registry will usually send you an information sheet and some documentation where you complete your banking details for dividends, your tax file number and preferences for receiving company information—namely, whether electronically or in hard copy form. If you elect to receive information and statements electronically, I strongly suggest you keep a copy on an external storage device. Another option is to print the documents and have both electronic and hard copies because this provides excellent security.

Notes

- Companies and share registries usually try to persuade investors to opt for electronic information because this eliminates delays and is far cheaper than hard copy especially for bulky documents like annual reports.

- Because the annual report is so expensive to produce, many companies have the information in summary form or as a chairman's address to shareholders. For the average investor, a full annual report is not usually warranted. As a shareholder, if you reduce company expenses, the benefits should flow back to you in the form of increased profitability.

Maintaining records

Another decision you need to make is whether you will keep your own records or leave this to others, such as your broker, share registry or even the ATO. All your transactions will be on file with your broker, and all dividend payment will be on file with the relevant share registry. This information is available to the ATO since your TFN is known to both your broker and the share registry. In fact, nowadays if you opt to submit an online income tax return, the ATO will already have many details pre-filled on your tax return so you don't need to submit any additional information other than capital gains or losses.

All these developments are very convenient, but I believe it is still important to maintain your own records so you can access them at any time. Some of the important information you may want to keep on file include:

- contract notes for all your trades

- share holding statements. If you've elected to join the CHESS system, you'll receive a CHESS holding statement for each different share you own with your HIN stated. If you're not in the CHESS system, you'll receive holding statements with your SRN stated. If your shareholding changes because you buy or sell shares or receive shares in lieu of dividends in a DRP, your holding statement will be updated

- dividend statements for all dividends received

- important company information such as shareholder briefing or newsletters and directors' reports or annual reports.

In addition, you may wish to keep on file summaries such as a trading summary, dividend summary and profit/loss summary (discussed in more detail later in this chapter).

Document filing system

If you elect to receive paper documents, I suggest you keep them in a metal hanging file cabinet or expanding paper file. I maintain the following files:

- A trading file, where I record all my trades and also copies of all contract notes

- A separate file for each of the shares I own, which contains all documents relevant to those shares (other than contract notes), such as dividend statements, DRP summaries and hard copies of any significant information I want to retain for future reference

- A single 'Sold Shares' file for all shares sold. Because I keep contract notes in a separate file, the only records I really need here are dividend statements. However, I often retain other information in this file for my own reference—for example, CHESS statements

- A file for my portfolio spreadsheet, my profit/loss spreadsheet and my dividend summaries (discussed later in this chapter).

Trading file

I maintain all trading information in one file. This is very useful because I can go back many years and check my buy and sell prices and number of shares traded. The contract note for each trade contains all the essential information about the trade and I file these contract notes in date order sequence in this file. I list a summary of all trades in date order on a single page in front of the contract notes and when the page is full I start another. The trading summary is of the format shown in table 14.1. This should be self-explanatory, but I've included some additional details in the 'Notes'.

Table 14.1: Trading summary

Date	Name	Code	Number	Price $	$ Bought	$ Sold

Notes

- The amount shown in the '$ Bought' and '$ Sold' columns is the net amount after trading costs have been included, rounded off to the nearest dollar.

- When I've participated in a share offer or buy back, I also record these transactions in the trading summary.

- I compile the summary manually but it could be formatted as a computer spreadsheet.

- Your broker should also have a record of all your trades but I like to keep my own summary.

- At the end of each financial year, I can use the trading summary to calculate taxable capital gains. I draw a red line under the last transaction each financial year and then go back to the previous red line and extract details of shares sold during the financial year. If any of these shares were received through participation in a DRP, I extract details from my DRP summary.

DRP summary

When you receive shares through a DRP, recording the date, number and price for each parcel of shares is important. Also, if you sell some (but not all) of your shares in a stock, you need to know which shares you sold and which you held because the parcel values will be different. If you're in the CHESS system, you'll receive a new CHESS statement every time the number of shares changes, but this statement won't show prices.

I file a DRP summary in the relevant file for each of my shares. The format of this summary is shown in table 14.2 and should be self-explanatory, but I've included some additional notes.

Table 14.2: DRP summary

Date	Number	Total number	Price	Cost	Total cost

Notes

- The 'Number' column shows the number of shares allocated in lieu of the cash dividend.

- The 'Total number' column shows the total number of shares now held after the allocation and this should match the number shown in the new CHESS statement and in your broker's records.

- The 'Price' column shows the allocation price of this parcel of shares.

- The 'Cost' column shows the allocation cost of this parcel, as shown in the dividend statement. This is equal to the allocation price multiplied by the number of shares received. It's seldom exactly equal to the amount of the dividend because you can't receive a fraction of a share. Although you didn't actually buy these shares, the accounting cost to you is the dollar amount of the cash dividend forgone by receiving these shares instead of cash.

- The 'Total cost' column shows the total cost of all shares received. If I sell some (but not all) of these shares, I record this as a separate transaction and adjust the quantity and total cost columns accordingly. The total cost is a very useful statistic because you can see at a glance your up-to-the-minute capital gains or losses on these shares.

Dividend summary

If you own a reasonable number of dividend-paying shares, it may be very useful (particularly at tax time or when calculating your profit/loss) to maintain a dividend summary for each financial year. You can do this manually or use a computer spreadsheet program that calculates new totals automatically after each new entry. When you receive a dividend, fill out one of the lines in the summary before you file the dividend statement.

A suitable layout for such a spreadsheet is shown in table 14.3.

Table 14.3: Dividend summary

Date	Shares	Code	Div. (uf)	Div. (f)	Franking credit
	Total				

Portfolio spreadsheet

A portfolio spreadsheet shows all the shares you own with current prices and values as well as total value. In some cases, it may also show the original purchase price and cost. If you keep records of your portfolio, you can compare the most current portfolio to a previous one and know immediately how your portfolio has fared. If you wish, you can also record a market index and compare your performance relative to the index. You can refer to and update your portfolio as often as you wish but if you are not a very active trader, once a week will probably suffice.

If you trade online, your broking site should have this facility available as a no extra cost feature. If you don't trade online but have access to the internet, some sites offer a portfolio facility. If you use this facility, clearly the site won't know your trades and you need to update the portfolio when you trade shares or receive shares through a DRP.

Even though I can access my portfolio on my broker's website, I still keep my own portfolio print out each time I update my portfolio. Duplicating data readily available may seem like a waste of time and effort, but there are several good reasons why I like to do this:

- Updating my spreadsheet each week focuses my attention on my shares on a regular basis. This is an important discipline for me because I'm not an active trader — rather, I'm a longer-term investor with many other interests and commitments apart from shares.

- I file the spreadsheets in date order sequence in a dedicated file. As each spreadsheet is only a single-page weekly printout, I can keep many years of data in a single file. This provides a very useful permanent record that I can refer back to at any time (and I've often needed to do so). I could also maintain the spreadsheet in an electronic file but I like to look at a hard copy.

- I can include additional information in the spreadsheet that's not in an online or broker's portfolio, such as dividend franking levels, stop loss levels and also any comments I want to make about the shares.

Table 14.4 (overleaf) shows a simplified portfolio spreadsheet with essential information included. However, I use a more complex spreadsheet and if you want to see the full version, please refer to my online investing book.

Table 14.4: Portfolio spreadsheet

Date	xxxx	All Ords	xxxx				
Name	Code	Number	Price ($)	Value ($)	Div type	Stop ($)	Comments
XYZ company	XYZ	12564	1.13	14197	DRP (ff)	1.02	Watch for trend reversal
Total				xxxxx			

Notes

- It is most convenient to list your shares in alphabetical order.

- At the top of the spreadsheet, include the date (shown in table 14.4 as xxxx) and also the value of the All Ords index at that date (also shown as xxxx in table 14.4). Each time you update the spreadsheet, you overwrite these.

- The 'Number' column is updated by overwriting when shares are bought, sold or received through a DRP. If all shares are sold, the line is removed and when new shares are bought a new line is added (in the appropriate place).

- The 'Price' column is updated by overwriting with new close-of-trade prices.

- The 'Value' column is calculated by the spreadsheet by multiplying the price by quantity.

- The 'Div type' column shows the dividend type using 'DRP' for dividend reinvestment plan, 'ff' for fully franked, '0.5 f' for 50% franked level (and so on) and 'uf' for unfranked. If this cell is blank, this indicates no dividend.

- The 'Stop' column shows stop loss levels I have set. I generally use 10% trailing stops and adjust my stops upward if the price rises but I don't adjust them downwards if the price falls. If the stop loss order has been placed with my broker, I indicate this with an asterisk (*) alongside the stop loss figure.

- In the 'Comments' column, I make any appropriate comments. In this case, I've added the comment 'Watch for trend reversal' because I think the chart is indicating that a change in sentiment may be in the offing.

- At the bottom of the spreadsheet, the total value for all my shares is calculated by the spreadsheet using the 'SUM' function.

- After I update the spreadsheet, I compare the total value of my portfolio to that shown on my online broking site. If they don't agree closely, I go back and check the number of shares and the prices to find the cause of the discrepancy.

- When I check my CHESS statement for any of my shares, I ensure the number of shares in the statement agrees exactly with the number shown in my spreadsheet. If there is any difference, I check until I find the reason for the discrepancy.

Reviewing performance

Reviewing is the process of comparing your performance to your goals and deciding whether anything needs to be changed. I can't overstate the importance of setting targets or goals (as outlined in chapter 6) and of having effective risk management strategies in place (as outlined in chapter 13) but having these is pointless unless you periodically review them.

Types of review

I suggest you consider three different types of review carried out at three different times:

1. reviewing each trade

2. regularly reviewing your shares and your portfolio

3. reviewing your portfolio over the longer term.

Reviewing each trade

I suggest you review each trade a short time after settlement. Hopefully, by now, I've convinced you that your trade should have been in accordance with a written trading plan. If your review shows that you've stuck to your plan, give yourself a pat on the back. However, if the trade wasn't in accordance with your plan, you need to ask yourself why. You might come up with reasons such as these:

- I panicked.

- I acted on impulse because I was feeling particularly optimistic (or pessimistic).

- I received a 'hot tip' that I wanted to act on immediately before the market wised up to it.

- I acted quickly because the market was very volatile and I wanted to get the best price.

- Because of other commitments, I didn't have enough time to carry out the necessary research before acting.

Being honest with yourself about why you made a trade that wasn't in accordance with your plan will help you to avoid making the same mistake in the future. And let's face it—if you have a plan and you didn't stick to it, you have erred. Most likely you've acted impulsively for some reason or other and, as I've said before, it's best to keep emotion out of the equation when you're trading shares.

Regularly reviewing your shares and your portfolio

Your planning should include the minimum time interval between reviews of your shares and your portfolio (refer to chapter 6). A thorough review of your shares and your portfolio should be a three-pronged approach:

1. Review the performance of each of your shares and your portfolio and compare their performance to a relevant market index.

2. Review the chart of each of you shares and so get a pictorial representation.

3. If these reviews show any sudden price rises or falls, try to ascertain the cause.

I review and update the price of the shares in my portfolio and the total value of the portfolio on a weekly basis. After updating my portfolio, I compare this week's portfolio value to last week's and calculate the percentage change in value. I also compare this to the change in the All Ords index and evaluate my performance relative to this market benchmark. Because I have a diversified portfolio of shares, my portfolio performance usually matches the market fairly closely but occasionally I do significantly better or worse than the market. If I do worse, I try to work out the reasons and decide if I need to take any action.

The percentage change in your portfolio or the index is calculated as follows:

$$\text{Percentage change} = \frac{\left(\text{This week's value} - \text{Last week's value}\right)}{\text{Last week's value}} \times 100$$

In the full spreadsheet I use, the calculation is programmed in, but I haven't shown this refinement in the simplified spreadsheet given in table 14.4. However, if you're acquainted with spreadsheets, you should have no problems working this out yourself.

After you have reviewed the numerical performance of all the shares in your portfolio as well as the overall performance of your portfolio, I suggest you look at the price chart for your shares and so get a pictorial impression. Your online broking site should have a charting facility, but if you're not using an online broker you can obtain charts from other online sites with charting facilities. Once you have logged on to the site, you can quickly examine the chart for each of your shares as well as the chart for the market index you are using.

You can use whatever time period you like but I use a six-monthly time period for initial investigation. This clearly shows price movements as well as the medium-term trend. If necessary, you can then look at a longer term chart over a year or two. Using charting techniques, you should be able to detect any warning signals or positive signals. You can make a note of these; I like to make notes in the 'Comments' column of my portfolio spreadsheet. If the chart shows up any strange price movements such as sudden rises or falls, these should be examined to try to ascertain the most probable cause. The first line of attack is to check if any company announcements could explain the change. Most broking sites allow you to access announcements and they are also posted on the ASX site. Sudden falls in price could be due to the shares going ex-dividend so this should also be checked.

Action

After reviewing the performance of your portfolio and the shares in it, you need to consider if some action is warranted. Three basic options are available to you:

1. Do nothing—hold on and continue to monitor the situation in the future.

2. Buy some more shares in one or more of the stocks you hold or in another stock.

3. Sell some (or all) of your shares in a stock if you're not happy with the future outlook of these.

Each of these options has pros and cons, and the decision is seldom a straightforward or easy one. It may actually be unpleasant if you need to sell some losing shares and so crystallise the loss. But, however unpleasant, you may need to 'bite the bullet' so you can get on with more productive investments and get your portfolio back on track.

Regularly reviewing your portfolio over the longer term

If your portfolio value changes gradually over a period of time, detecting longer term trends can become difficult, so it's worthwhile checking your portfolio performance over the longer term. I think every six months is appropriate but you may prefer to do it annually. Unfortunately, you can't just look up a chart of your portfolio as you can with your shares and so see at a glance the changes over the period. However, you can keep a spreadsheet where you record your portfolio values weekly (or every time you obtain them). At the end of the longer term, you can use the spreadsheet charting facility to create a chart of the portfolio value and so obtain a visual impression of trends.

If you wish, you can also work out your total profitability over the longer term. From the initial and final portfolio values you can obtain your capital gain (or loss). You can then add in the dividends received in the period and so obtain your total profit (or loss) as the sum of capital gains and dividends. You can also calculate the average capital invested and so obtain the percentage return on capital.

Improving portfolio performance

Clearly, if the performance of your portfolio is below your expectations, you need to consider the reasons for this and consider how you might be able to do better in the future. If you're achieving or surpassing your targets, you may still wish to consider whether your strategies could be fine-tuned for even better performance. When you do this, try to be dispassionate and, in effect, become a self-auditor. A good way of improving portfolio performance is to ask yourself several questions:

Firstly, look at your total portfolio value and ask:

'If I owned no shares but had this amount of share investment capital available, what would my ideal portfolio be?'

Then look at each parcel of shares in turn and ask:

'If I didn't already own these shares, would I buy them today?'

If the answer to this question is 'No', then ask:

'If I sold these shares and had this amount of cash, what shares would I buy instead?'

Asking and answering these questions will help you to realistically review your portfolio and so continually improve your profitability and return on capital invested. If your performance has been below expectations, self-flagellation is pointless, and regret over poor decisions can't alter them. Instead, try to learn from each experience and, if you have made a mistake, try to avoid repeating the same mistake in the future.

It might help to remember some stock market sayings:

Anyone can make money on the stock market with the wisdom of hindsight!

And another one:

No-one can make every share trade a profitable one!

367

As long as you are making decisions that conform to your systematic approach, accept that not all your investing decisions will result in profits and move on. Also accept that the sharemarket goes through down periods that you won't be able to control and that can result in losses before the gains eventually re-establish.

Learning exercises

14.1 What are the essential differences between a systematic and an ad-hoc approach to share investing?

14.2 What's the essential difference between monitoring and reviewing?

14.3
   a. In the context of share investing, what's meant by a stimulus?

   b. What typical stimuli might occur?

   c. If you're using an ad-hoc approach, what might be your likely response to a stimulus?

   d. If you're using a systematic approach, when you receive a stimulus how should you respond to it?

14.4 What are three important reasons you need to maintain good records for your shares?

14.5 What important information are you likely to receive for shares in your portfolio from your broker or share registry?

14.6 Suggest suitable files you could set up and maintain for your share trading and investing information.

14.7 In addition to filing contract notes, what are the benefits of compiling a trading summary?

14.8 In addition to filing dividend statements, what are the benefits of compiling and filing a DRP summary for shares received through the DRP?

14.9 You have a written trading plan that you've followed but your last two trades have been losing trades. What should you do?

14.10
   a. What three options are available to you after reviewing your portfolio?

   b. What are three different types of review you can carry out and at what times would you do each of them?

14.11 What are three useful questions to ask yourself when you're evaluating your portfolio and seeking ways to improve performance?

14.12 What are three ways the capital invested in a share portfolio can be interpreted?

14.13 Your share portfolio had a value of $115 632 last week and your benchmark index was 7326. This week your portfolio value was $117 046 and the index was 7404. What was the percentage change in your portfolio and the index? How did your portfolio perform relative to the index?

Learning exercises solutions

14.1 A systematic approach is one that follows a plan you've devised before making any trades. Then all trades you make are in accordance with your plan. You regularly monitor and review performance and decide on any actions you need to take. Finally you may need to tweak your strategies to improve with longer term performance. An ad-hoc approach is one that doesn't follow a plan but is based on 'gut feeling', emotions or knee-jerk reactions.

14.2 Monitoring is the process of measuring results and keeping appropriate records. Reviewing is the process of evaluating performance, identifying any deficiencies or areas for improvement and then taking appropriate action.

14.3

   a. A stimulus is a change of some type that provokes you into considering a response.

   b. A stimulus could be a 'hot tip' or media report, receiving or needing cash, a change in market sentiment that invokes a rush of optimism or pessimism or simply a change in mood.

   c. If you're using an ad-hoc approach, you'll probably act (or decide not to act) without careful or rational consideration.

   d. In a systematic approach, you don't react to a stimulus in a knee-jerk fashion. Instead, you refer to your plan and see whether or not the stimulus fits into it and so decide rationally whether or not you will take any action.

14.4 Three main reasons for keeping good records are:

   1. You need relevant information about shares you own or have traded so you can refer to this when you're evaluating your performance.

   2. Income tax law requires you to maintain complete and accurate records of all your income from trading and from dividends received.

   3. If shares are part of your estate, your executors need clear records of all your share transactions for these shares.

14.5   Likely important information includes:

» contract notes for your trades

» share holding statements

» dividend statements

» company newsletters, updates or directors' reports, notification of AGMs or other meetings with proxy forms for absentee voting purposes and annual reports or abridged annual reports (unless you elect not to receive them).

14.6   Suggested files include:

» a trading file with records all trades and copies of all contract notes

» a separate file for each of the shares in your portfolio

» a 'Sold shares' file that contains important information about shares you've sold

» bank statements for share accounts

» a file for portfolio spreadsheets, for P/L spreadsheets and for dividend summaries.

14.7   The benefits of compiling a trading summary are:

» You have a one- or two-page summary that's easier and quicker to refer to than wading through contract notes.

» You can easily check that bank account deposits and withdrawals align with your contract notes.

» It's an easy and quick point of reference whenever you're working out your P/L or when compiling your capital gains tax information.

14.8   The benefits of a DRP summary include:

» If you hold some shares over a number of years and receive new shares twice each year through the DRP, keeping a one-sheet summary showing each new parcel of shares acquired and the acquisition cost is very useful.

» If you sell some (but not all) of your shares in this company, you need to know which shares you've sold and which you've held because the parcel values will be different.

» Your executors need these details going back to the time of first allotment for any shares that are part of your estate.

14.9 You should continue to follow your plan unless your losing trades have highlighted some deficiency in your plan that can be rectified.

14.10

a. When you review your portfolio, you have three basic options available to you:

1. Do nothing —simply hold on and continue to monitor the situation.

2. Buy some more shares in one or more of the stocks you hold.

3. Sell some (or all) of your shares if you're not happy with the future outlook.

b. Three different types of review carried out at three different times are:

1. After each trade.

2. When you update your portfolio spreadsheet—for example, weekly.

3. When you review your long-term performance— every six or twelve months.

14.11 For your total portfolio, ask:

'If I owned no shares but had this amount of capital to spend on shares, what would my ideal portfolio be?'

For each parcel of shares ask:

'If I didn't already own these shares, would I buy them today?'

If the answer to this question is 'No', ask:

'If I sold these shares and had this amount of money in cash, what shares would I buy instead?'

14.12 The three ways capital invested can be interpreted are:

1. the initial capital invested (that is, at the start of the period)

2. the final capital invested (that is, at the end of the period)

3. the average capital invested (that is, the average value over the period).

14.13 The change in your portfolio value is $1414.

The percentage change is $(1414 \div 115\,632) \times 100 = \mathbf{1.22\%}$.

The change in the index = 78 points.

The percentage change is $(78 \div 7326) \times 100 = \mathbf{1.065\%}$.

Therefore, your portfolio **slightly outperformed** the index.

Chapter 15

Wrapping
it all up

In this chapter, I highlight some of the key points and important aspects of share investing and trading strategies from the previous chapters.

Can all traders win?

Can all traders who 'play the market' win or do the winners gain at the expense of the losers? Another way of looking at this question is to ask, 'Is share trading a zero-sum game?' A zero-sum game is one where the total losses and total gains by the players balances out so the total gain (or loss) is zero. That's to say, if a player wins is that only at the expense of another player who loses? A typical example is a poker game, where each player comes into the game with a certain amount of cash and there's no fee for playing.

Consider such a game with four players, Tom, Dick, Harry and Jane, where each player has $100 in cash. After a while the situation is:

- Tom has made a profit of $60 and so has $160.

- Dick has made a loss of $20 and so has $80.

- Harry has made a loss of $40 and so has $60.

How much is Jane winning or losing? To work this out add up Tom, Dick and Harry's cash, which is $160 + 80 + 60 = \$300$. Therefore, Jane has $100 and must be breaking even, making neither a loss nor a profit.

Another way to work this out is to total the profits and losses made by Tom, Dick and Harry: $60 - 20 - 40 = 0$.

Since the game is a zero-sum game, Jane must be making zero profit (breaking even). Because Jane has broken even, Tom's wins must be balanced by Dick and Harry's losses. And so it is since Tom has won $60 at the expense of Dick who has lost $20 and Harry who has lost $40.

What happens if another player enters the game with more funds or if one of the existing players digs deeper and increases their cash pool? The answer is all that has happened is that the cash pool has increased but the game remains a zero-sum game and the wins and losses balance at a higher level.

Application to share trading

Is share trading any different or is it also a zero-sum game? That is, do all the capital gains made on the winning share trades balance all the capital losses on the losing trades? The answer is 'yes' if the total cash pool remains the same. Actually, because traders pay brokerage, the cash pool will diminish unless it is topped up by the influx of additional capital.

Three basic scenarios for traders are outlined in table 15.1.

You can see that if a share price (or the market as a whole) is trending up, the capital invested in that share (or the market) must be increasing. This means that there must be a net capital inflow into that share (or the market). Conversely, if a share price (or the market) is trending down, there must be a net capital outflow. When a share price (or the market) is trending sideways, the capital invested remains the same.

Table 15.1 Trading gains or losses

Price trend	Overall trading profit	Trades	Market cap (capital invested)
Uptrend	Positive	More profitable trades than unprofitable ones	Increases—total dollars invested increases
Sideways	Zero	Profitable trades balance unprofitable ones	Steady—total dollars invested remains the same
Downtrend	Negative	More unprofitable trades than profitable ones	Decreases— total dollars invested decreases

It's a rather sobering thought that when shares (or markets) are trending sideways, trading is a zero-sum game and the total trading profits and losses balance. In this situation, when you're thinking of buying shares because you expect the price will rise, you might want to consider that other traders are selling those shares because they think the price will fall. Conversely, when you're thinking of selling because you expect the price to fall, other traders are buying because they think the price will rise. So viewed objectively, you have a 50% chance of being correct when you trade.

Beating the market

First-time share investors may think it should be relatively easy to beat the market. All that is needed is a better system or a somewhat cleverer approach than the average trader. In fact, beating the market is very difficult because of a market truism:

The market is always right.

The reason for this is that share prices are determined by the market and even if the market is irrational, share prices always move in accordance with market trends. Therefore, the market is always right.

You can also see why if you imagine you own a property that you decide to sell. You get several valuations and they all indicate that the property is worth about $800 000. You agree with this valuation because you paid $750 000 for it several years ago and subsequently spent $50 000 improving it. You place the property on the market at this price and you get several offers but the highest one is $700 000. So what is your property actually worth? The fact is that any commodity, be it property, shares or anything else, is worth only what a willing buyer will pay for it. So in this example, if the best offer you can get on your property is $700 000, that is the value of your property. The market has decided and the market is right because no amount of rational argument based on what you paid for the property and the money you spent on it has any sway if the highest bidder is prepared to pay only $700 000.

Considering the sharemarket, imagine you hold some shares that you think are worth a certain amount because you believe the company is well managed, has a good product, has bright future prospects, or whatever other positives you see. But if the share price is trending down, clearly the market doesn't share your opinion about those shares. Remember that the market is always right; so stubbornly holding those shares (or even buying some more) because you think the market is wrong is a recipe for disaster. I'm not saying a contrarian strategy won't ever pay off, but the odds are against it. In the long run, working the odds in your favour is most likely to produce the best results and going against the probabilities will lose.

Improving the odds

As I've said, consistently beating the market is very difficult—especially over the longer term—so you are doing well if your returns aren't less than market returns. If you follow the principles I've outlined in this book, you may be able to swing the odds a little more in your favour. The most important trading principle that will help you to do this is:

> *Buy in an uptrend, sell in a downtrend and sit on the fence in a sidetrend until a trend change is clearly evident.*

Irrational optimism or pessimism

As I've pointed out in previous chapters, a trap to be aware of in the market is the emotional aspect that affects traders who get 'carried away' with irrational optimism or pessimism and drive share prices to unsustainable levels. As an example, consider an IPO that issues one million shares at a price of $1. The offer is taken up by 1000 investors who subscribe to

1000 shares each. After listing, the price rises and all investors sell when they've made 20% profit. The price continues to rise and the investors who subsequently bought 1000 shares also sell when they're making 20% profit. Table 15.2 shows the result if this sequence continues for 10 trades.

Table 15.2: Sequential trades with 20% profit

Trade number	Buy price ($)	Sell price ($)	% Profit	Market cap of the stock ($M)
1	1.00	1.20	20	1.2
2	1.20	1.44	20	1.44
3	1.44	1.73	20	1.73
4	1.73	2.07	20	2.07
5	2.07	2.49	20	2.49
6	2.49	2.99	20	2.99
7	2.99	3.58	20	3.58
8	3.58	4.30	20	4.3
9	4.30	5.16	20	5.16
10	5.16	6.19	20	6.19

You can see that if all trades result in a 20% profit, after 10 trades the share price has risen from $1.00 to $6.19 and the market cap of the stock has risen from $1 million to $6.19 million.

Does this process have to stop, or can it keep going on with each successive trader making 20% profit on the same shares? In theory it can, provided buyers are always prepared to match the sellers prices. However, after 10 trades the price has risen more than six-fold. After 20 trades, the price would rise more than 38-fold and after 50 trades the price would rise 9100 times with each share initially valued at $1 share trading for $9100!

In real-life situations, if a share price has been driven up by irrational optimism and not by sustainable profits, inevitably some traders will lose their nerve and they'll sell. As soon as there's a hint of a change in sentiment, the price will fall and the uptrend will most likely change to a downtrend. The downtrend can accelerate quickly if sellers panic and the trend gains momentum. If the price ends up falling back to the original issue price, this indeed would be a zero-sum game and some traders will make large losses—equal to the gains made by the winning traders.

This might sound like a far-fetched scenario but it has occurred in the past. Tulip mania in the 17th century due to a shortage of tulip bulbs caused their prices to skyrocket to astronomical levels before collapsing. During the 'South Sea bubble', some early investors (including Isaac Newton, it's said) lost huge sums when the bubble burst. And I've already mentioned an Australian example from the 1960s, when mining company Poseidon announced a promising nickel find. At the time, its shares were trading at 80¢, but within a few months, accompanied by a blaze of publicity, the share price rose to around $280 as a buying frenzy gathered momentum. Inevitably, the bubble burst and the share price plummeted back down again in panic selling. The company never did make a profit from its nickel find and within a few years was delisted!

While these extreme examples are rare, an element of irrational optimism or pessimism is often a feature of sharemarkets today when emotions drive traders to buy because of the 'fear of missing out' (FOMO) or when sellers rush to sell because panic sets in. These emotions are the cause of high volatility and overshoot and undershoot. The best way of ensuring you don't get 'sucked in' is to sit tight and avoid 'following the herd' when the market acts in an irrational manner.

Notes

- You might argue that if the market is always right, you should follow the market even in times of irrationality. The problem with trying to do this is that it's very difficult to predict irrationality and to take advantage of it, especially for the average investor. If you try to do so, you will most likely get your fingers burnt. Remember that irrationality is a 'knee jerk' response (otherwise known as the 'fight or flight' response) and is only a short-term reaction. Rational behaviour always triumphs in the longer term.

- You might think that panic trading isn't common nowadays and that people are more rational in their behaviour but, in fact, panic trading behaviour driven by FOMO is still as prevalent today as it was in the past. As the COVID-19 epidemic spread to Australia in early 2020, customers were emptying the shelves in supermarkets of many items including (of all things) toilet paper!

Remembering the difference between shares and gambling

In a horse race, you make your selection before the race starts and you can't change your choice or adjust your bet once you've placed it. So the buy decision is all-important and most punters spend a lot of time studying form and agonising over which horse to back. Once the race starts, if the horse gets off to a bad start, the punter can't do anything about it. On the other hand, you can think of the sharemarket as a perpetual race where the horses keep going round and round the track and where you can vary your bet as the race progresses. Now you can change your mind and alter your strategy at any time. In this situation, the sell decision becomes very important because it enables you to minimise your losses if you have backed what will clearly be a loser. The fact is that no matter how sophisticated your selection process or how much time you spend on it, you are never going to be right all the time.

So an essential difference between gambling and share trading is that with gambling you can't manage your bet once you have placed it. On the other hand, with shares you do have the opportunity to manage your trade after you have placed it. Indeed, this is the most important aspect of share trading and investing — what you do with the shares after you have bought them. You need to decide if you will sell or hold and, if you decide to sell, when you should do so and what minimum price you will set.

I believe the average share investor believes that success depends on making a good selection of shares in the first place. If the portfolio does well, they believe it's because their selection of shares was good and, conversely, if it does poorly, the shares chosen must not have been very good. While it is certainly true that having a good selection of shares in your portfolio is important, it is also true that success depends as much (or even more) on what you do with those shares after you have set up your portfolio. In other words, portfolio management is just as important (or even more) than portfolio selection.

Trading stake

A staking system sometimes advocated for punters goes like this:

> Plan to make a certain profit by punting. Taking account of the odds, place a wager on the horse of your choice so you can make your planned profit. For example, let's assume you plan to make $20 profit and the odds are 2:1, so you'll wager $10 on your first bet. If you lose, you raise the amount of your stake on the next bet so the amount you'll win is your planned profit plus the amount of your loss on the previous bet, namely $10. That is, you need to stake enough to be able to make $30 profit from your next wager. Should you lose again, the process continues until eventually, you'll pick a winner and recoup all your losses and make your planned overall profit of $20.

In theory, this system is ironclad provided you have an unlimited amount of capital and nerves of steel.

You can easily apply the same staking system to share trading. You can plan to make, say, $1000 profit from a share trade and buy a parcel of shares of value, say, $5000 and set a profit stop of 20% and a stop loss of 10%. If the price falls and your stop loss activates, you lose $500, so you raise the planned profit on your next trade to $1500 to make your planned profit and recoup your loss on the previous trade. Each time you fail to make your planned profit, you raise your parcel value on the next trade accordingly until eventually you recoup all your losses and make your original planned profit.

While this staking system appears infallible for both punting and shares, the flaw with it is that if you have a run of losers, you end up staking large amounts of capital to make relatively small profits. At this point, you can easily run out of capital or lose your nerve. Indeed, as I demonstrated in chapter 13, sequential trading with increasing parcel values has an additional inbuilt risk. In order to avoid the additional risk, you need to keep the parcel value of your trades approximately the same.

Winning with share investing

Is share investing intrinsically different from share trading or is it also a zero-sum game? Remember the difference between investing and trading is that investors don't trade frequently but maintain a share portfolio over a relatively long period of time. So the question is: can all share investors show profits over the longer term or do those who profit do so only at the expense of those who don't? The answer is that all share investors can show a profit over time depending on the market. If the market is rising, total market cap is increasing and this means more capital is flowing into the market. When this happens, the value of the majority of the shares held by investors in the market is also rising. So, in theory, all investors already in the market should be making capital gains.

Naturally, some shares and some sectors do better than others but overall this demonstrates the benefit of being a long-term investor and why frequent trading is a wealth hazard. Another benefit of being a longer term investor is that if you hold a good proportion of dividend-paying shares, you obtain the income from them on a regular basis and this boosts your total profit. So provided the market isn't in a long-term bear phase, longer term investors with diversified portfolios should be able to show good profits from shares.

Contradictory strategies

Many different share investing and trading strategies have been devised over the years and, interestingly, many of these strategies contradict one another. It's even more interesting that I've found that you can follow a strategy and make a profit, and follow the opposite strategy and still make a profit! On the other hand, you might follow a strategy and make a loss but still make a loss when you follow the opposite strategy.

The conclusions from this are:

- In the sharemarket, different strategies work in different situations and no single strategy is best in all situations.

- It's not necessarily the strategy that's so critical. What's more important is that you follow the strategy through thick and thin.

It's said that real wisdom comes from asking questions and querying accepted knowledge rather than from believing what others tell you. Indeed, it's the only way progress in knowledge and technology can occur. So I suggest you view with scepticism any claim of an infallible system for making profits with shares. Remember that in a bull market everyone can make good profits from shares but the real test of a system is how well it works in sideways-trending or down-trending markets. Also bear in mind that you can demonstrate good results from any system with the wisdom of hindsight. The real test of a system is not how well it has performed in the past but how well it performs in the future.

To illustrate my point about contradictory strategies, I've listed in table 15.3 some strategies for share investing or trading you might encounter and the contradictory strategy. After you've considered them, you can decide which makes more sense to you and which ones you might want to adopt.

Table 15.3: Strategy versus contradictory strategy

Strategy	Contradictory strategy
'Follow the herd' because the market's always right. Most investors are informed and, therefore, you should go with the flow. For example, buy shares that are the 'flavour of the month' and sell them when the market's abandoning them. Buy when everyone else is buying and sell when everyone else is selling.	Be contrarian and 'do your own thing'—it's the only way you can beat the market. Many investors are uninformed and are simply following the herd. Consider buying shares that are out of favour and selling them if they become popular and the price rises. Consider selling when everyone else is buying and buying when everyone else is selling.
Stick to quality shares and avoid speculative ones.	You can make higher capital gains from speculative shares than from blue chips.
Use technical analysis—it can be used with charting to identify buying and selling opportunities.	Ignore technical analysis—it has the same scientific credibility as astrology or tarot cards. The future's unknown and you can't use past performance to predict the future.
Use fundamental analysis— shares with good fundamentals will prove to be good investments in the long run.	Ignore fundamental analysis—the market is moved by people, not financial statements.
Analyse shares for purchase very carefully—profitable share investing depends on good share selection.	You don't need to agonise too much over which shares to buy—a randomly chosen portfolio often performs as well as a carefully chosen one. Profitable share investing depends on good portfolio management rather than good share selection.

Strategy	Contradictory strategy
You need to follow the market frequently and trade often in order to make good profits.	The more you trade, the less profit you'll make. A 'bottom drawer' approach often does better in the long run.
Diversify your portfolio with many different shares in different sectors.	Concentrate your portfolio with a small number of different shares or sectors. That is about the only way you can beat the market.
Trade geared instruments such as warrants, option and CFDs or use a margin loan to increase your leverage so as to get a better return on your capital invested.	Gearing your investment can improve return on your capital invested if you get it right but it increases the level of risk and will magnify your losses if you get it wrong.
Seek as much advice as you can from advisors and other 'experts' and follow their advice. The extra profit you make will more than cover the fees.	There's no such thing as a sharemarket 'expert'. You're better off relying on your own judgement and knowledge and saving the advisor's fees.
Set stop losses for all your shares after you purchase them and stick to them rigidly.	Stop losses have disadvantages as well as advantages and you need to judge each situation on its own merits.
Use profit stops and take profits as often as you can. Cash is king and once the money is in your bank account, you can't lose it if the price falls.	You shouldn't use profit stops because they often mean selling in a rising market and that's not a good strategy. Cash in the bank is wasted capital and just 'marking time' because it will produce little (or no) return.
As you make profitable trades, reinvest all your capital on the next trade. This will magnify your profitability and return on capital.	Trading sequentially increases your level of risk and the loss you will incur if the trade goes against you.
Buy a share when the price is close to the 52-week low. You will make most capital gain when the price rises.	Buy shares when the price is close to the 52-week high. This indicates that the shares are in favour with investors and could easily hit new highs.
You need heaps of information in order to make good investing decisions.	Too much information can slow down the decision-making process and lead to 'paralysis by analysis'.
The more sophisticated and complex your system, the greater the probability that it will be successful.	Some of the best investing strategies are based on a few basic principles only. Complexity can just muddy the waters and be distracting.

Key principles you may find helpful

As you'll see from table 15.3, no strategy is guaranteed to work best in all situations. However, some principles apply to most share investing situations and can tip the balance of probabilities in your favour. I'll conclude by summarising some of these principles.

My useful principles of share investing are:

1. *Plan before you trade.* Know your risk profile and include this in your planning. Have a written trading plan and stick to it. Set realistic goals. Monitor your performance on a regular basis and modify your portfolio and your plans according to how well you're performing.

2. *Practise good cash management for your trades and for your portfolio.* Use the 1% rule or at most a 2% rule to limit the possible downside loss on any shares you buy or own. Always keep some cash in reserve. Consider using stop loss orders with your broker or set your own limits and monitor prices regularly. Maintain an approximately constant parcel value for your trades and your portfolio.

3. *Buy in an uptrend and sell in a downtrend.* Don't buy in a downtrend or sell in an uptrend. In an uptrend let your profits run and don't sell unless the price starts to downtrend.

4. *Don't make the assumption that because shares seem cheap or are hitting new lows the price won't fall any further.* Beware the 'dead cat' bounce after a share price falls. Don't assume that because shares hit new highs they're now a sell and the price won't rise further.

5. *Don't equate a good product with a good share investment.* In other words, don't buy simply because you like the business or the product. A company can have a great product in a growth market but that doesn't guarantee high and growing profits. In some cases, shares in a company with a great product can perform poorly. This is because many other factors influence company profitability other than the market for the product.

6. *When you're trying to decide whether or not to sell shares, ignore what you paid for them.* Base your decision on future performance potential and not on hope or wishful thinking. Don't hang onto losers in the hope that they'll turn into winners or because you want to avoid the pain of a crystallised loss.

7. *Don't 'put all your eggs in one basket' (or two, for that matter).* Diversify your portfolio with at least five different shares (and preferably 10) in different sectors.

8. *Generally avoid shares with unusually high or low PEs.* Very high PEs can't be justified in the long run and usually precede a price fall. Very low PEs usually indicate something is wrong and at least that the shares are out of favour.

9. *If you're a long-term investor, consider basing your portfolio on shares that are making profits and are paying good dividends.* If you wish to speculate, allocate no more than 10% of your trading capital for this purpose.

10. *Use both fundamental and technical analysis to guide your investing decisions.* They don't have to be considered mutually exclusive and can be used together for the best trading decisions.

11. *The market is always right.* Don't try to make the market see things your way because it won't. Shares you like won't necessarily be good investments and shares you don't like won't necessarily prove to be 'dogs'.

12. *Look forward, not backward.* Everyone can make a fortune on the sharemarket with the wisdom of 20/20 hindsight. Future potential is far more important than past history. Use past performance as a guide but don't assume it will necessarily continue into the future.

13. *If you make a loss trade don't agonise over it.* Everyone has some loss trades and even the most experienced share traders and investors don't get it right all the time. If you've stuck to your trading plan, congratulate yourself and treat the loss as an experience.

14. *Try to be as dispassionate as you can about your investment decisions*. Emotionally motivated and 'gut-feel' decisions are seldom good ones with shares.

15. *Develop a system to keep track of all your trades and investment information*. Maintain a file of all relevant documents and data in an orderly fashion.

16. *Don't act on a 'tip' without investigating it yourself*. This applies regardless of whether you receive the tip from an 'expert', relative, friend, taxi driver, hairdresser, or any other source. True insider knowledge is very rare with shares and, indeed, acting on insider knowledge for financial benefit is illegal.

17. *Don't get unduly stressed if an event occurs either in Australia or in some other country that causes our market to dive*. Be secure in the knowledge that the market is resilient and will recover sooner or later and so save yourself unnecessary anguish. Just ride the downs with the 'ups' knowing that this is a feature of all sharemarkets.

Note

These principles aren't necessarily stated in order of importance.

Working with the best system for you

Many people are trying to make money from the sharemarket. Most do so by investing or trading shares or other instruments, but others do so by offering advice, or by providing an investment service and by charging a subscriber a substantial amount to access some 'special' system they have devised and that they claim produces superior returns. So if you're already a share investor or considering becoming one, a really important question boils down to this:

Is there a system or strategy that I can use that will consistently produce returns that are better than those produced by other systems or strategies or indeed the market in general?

I believe that the answer to this question is 'no' for the simple reason that if a system or strategy was devised that always produced superior returns, inevitably everyone would find out about it and use it. And, as we've seen, it's impossible for all investors and traders either in a share or in the market as a whole to consistently beat the market. If your shares do as well as the market, you're doing as well as you can reasonably expect. The best way to match the market is to have a well-balanced portfolio, not to trade too often but to hold on and ride out the inevitable market fluctuations.

Your aim should be to tip the probabilities in your favour so you make more profit from your winners than the losses you incur on your losers. As I showed you in chapters 10 and 13, you can improve the likelihood of success by adopting good trading and risk management strategies. If you studied learning exercise 13.19, you'll have seen that you can make capital gains in a sideways trending market if you adopt suitable trading and cash management strategies. At the end of this chapter, learning exercise 15.14 demonstrates that you can make capital gains with shares even when the market is trending down, provided you adopt a simple trading strategy that includes the use of stop losses.

And, finally, remember that many Australian companies pay a good dividend on their shares that is much better than the interest you might receive from a bank or other financial institution. Even if the market is very volatile, the dividend can provide a bulwark of stability and income. In many cases, you may have the option of joining a DRP and if you decide to forgo the dividend income and take it in shares, the value of your shareholding will increase in a compound manner that provides an additional boost to your portfolio over the longer term.

Learning exercises

15.1 Is share trading a zero-sum game? In what circumstances is it possible for most traders to make a profit?

15.2 What's a likely cause of panic selling and how can you avoid being caught up in it?

15.3 Consider the following strategy: 'I plan to make $1000 profit on my first trade. If I make this profit, I continue trading but if I don't I'll add my loss to my planned profit of $1000 and increase my parcel value on the next trade. I'll continue this process until eventually I must end up making an overall profit of $1000 from share trading.'

Can you see anything wrong with this strategy; should you consider adopting it?

15.4 Explain why contradictory strategies might each produce a good result on the sharemarket.

15.5 When you receive a 'hot tip' on the sharemarket, what should you do?

15.6 Is there a downside to obtaining all the information you possibly can before making share trading or investing decisions?

15.7 You fancy some shares and you've been keeping a close watch on their price, which has fallen from previous highs. When the price falls to what you think is a 'bargain basement' level, you decide to jump in. Is this the best strategy or can you think of a better one?

15.8 A listed company has a great product and ample evidence indicates a growing market for it. Should you buy shares on the expectation that the company's bound to make good profits in the future? Should you consider anything else?

15.9 What is the essential difference between share trading and gambling?

15.10 Why is it generally not a good idea to invest in shares that have a very high or very low PE compared to the market average?

15.11 What types of shares should you consider for a long-term core portfolio? If you want to trade speculatively, how much of your investing capital should you devote for this purpose?

15.12

    a. Why are shares that pay a consistent dividend generally good for long-term investing?

    b. What's the benefit of fully franked dividends?

    c. What's an additional compounding benefit of taking dividends in shares (through a DRP), rather than getting a cash payment?

15.13 Why should you consider the future potential of a share rather than just past performance?

15.14 You invest $40 000 equally spread over eight shares (labelled A through to H) during a bear market. A year later, three shares go up in price and five go down in price as follows:

- A: +50%

- B: +20%

- C: +10%

- D: −20%

- E: −30%

- F: −40%

- G: −50%

- H: −60%

    Neglect trading costs and work out:

    a. The percentage return on capital invested if you adopted a buy and hold strategy.

    b. The percentage change in the market if these shares typify the overall market.

    c. The percentage return on capital invested if you set a 10% stop loss level for all shares. Draw conclusions.

    d. Can you apply a 1% percentage rule to this portfolio? If not, what percentage rule can you apply?

Learning exercises solutions

15.1 Share trading is a zero-sum game when shares are trending sideways. It's possible for most traders to make a profit when prices are uptrending.

15.2 Panic selling is likely to occur when share prices rise to unsustainably high levels because of irrational optimism and then start to drop. You can avoid being caught up in it by ensuring that you don't buy shares with very high PEs or shares with a high price based purely on 'blue sky' potential.

15.3 In theory, nothing is wrong with this strategy, provided that you have an unlimited cash pool and nerves of steel should you incur a run of losses.

15.4 Contradictory strategies might produce a good result on the sharemarket because each strategy might work best in different circumstances and with different types of shares.

15.5 When you receive a 'hot tip' on the sharemarket, you shouldn't act on it until you've conducted your own research and satisfied yourself that it conforms to your trading criteria.

15.6 The danger is that you can end up with information overload or 'paralysis by analysis'. It is a mistake to think that complexity always improves results; often, focusing on a few key parameters is the best strategy.

15.7 It's usually dangerous to assume prices can't fall below what appears to be 'bargain basement' level and you shouldn't buy unless you're convinced a true trend reversal has taken place. Beware of the 'dead cat' bounce.

15.8 It's dangerous to equate a great product with future profits. Profitability depends as much on good management as a good product and you should look for evidence that the company is managed well—particularly with regard to cash management.

15.9 The essential difference is that with gambling you cannot alter your bet in any way after you have placed it, whereas with shares you have the opportunity to manage your trade later and cut your losses or improve your profitability.

15.10 If the PE is too high, the company is trading on 'blue sky' potential and if the potential doesn't eventuate, the share price can plummet. A PE being too low is a sign of investor disenchantment with the company and there's usually a good reason for it.

15.11 I believe that the best types of shares for a long-term core portfolio are blue or green chip shares that pay good consistent dividends, preferably fully franked. If you want to trade speculatively, I suggest you devote no more than 10% of your investing capital for this purpose.

15.12

    a. Consistent dividend-paying shares are generally good for long-term investing because this indicates consistent profitability and receiving a dividend increases your profit and helps to offset any price drops.

    b. The benefit of getting fully franked dividends is that the franking credits are treated favourably so your after-tax income is higher.

    c. The additional compounding benefit of taking dividends in shares is that you get double compounding because dividends are paid on the shares you received from previous dividends.

15.13 You should always consider the future potential of a share rather than just considering past performance because the sharemarket is forward-looking and more emphasis is placed on future potential than past results. Remember—today's investor can't profit from yesterday's earnings.

15.14 You invested $5000 in each of the eight shares. The table overleaf summarises the situation for options (a) and (c) after one year.

    a. A buy and hold strategy would have resulted in a loss of $6000 for $40000 invested, which is a **15% loss**.

    b. If the market is typified by these shares, it would have dropped in value by **15%**.

c. Using a 10% stop loss, you would have sold five of these shares and held only three at the end of the year. Overall you would have made a capital gain of $1500 on $40 000 invested, which represents a return of **3.75%**—in other words, you beat the market by **18.75%**.

Conclusions:

» You can make a profit in a down-trending market provided you set stop losses (and act on them).

» Only three shares out of the eight chosen were winners, so you were right in your selection only 37.5% of the time, yet using a stop loss meant you still made a capital gain that year and did 18.75% better than the market.

Stock	($) invested	Price move	$ P/L buy and hold strategy (a)	Hold or sell trading strategy (c)	$ P/L trading strategy (c)
A	5000	+50%	2500	H	2500
B	5000	+20%	1000	H	1000
C	5000	+10%	500	H	500
D	5000	−20%	−1000	S	−500
E	5000	−30%	−1500	S	−500
F	5000	−40%	−2000	S	−500
G	5000	−50%	−2500	S	−500
H	5000	−60%	−3000	S	−500
Total	40000	Total	−6000	Total	1500

d. You can't apply a 1% rule to this portfolio with a 10% stop loss because the portfolio only has eight shares and you need 10. The maximum loss allowed by the 1% rule would be 1% of $40 000, which is $400. In fact, the loss of $500 on each loss trade means using a **1.25%** rule.

Index

Also available from Roger Kinsky...

CPSIA information can be obtained
at www.ICGtesting.com
Printed in the USA
LVHW052039071120
671037LV00008B/154